"What do conservative Christian male church leaders really think about ordained women, and why? It's an important question almost wholly unexplored, until now. In this significant new work, readers can learn from male clergy's rich biographical stories and reflections and, through Alex Fry's sensitive analysis, gain both theoretical and practical insights."

Professor Abby Day, *Goldsmiths, University of London and author of* The Religious Lives of Older Laywomen: The Last Active Anglican Generation

"This careful and thoughtful book analyses extended interviews about the ordination of women with three groups of Anglican male clergy. Tellingly, clergy often displayed opposition to feminism, and gender stereotyping alongside their opposition to women as clergy. Dr Fry's judicious conclusion is that 'given the Church of England's established position in the life of the nation, it is appropriate to more directly address the patriarchy that evidently exists within its structures'. Well worth buying."

Canon Robin Gill, *Emeritus Professor of Applied Theology, University of Kent*

"Fry takes the reader through detailed research findings, demonstrating how clergymen interact with clergywomen and the Church of England. Using concepts such as intersectionality, he is able to hold up a lens which provides insights which will inform the way clergy see themselves. The nuance provided by this depth and breadth of analysis is intriguing. This book will be of particular interest to church leaders today."

Mandy Robbins, *Professor of Psychology, Wrexham Glyndŵr University and co-author of* The Long Diaconate 1987: 1994

Gender Inequality in the Ordained Ministry of the Church of England

This book offers a fresh social scientific analysis of how theologically conservative male clergy respond to the ordination of women to the priesthood and their consecration as bishops within the Church of England. The question of women's place in the formal structures of England's Established Church remains contested. For many, to prevent women from occupying such offices is often understood to be a matter of inequality, whereas those who oppose their ordination see it as a matter of obedience to God's will. Tensions have become heightened in a culture that increasingly promotes the rights of individuals who have historically been marginalised and that challenges traditional social roles. This volume explores the gender attitudes held by clergy in the Anglo-Catholic and evangelical traditions of the Church and considers how these gender attitudes shape the way they think about women's ordination and how they interact with female colleagues. It also considers the contribution of a range of social phenomena to the formation of these gender attitudes. The author draws on and develops a variety of sociological and psychological theories that help to explain the processes that lead to the formation of clergy attitudes towards gender more broadly.

Alex Fry completed his PhD in the Department of Theology and Religion at Durham University, UK. He is a Senior Lecturer in the Sociology of Health and Illness at the University of Bournemouth, UK.

Routledge Studies in Religion

Domestic Demons and the Intimate Uncanny
Edited by Thomas G. Kirsch, Kirsten Mahlke and Rijk van Dijk

Jews and Muslims in London and Amsterdam
Conflict and Cooperation, 1990–2020
Sipco J. Vellenga and Gerard A. Wiegers

Alternative Spirituality, Counterculture, and European Rainbow Gatherings
Pachamama, I'm Coming Home
Katri Ratia

Religious Freedom and the Global Regulation of Ayahuasca
Edited by Beatriz Labate and Clancy Cavnar

Interreligious Encounters in Europe
Sites, Materialities and Practices
Edited by Jan Winkler, Laura Haddad, Julia Martínez-Ariño and Giulia Mezzetti

Modern Debates on Prophecy and Prophethood in Islam
Muhammad Iqbal & Said Nursi
Mahsheed Ansari

Religious Responses to the Pandemic and Crises
Isolation, Survival, and #Covidchaos
Edited by Sravana Borkataky-Varma, Christian A. Eberhart, and Marianne Bjelland Kartzow

Gender Inequality in the Ordained Ministry of the Church of England
Examining Conservative Male Clergy Responses to Women Priests and Bishops
Alex D. J. Fry

For more information about this series, please visit: https://www.routledge.com/religion/series/SE0669

Gender Inequality in the Ordained Ministry of the Church of England

Examining Conservative Male Clergy Responses to Women Priests and Bishops

Alex D. J. Fry

LONDON AND NEW YORK

First published 2024
by Routledge
4 Park Square, Milton Park, Abingdon, Oxon OX14 4RN

and by Routledge
605 Third Avenue, New York, NY 10158

Routledge is an imprint of the Taylor & Francis Group, an informa business

© 2024 Alex Fry

The right of Alex Fry to be identified as author of this work has been asserted in accordance with sections 77 and 78 of the Copyright, Designs and Patents Act 1988.

All rights reserved. No part of this book may be reprinted or reproduced or utilised in any form or by any electronic, mechanical, or other means, now known or hereafter invented, including photocopying and recording, or in any information storage or retrieval system, without permission in writing from the publishers.

Trademark notice: Product or corporate names may be trademarks or registered trademarks, and are used only for identification and explanation without intent to infringe.

British Library Cataloguing-in-Publication Data
A catalogue record for this book is available from the British Library

ISBN: 978-0-367-53426-4 (hbk)
ISBN: 978-0-367-53427-1 (pbk)
ISBN: 978-1-003-08191-3 (ebk)

DOI: 10.4324/9781003081913

Typeset in Sabon
by MPS Limited, Dehradun

For Helen

Contents

Acknowledgements		*x*
Foreword		*xii*
Preface		*xiv*
1	Introduction	1
2	The Church of England and gender in historical perspective	26
3	Clerical sexism	52
4	Empathy, intersectionality, and gender schemata	79
5	Contact and contact avoidance	102
6	Schism and clergy capital	128
7	Gender attitudes in (inter)national perspective	146
8	Summary, reflections, and implications	172
9	Conclusion	191
	Bibliography	*201*
	Index	*217*

Acknowledgements

There have been, unsurprisingly, many people who have supported the process that has led up to the writing and publication of this monograph, and even more people supporting the doctoral research on which it is based. I am immensely grateful to colleagues, family, and friends who have, in a wide variety of ways, helped make this work possible.

To start at the start, I am grateful to Mathew Guest and Jocelyn Bryan for their encouragement, advice, and feedback during their supervision of my PhD at Durham University (and indeed during the years proceeding from it). Their genuine interest in my research and academic career has significantly supported my progress during my doctoral research, and their generosity of spirit has been highly valuable during my early, formative years in academia. I am also grateful to my PhD examiners, Sarah-Jane Page and Robert Song, who engaged thoughtfully and thoroughly with my thesis, asking me incisive and insightful questions during the viva. They have also been supportive in the immediate years post-PhD, and I will remember for some time to come my delight when Sarah announced that I had passed the viva and when Robert commented, "Well, I learned a lot", both of which were, naturally, taken as significant complements.

During my time as a research student at Durham University, the warm and hospitable environment of St John's College helped foster many fond memories, especially under the leadership of David Wilkinson (the then Principal), Mark Ogden (the then Senior Tutor) and Susie Curtis (the then Chaplain). St John's provided plentiful opportunities to pursue academic interests as well as spaces of retreat from the demands of the PhD, making sure to take an interest in the whole person—an important mainstay of academic life, even if often forgotten by the research students themselves!

Numerous conversations during my research will have informed my own thinking and refining of ideas. This includes conversations in Durham University's Department of Theology and Religion as well as at the conferences I frequently attended, such as the European Association for the Study of Religions. However, two conversations stand out in particular. First, there was my conversation with Nancy Nason-Clark at the 2017 meeting of the Society for the Scientific Study of Religion, in Washington,

Acknowledgements xi

D.C. Second there was my conversation with Linda Woodhead in Las Vegas at the 2018 meeting of the SSSR. Both conversations were full of scholarly wisdom and energised me, particularly during the data analysis stage of my work. I would also like to express my appreciation to Nancy for agreeing to write the foreword for this monograph. On a similar note, I would like to thank Abby Day, Robin Gill, and Mandy Robbins for their endorsements, particularly for taking time out to read and write about the monograph when there are many demands on their time.

Of course, there are many beyond my professional sphere who have provided all kinds of support during the research and the writing of this monograph. First and foremost, I would like to thank my wife, Helen Colpus-Fry, who I was so incredibly fortunate to meet during my time as a doctoral student. With her own background in sociological study, Helen's interest, encouragement and, perhaps most importantly of all, grounded outlook have been of paramount importance to me. This book is dedicated to her.

I would also like to thank my parents, Kevin and Caroline Fry, for all their support during my education. It was their financial support during my undergraduate and taught postgraduate degrees that allowed me to pursue my intellectual interests in religion and the big questions of this world. As if that was not enough, they were more than happy for me to continue using the family home as a base (free of charge) when undertaking fieldwork, and also provided me with access to a car, which allowed me to travel freely for participant interviews.

I would like to thank those friends who have taken an interest in this work. I would especially like to thank Mark Povey, who has his own interests in the social sciences, for asking thought-provoking questions in the writing of the monograph, and Mike White for reading over an early draft of the introduction and offering comments on its writing style from the perspective of someone beyond the world of academia.

This research was generously funded by: the St Luke's College Foundation; the Barry Scholarship in Divinity (Durham University); the Foundation of St Matthias; the Whitecourt Charitable Trust; the Latimer Trust; and the St Hild and St Bede Trust. I am incredibly grateful for these grants as well as for the travel grants received during my research for travel, awarded by the Society for the Scientific Study of Religion, St John's College, Durham, and the Faculty of Arts and Humanities, Durham University.

Foreword

During the 2017 annual meeting of the Society for the Scientific Study of Religion, held in Washington, D.C., Alex Fry and I sat down to discuss his passion for understanding the debate on the ordination of women to the priesthood in the Church of England, and the clergy who find themselves scattered along the continuum of attitudes towards it.

Since then, he has put words into action and crafted a convincing and compelling series of arguments as to why resistance to the ordination of women to the priesthood and episcopate persists despite legislative changes within the Church of England that permit women's ordination and the example of many ordained women currently ministering in parishes across England and indeed around the world.

Over 40 years ago, I completed a PhD at the London School of Economics and Political Science where I analyzed the experiences and opinions of clergy towards the ministry and ordination of women, a time when the debates within the Church of England were raging. At that point in history, social scientists studying religion were in the early days of trying to disentangle the rhetoric from the reality surrounding the debate, to focus attention on ordinary priests and pastors, not solely on those whose reactions seemed at times bordering on the hysterical, and to understand why so much emotion, angst, and anger was expressed toward women who felt a call of God on their lives and towards others (both men and women) who were desirous of walking alongside them on their ministry journey. All of these years later, questions still remain.

Alex Fry helps us to tease apart this persistent issue, involving both beliefs and practices, from a broad angle and multiple perspectives. His analysis is replete with theological, historical, and social psychological theories and contexts which he ever so skillfully interweaves within a sociological framework and grassroots fieldwork.

I invite you to read this book with an expectation that it will challenge some of your preconceived notions about those priests and pastors who persist in perpetuating ideas about sex and gender that thwart action in response to a call of God on the lives of women seeking ordained priesthood.

I trust his book will receive wide attention, thoughtful consideration, and perhaps, even, lead to changed actions and attitudes.

Nancy Nason-Clark, PhD, FRSC
Professor Emerita
Department of Sociology
University of New Brunswick
Fredericton, NB, Canada

Preface

The question of why people believe what they do and behave as they do is highly salient, especially when these beliefs and behaviours concern religion. Historians and sociologists have argued that during the second half of the twentieth century, historical Christian beliefs and practices declined in the UK. A worldview that was once taken for granted is no longer so. Scholars have attributed this to the poststructuralist turn, where the individual possesses greater autonomy in the formation of their identity than was previously the case. It is also widely acknowledged that this has been accompanied by globalisation, exposing individuals to ways of understanding the world that are prominent in other countries and indeed continents.

A persistent controversy in this milieu concerns the rights of women. Although the question of gender (in)equality has by no means been confined to discussions of religion, religious groups, networks, and organisations have nevertheless been frequently implicated in it. This is true of both religious traditions that have had a clear historical presence in the UK and those that have had a smaller (even if growing) presence. The Church of England has found itself caught up in such debates, particularly since the rise of the so-called second wave of feminism, which emerged before the Church's decisions to ordain women as deacons and priests and to consecrate them as bishops. Many within and without the Church of England have struggled to understand why it has been slow to afford women the same opportunities within its hierarchy as men and to understand why some within the Church still resist such developments.

Those who oppose the ordination of women and their consecration as bishops regularly make theological claims to support their stance. I was previously an undergraduate student of Theology & Religion at the University of Manchester and a taught postgraduate student of the same at King's College London. During my studies, I came to realise that individuals could explore the same theological sources—not least those employed in debates about gender roles in religious contexts—and sometimes even utilise the same or similar interpretive methods but reach quite different conclusions about their meaning or applications for the Church in the present. I also noted that where differences of opinion occurred, they were often between those of different

Preface xv

traditions, perhaps sometimes owing to the fact that the makeup of my peer groups was international. However, even between those immersed in religious traditions common in the UK, clear differences of opinion existed when interpreting theological sources.

It is this realisation that has led me to ask what difference social context makes to one's stance on the role of women within the local church and denominational hierarchies. Although the insight that social factors come to shape our religious beliefs is hardly a novel idea, research that specifically and systematically explores the influences on those who oppose women's ordination has been lacking in recent years, despite the recent historic development of the Church of England's first women bishops and continued controversies surrounding the Church and gender inequality. I therefore embarked upon doctoral study at the Durham University to address this gap in knowledge and it is my PhD dissertation that has led to this monograph, in which I have developed and expanded my doctoral research.

I have sought to offer a detailed account of the various strands of social factors that collectively shape gender attitudes amongst male clergy from theologically conservative traditions within the Church of England. This, I hope, has meant resisting overly simplistic claims, particularly those that caricature and 'other' human beings, including those who possess outlooks that I disagree with. Therefore, the chapters that follow contain information that is best read alongside that which is presented in the other chapters, as the chapters often build upon each other to offer a more nuanced and textured account of clergy gender attitudes and their formation.

It is also my hope that the analysis and implications provided in the subsequent pages will prove useful to both academia and the Church, not least the Church of England. With regards to the former, I have sought to show how interdisciplinary social scientific study that integrates complementary theoretical lenses can lead to higher levels of explanatory power and provide a highly nuanced account of gender attitude formation that requires engagement with different bodies of knowledge. With regards to the latter, I have sought to show that how one interprets biblical texts and Church tradition about women is not simply a matter of fidelity (whether to text or tradition) but is significantly shaped by a plurality of social factors. At an individual level, this ought to lead to greater reflection on the origins of our beliefs and practices on the matter of gender roles and the holding of Church offices. At an institutional level, this should lead to revised practices regarding the ordaining and consecrating of women clergy and the provisions currently in place for those who oppose this.

I am aware that, as I write these words, the Church of England has recently assembled a new standing commission. This commission will consider the arrangements introduced when women were first permitted to become bishops in 2014, including those designed to appease factions opposed to this development. I have provided much evidence that the current state of affairs is highly problematic. Although many of the attitudes outlined may not surprise those who have been on their receiving end, I trust it will be useful to have identified multiple sources of such experiences and equally as useful to suggest a way forward for effectively addressing these attitudes, one that is rooted in evidence provided by those who hold them.

Alex D. J. Fry, PhD, AKC, FHEA
Bournemouth University
June 2023

1 Introduction

Introduction

Amongst the English population, gender attitudes are not exactly homogenous. In England, traditional stereotypes that rely on distinct spheres for men and women often sit alongside ideals that reject such binaries. However, in recent years, there have been several high-profile events that, although sometimes anecdotal, are testament to an assumed value of gender equality. For instance, the 2010 Equality Act consolidated and expanded on legislation dating back to the 1970s, to prevent discrimination against women (Legislation, 2010). Another example was seen in 2014 when Members of Parliament (MPs) and celebrities donned t-shirts with the slogan "This is what a feminist looks like" as part of a national campaign to promote women's rights. Then in 2017, the gender pay gap between presenters working for the British Broadcasting Corporation (BBC) came to light, leading to increased demand for employers to publish the pay gaps between the men and women that they employ.

In this respect, the UK context echoes wider European priorities where the concept of human equality has been intrinsic to the European Union (EU) since its founding. In 2006, the European Institute for Gender Equality was formed with the sole remit of establishing gender equality throughout its member states (European Union, 2006). It compares the levels of gender equality across Europe with the Gender Equality Index. In 2019, the UK ranked fifth out of the (then) 28 EU member states, based on an assessment of measures such as access to healthcare, education, occupation, and income (European Institute for Gender Equality, 2020).

However, there is a paradox. For half a millennium, the Church of England (CofE) has been the Established Church in England, meaning that it is formally recognised by the Government of the United Kingdom as a national institution and is supported by the civic authority. In particular, the House of Lords—the upper chamber in the Houses of Parliament—has up to 26 bishops at any one time, who contribute to legislative processes. Monarchs must also be consecrated by the leading cleric in the CofE, the Archbishop of Canterbury, and the CofE receives tax breaks for its historic buildings. In other words, the Established Church enjoys a privileged position within England's national life.[1]

DOI: 10.4324/9781003081913-1

2 Introduction

Why is this paradoxical? The CofE has historically prevented women from entering its ordained ranks. Whilst it does now allow women to be ordained, it does not allow them to be so on the same terms as men because there are still factions of the Church that oppose this development (see Fry, 2021a, 2021b). To put this another way, England's Established Church enjoys a privileged position despite neglecting to reflect the country's assumed value of gender equality. This paradox is problematic for several reasons.

Firstly, as the Established Church, the CofE exists to provide pastoral care for all who reside in England. However, there is an evident disparity between the Church and much of wider society on a matter that is typically understood as fundamental to people's identity. This undermines the Church's ability to offer pastoral care effectively. Secondly, there has been a steady decline in the number of people affiliated with the CofE since the arrival of (what is often called) second-wave feminism (Day, 2017).[2] This has been attributed—amongst other things—to the dissonance between women who are experiencing new opportunities in the public domain and the historically socially conservative CofE, whose engagement with questions of gender equality has lagged behind those of the English people as a whole. In other words, the Church's actions on this matter have contributed to its failure to represent the beliefs of the English population (Brown and Woodhead, 2016). Thirdly, as a religious organisation, it is exempt from gender equality legislation that is imposed on many other national institutions within the country (Maltby, 1998). Were the CofE not established as a national institution, this would be less problematic. As it stands, however, the Church is not held to the same standards of equality as other national institutions.

There exists another paradox. Women make up a larger percentage of the churchgoing population than men in the UK (Hackett et al., 2016). Recent figures also indicate that more women than men are choosing to affirm their faith by receiving the rite (i.e., religious ceremony) of Confirmation[3] in the CofE (Research and Statistics, 2019). The UK Office for National Statistics (2013) also reports that between 2001 and 2011, women in most age brackets were more religious than men. These phenomena are curious and counter-intuitive and so highlight the need to better understand the gender attitudes of those within the Church. This monograph has been written to offer detailed insight into just that. Before I expand on this, a greater appreciation of the current state of affairs will be instructive. This can be achieved through understanding how the CofE functions, the development of its stance on questions of gender, and the opportunities it provides for women within its ordained structures.

The structure and make-up of the CofE

In addition to being established, the CofE is also an episcopal church. This means that it is hierarchical, consisting of deacon, priest, and bishop. The term 'episcopal' derives from the ancient Greek word ἐπισκοπή, used in the

New Testament, and may be translated as 'overseer'. Within the three-fold ministry of the CofE, a deacon is normally someone in their first year of ordained ministry, preparing for the priesthood. In this sense, it is the lowest rung in the ordained hierarchy. Deacons are servants with a particular remit to meet the needs of vulnerable members in the communities they are sent to serve. All priests start their ordained life as deacons.

Whilst pre-Reformation language is used to denote the position of priesthood, in Anglican usage it refers to the role of the early Church's πρεσβύτερος or presbyter. The priest is the Church's representative to God and to society. They proclaim the Christian faith in the communities that they serve. After a deacon is ordained priest, they often continue in their current post—as assistant curates[4]—under the oversight of a more experienced priest for a further two to three years as they continue their ministerial training. However, after this period, they often go on to lead their own churches as incumbents[5] or become chaplains in a variety of contexts. A key distinction between deacon and priest is that the latter presides at the altar to consecrate the bread and wine used in the Eucharist.[6] A bishop is the most senior clergyperson in a diocese[7] and is responsible for overseeing the churches under their care. This includes pastoral oversight of the clergy and playing an authoritative role in directing the Church's ministry, including licensing clergy to parishes and, where appropriate, discipline (Church of England Glossary, 2018a).

The CofE is theologically diverse. Whilst it can be overly simplistic to define its various traditions too exactly, studies indicate that many clergy and laity (i.e., non-ordained persons) do identify with particular subsets of Anglicanism. For example, Village (2013) refers to the CofE as constituting evangelicals, Anglo-Catholics, and those who are broad church, a description that has benefited from empirical weight (see Francis, Robbins and Astley, 2005). However, even within these traditions, there is diversity. The evangelical tradition is often understood to consist of those Christians who believe in: (i) the exclusive authority of the Bible; (ii) the need for personal conversion; (iii) Jesus' death on the cross to bear the guilt of sinful humanity; and (iv) social activism, as key components of faith (Bebbington, 1989). Charismatic expressions of evangelicalism emerged in some quarters during the twentieth century. They have been well documented as has the liberal/ conservative divide that emerged within the evangelical tradition during this period (see e.g., Bebbington, 1989).

The charismatic movement has also found expression in Anglo-Catholicism (Maiden, 2018). The Anglo-Catholic tradition has been described as possessing an "antipathy" towards women priests (Church of England Glossary, 2018b). However, it can be divided between traditional and liberal catholics. Traditional catholics emerged as the result of the Oxford Movement and are theologically more inclined to incorporate traditional Roman Catholic theology into their own thinking. Liberal catholics emerged in the twentieth century, are more affirming of women's ordination, and stress the need for

4   *Introduction*

theological reflection on the contemporary implications of Roman Catholic teaching (Furlong, 2000).

The broad church tradition is often referred to as the central tradition (Hylson-Smith, 1993) or the via media (the middle way). It can be situated somewhere between the catholic and evangelical wings of the CofE (McGrath, 1993). It developed as a reaction to the introduction of Anglo-Catholicism during the nineteenth century (Chadwick, 1972), and those situated within this tradition have typically been affirming of women's ordained ministry (see Nason-Clark, 1987a).

Opponents of women's ordination tend to be situated in either conservative evangelicalism or traditional Anglo-Catholicism. Whilst those who usually disagree with the ordination of women tend not to oppose their entry into the diaconate (i.e., ordination as deacons), there are mixed views over what other roles are (in)appropriate for women to hold. For example, evangelicals who possess more traditional theologies of gender roles may not oppose the ordination of women as priests per se. Rather, they may disagree that it is appropriate for a woman to lead a church as an incumbent or become a bishop because they believe that Judeo-Christian scripture prohibits women from teaching or leading men in a church context.

For such persons, it may be acceptable for women to be priests on the proviso that they are chaplains in contexts that do not require them to preach to men. Opposition to women's ordination within this tradition, therefore, stems from the fact that most women are ordained in the CofE on the assumption that they will lead churches and/or preach to men. By way of contrast, traditional catholics within the CofE may have no objection to women teaching or leading men. Instead, they might object to a woman presiding at Communion and so take issue with the priesting of women because standing in the place of the male Christ at the altar is thought to be an intrinsic part of priesthood, as is the administration of other sacraments.[8] It is within this institutional context that debates concerning the appropriate roles for men and women within the Church, the family unit, and wider society have emerged.

The development of women's ordination

When charting the development of women's ordination within the CofE, the most appropriate place to start is the introduction of women deaconesses because this was the first formalised office that women could hold. The idea of the deaconess came to the fore in the latter half of the nineteenth century over concerns that the Established Church was failing to engage the working class. At that time, the Church believed that it was necessary to introduce an additional order into the hierarchy to include the working class more fully into the life of the CofE. However, because this was thought to require a less educated cohort of ministers, members of the clergy were concerned that the introduction of permanent deacons would compromise the social status of the clergy (Young, 2015).

Introduction 5

The solution was to introduce an "inferior office" (Young, 2015, p. 66) as it was called by some of the clergy, culminating in the introduction of a fourth order, namely that of the deaconess in 1862. A deaconess' role was more limited than that of a male deacon. The former could lead worship services, offer pastoral care, teach the Christian faith, and prepare devotees for receiving sacraments such as baptism[9] or Communion, but only under the oversight of a male priest (Young, 2015).

The next significant step towards the ordination of women was in 1975 when the CofE's governing body, the General Synod,[10] passed a motion stating that there was no fundamental objection to ordaining women as priests (Barticioti, 2016). However, attempts to pass a motion for ordaining women were unsuccessful and it was not until 1987 when women could first be ordained as permanent deacons. It was then an additional five years before the General Synod approved the ordination of women to the priesthood (Francis and Robbins, 1999). As a result of the 1992 Synod, nearly four hundred dissenting priests left the CofE (Goodchild, 2002). However, no provisions were made for women to become bishops at that time, and male clergy were able to resist women's ordination by refusing to be ordained by a bishop who also ordained women. Congregations that opposed women's ordination as priests were also permitted to pass 'resolutions', which prohibited women from either presiding at Communion or becoming their incumbent (Maltby, 1998).

It was not until 2012 that the General Synod voted on whether to consecrate women as bishops, but the motion failed to win a majority in the House of Laity. The motion was then brought back to the Synod in 2014 and won the necessary two-thirds majority in each of the houses (Brown, 2014). However, provisions were put in place for priests who do not accept the authority of a woman bishop. Such clergy can elect to go under the episcopal oversight of a gender traditionalist (male) bishop, who believes that men and women ought to occupy traditional gender roles, particularly in the Church. At present, there are approximately 20,000 active clergy in the CofE, but only 33% are female. With respect to stipendiary (i.e., paid) clergy, only 32% are female (Research & Statistics, 2020). At the time of writing, there are 27 women bishops in the CofE and 80 male bishops and archbishops, with other bishop posts currently vacant.[11]

Developments in research

Much research on the subject is at least 25 years old and was published during the debates surrounding ordaining women to the diaconate and the priesthood. Many of the clergy partaking in these studies were men and women could only be deaconesses or deacons at that time (e.g., see Nason-Clark, 1984). Research argued that clergy attitudes towards women could be understood as sexist and that newly ordained women (beyond the CofE) were facing challenging barriers within their own institutions (Nason-Clark, 1987a, 1987b).

6   Introduction

Other research charted the submission of women within the CofE and argued that the introduction of a distinctive diaconate for women is evidence of their subjugation within the Established Church, not least because, at this point, they were not permitted to become priests. It also concluded that, whilst the majority of clergy were in favour of the ordination of women, they possessed much power over the future of the women who might later become priests, even though these men would not be practically impacted by such changes. It is therefore unsurprising that women deacons viewed themselves as being in a struggle against male power in a male-dominated institution (Aldridge, 1987, 1989, 1992).

It was also posited that Anglican clergy understood themselves as having inherited elite status through their ordination and so possessed high levels of social status because of their ancient profession (Aldridge, 1993). However, whilst these insights provided useful information at the time, significantly shaping the course of research on the CofE, much has changed since then, despite gender inequality persisting within society. The CofE now has women occupying all three levels of its ordained hierarchy and their roles in the occupational sphere have also grown since that time. Social scientific understandings of sexism have also developed significantly and theories not previously available have since evinced their utility as effective analytical tools in related areas of research.

Research since then has explored the impact of women's ordination. For instance, female clergy reported the barriers that they had to overcome in the pursuit of their priestly ministries, including issues surrounding inclusive language, roles and responsibilities, and their happiness with the Church's handling of women's ordination (Francis and Robbins, 1999). Later research explored how clergy attitudes towards women's ordination had changed ten years after the General Synod approved the motion to ordain women as priests, positing that no substantial change had occurred (Jones, 2004). It has also explored the possibility of whether one's social identity leads to opposition to women's ordination (Sani and Reicher, 1999, 2000).

More recent studies have explored how women priests navigate motherhood and clergy dress, and how clergy husbands (in opposite-sex marriages) inhabit a gendered privilege not afforded to clergy wives (Page, 2010, 2014, 2017). Other researchers have also explored the experiences of women priests in relatively recent years (Bagilhole, 2003, 2006; Greene and Robbins, 2015; Robbins and Greene, 2018). However, these more recent works, whilst providing useful insight into gender concerns within the Church, do not systematically review the current gender values of the clergy or the attitudes they hold towards women.

Given the amount of social change that has occurred since most of this research was undertaken, an assessment of clergy attitudes is long overdue. Whilst some of the earlier studies explored clergy attitudes towards the advent of women's ordination, there have been very few studies that have sought to understand the social psychological factors that lie behind these attitudes, nor the broader socio-historical context in which they have been formed. Many of those that do have not been published recently and leave the evangelical tradition unexplored (e.g., see Sani and Reicher, 2000). At present, however, it is this tradition that is the most resistant to Anglican decline (Brierley, 2018), meaning that its share of English Anglicans is becoming larger.

The CofE remains a male-dominated institution, where men occupy most of its senior positions. It is therefore particularly surprising that no extended efforts have been made to gauge what lies behind their objections to, or affirmations of, women's ordination in recent years. That men have had the power to prohibit or permit women to have a place in the hierarchy of the Established Church (see Aldridge, 1989) ought to make such enquiry a priority.

Aims of this monograph

There remains comparatively little research that has sought to understand why traditionalist gender values remain in the CofE. There is also a lack of research that has sought to specifically understand whether the historic introduction of women to the Church's most senior positions and changing gender norms within English society have had an impact on gender attitudes within the Established Church. In this monograph, I address this lack by offering an up-to-date analysis of how gender attitudes in the CofE are being shaped by a variety of social phenomena. In doing so, the contours of the debate concerning gender within the CofE will become significantly widened, offering a detailed and interdisciplinary social scientific perspective. Consequently, it will provide an analysis with convincing levels of explanatory power.

Attitudes and values

First, though, a brief note on definitions will be instructive. Thus far I have referred to gender attitudes and gender values. Attitudes have been a significant area of study within social psychology. They can be defined as an evaluation of something (or someone) that can range from extremely positive to extremely negative (Wood, 2000). Individuals can also possess ambivalent attitudes towards a phenomenon (Wood, 2000). Attitudes have three components, namely belief, emotion, and behavioural intention (Carlson, Martin and Buskist, 2000); the last of these can also impact behaviour (Krosnick and Petty, 1995).

The concept of values has been debated amongst social scientists and has suffered from various shortcomings (see Martin and Lembo, 2020). They are often thought to be more abstract ideas and ideals and so are not necessarily reflected in people's behaviour (Hitlin and Piliavin, 2004). That there is currently little research on "the processes through which values operate within and across interactions" (Hitlin and Piliavin, 2004, p. 362) indicates

8 Introduction

that the concept is of limited use for the present purpose. This is because participants' data includes a combination of speech (including reports of behaviour) and observation as they relate to institutions and group dynamics.[12]

This monograph is concerned with a range of facets related to gender exhibited by those within the Established Church.[13] The focus will be on gender attitudes because this well-evidenced concept encompasses important aspects of values as typically understood, whilst providing more convincing levels of explanatory power for the data. It encompasses the broad phenomenon of belief, which is not limited to the notion of a value, but nonetheless includes it in the context of this study, as participants articulated theological beliefs that demanded adherence to certain ideals. Such adherence has behavioural implications for my participants, making attitudes the more appropriate area of analysis. Nevertheless, when discussing gender attitudes, I will inevitably be touching on values. Likewise, when discussing values, I will be touching on the belief component of attitudes. It will also be necessary at times to discuss gender values held by different groups to assess the gender attitudes held by my participants.

I will identify historical, sociological, and social psychological factors that shape (i.e., contribute to) the attitudes held by those within the CofE through an in-depth and systematic review. The focus of this monograph will be on the gender attitudes of men because: (i) there has been a particular absence of studies on male gender attitudes in the Established Church in recent years; and (ii) men have much influence over the lived realities of women within the CofE. I will focus on those held by ordained men within the Church given that: (i) it is male clergy more so than male laity that steers the CofE's position on women's ordination (two of the three houses in the General Synod are made up of clergy); and (ii) it is clergy who are more directly impacted by the recent decision to consecrate women as bishops, as they are responsible to their bishop, who influences the culture of the diocese they work in.

More specifically, I will explore the gender attitudes of those within the evangelical and Anglo-Catholic traditions. It is most often clergy within these traditions who hold gender values that are at odds with those of wider English society. If one is to better understand why these differences exist, it is necessary to focus on clergy within these branches of the Established Church. Whilst the evangelical tradition is broad, exhibiting a great diversity of expressions (e.g., see Steensland and Goff, 2014), the conservative evangelical tradition has been particularly resistant to women's ordination within the CofE (e.g., see Jones, 2004). It maintains this stance today and so this monograph reports research conducted amongst this tradition. By way of contrast, the charismatic evangelical tradition is typically conservative, yet historically comparatively less traditionalist on the matter of women's ministry (Guest, Olson and Wolffe, 2012). Hence, the gender attitudes held by clergy within this tradition will also be explored to offer a comparison between two evangelicalisms. This will afford greater depth and nuance.

Sex and gender

Debates over the ordination of women within the CofE have typically assumed that males and females are biologically clear and distinct categories. It is therefore unsurprising that the data gathered for analysis in this monograph contain the assumption that the nature of the traditional biological categories of 'man' and 'woman' as binary sexes are self-evident, even when assumptions about gender are more flexible.[14] There was no consideration amongst my participants of those who do not biologically fit into such a binary and rarely of those who are not cisgender. When I discuss gender attitudes, therefore, I am specifically concerned with the attitudes that the clergy interviewed have towards adult males ('men') and adult females ('women') who fit the traditional mould, with respect to the roles that participants feel adult males and females ought to occupy within society. I am not exploring attitudes towards persons who are intersex or who do not possess a cisgender identity. This means that when I discuss sex-related prejudice (i.e., sexism), I refer specifically to attitudes towards those who fit within the male–female binary but will focus on prejudicial attitudes towards women. This will be unpacked further in the third chapter. Having already anticipated methodological considerations through a discussion of this monograph's scope, I will now offer more detail on the methodological underpinnings and assumptions that lie behind this project.

Methodology

Participant selection

I have already outlined the traditions that will be studied in this monograph. However, there is more to discuss on this front. Firstly, there is the matter of participant selection. I opted to conduct the research in a single diocese to achieve representative results, given that participants would be exposed to the same regional culture. I settled on a particular diocese because it had a mixture of urban, suburban, and rural areas, meaning that interviews would be conducted in a context that was more representative of the CofE as a whole. For this reason, I also opted for a diocese that had the breadth of Anglican traditions. It was also chosen because of its perceived liberal theological positioning. The diocese has had a succession of bishops whose theology has been thought of as contrary to historically orthodox (i.e., traditionally accepted) teaching. The diocese is also typically understood to embody this. It was thought that this diocese would thus provide the necessary context to more clearly see how theologically conservative male clergy think and behave in an environment that has a distinct theological culture to their own. In this sense, it mirrors the fact that gender traditionalists in the CofE are operating in a denomination that has distinct gender values to their own.

With respect to conservative evangelicalism, I decided to study a group called Reform.[15] This is because it emerged partly in protest to women's

10 *Introduction*

ordination to the priesthood, in 1993 (Jones, 2004). The majority of those interviewed in this group who reflected on their tradition self-identified as 'conservative evangelical'. This is also the term employed by scholarship to refer to the evangelicalism that has resisted women's ordination (e.g., see Bebbington, 1989). Members of this group were initially contacted through the Chair of the Reform group in the diocese and then through recommendations from those who became participants. In total 14 partook in this research, one of whom was not formally a member but was active within the group whilst considering membership.

The largest established charismatic evangelical group within the CofE is a loose network of affiliated members called New Wine. Participants in this tradition were initially sought through their church's membership of this network and then through recommendations from participants. A total of 14 participants accepted invitations to contribute to the study. Whilst this group had some affiliation with charismatic evangelicalism, the majority reported that their churchmanship had become broader over time, incorporating elements of other traditions into their own theology and religious practices.

Traditional Anglo-Catholic participants were initially invited to contribute to the research based on their membership of Forward in Faith. This group was established in protest to the ordination of women as priests and based its theological objections on Roman Catholic theology of ordination. Additional Anglo-Catholics without membership of this group were contacted on the recommendations of those who accepted my initial invitation. A total of 13 participants within this tradition have informed the research in this monograph, six of whom were members of Forward in Faith.

All the names used throughout are pseudonyms. The name of the diocese also remains undisclosed for the purposes of research ethics, as are the specific churches that the clergy belonged to. This process ensured a level of candour amongst those taking part, as will be evinced by the data analysed in subsequent chapters. The participants varied significantly in age, the youngest being in their 30s and the oldest in their 80s. The quotations selected for analysis in the coming chapters were chosen because, unless otherwise stated, they were representative of their respective group, allowing me to explore the attitudes common within each group.

Data collection and analysis

Semi-structured interviews were conducted one-to-one and lasted a modal average of 75 minutes. The questions I asked were designed to discuss four main aspects of participants' lives. First, I asked them to provide some information on their family upbringing before describing the period of their lives when they first felt a vocation to ordination. Second, I asked participants about their time in ordination training. Third, there were questions designed to understand their theological positions and their attitudes on a range of topics related to gender and sex. Finally, I asked those interviewed to discuss their experiences of working with others in the CofE who were from different traditions to them and about their engagement with their local communities. Interviews were supplemented with structured observations, such as attendance at church services when invited by my participants. They were also supplemented through ethnographic observations, such as noting the books that participants had in their studies. I then asked further questions in light of these observations.

Such qualitative methods possess the ability to capture participants' subjective interpretations of the questions asked and nuances in their answers (see Burman, 1994). Questions were designed to be open-ended, and space was given to allow for unplanned follow-up questions, whether for clarity or to capture greater detail. In doing so, my own influence on the research process was reduced. To achieve data saturation, I kept interviewing participants from each group until I found that the same ideas were being repeated in participants' answers and new data failed to provide additional information (see Grady, 1998).

Thematic narrative analysis was employed to interpret the data. Narrative analysis has been adopted for two reasons. Firstly, all human beings construct narratives to make sense of the world around them and of their life experiences (Riessman, 2005). Secondly, the narratives people construct aid one to find sequential relationships in their life experiences (Bryan, 2016). Thus, if one's life experiences shape their attitudes towards gender—as I will be assuming—an examination of participants' narratives more readily enables me to understand the factors that shape their gender attitudes. To achieve this, the questions asked concerned different stages in my participants' lives as they related to their faith and vocation to ordination, in chronological order.

I employed a *thematic* narrative analysis because it possesses the efficacy to help one identify themes across a data set (Braun and Clarke, n.d., para. 5; Braun and Clarke, 2006), enabling me to find similarities in each group of participants. This is precisely what is required in this study because I interviewed individuals of shared religious traditions to understand the factors that have shaped the gender attitudes of each group as a whole. This approach also enabled me to more sharply identify differences between the traditions explored. This provides a more panoramic understanding of gender attitudes across the three traditions, highlighting the diversity that exists amongst theologically conservative traditions within the CofE. I have also adopted an inductive approach, applying any interpretive lens to the data after it had been collected. This has allowed for an interpretation of the data that more naturally fits it, rather than steering the results to fit a specific theory (see Clarke, Braun and Hayfield, 2015).

Coding of the interview data occurred in two phases (see Saldaña, 2009). First, I employed descriptive coding, summarising the data using language

12   *Introduction*

found within the transcripts. This limited the extent to which I imposed meaning onto participants' data because it is labelled using their own choice of language. Second, I employed pattern coding, grouping data that was conceptually related even when the language was not identical. This was to identify relationships between different codes that were not immediately obvious through descriptive coding. I also employed focused coding, identifying the most common codes. Themes were identified by grouping relevant codes together. By identifying the most common codes, the most prominent themes became apparent. I also took notes during the structured observations to record what I observed. These were analysed using process coding to capture actions, before employing pattern and focused coding. I then identified themes as with the interview data.

Epistemology

I adopt a critical realist outlook; I believe that one interacts with phenomena that exist independently of the one perceiving them, given that the social world is not merely a construction. Equally, I affirm the insight of poststructuralism—that one engages with the world exterior to oneself through a process of interpretation (see Sayer, 2000). Critical realism therefore strikes the balance between a reflexive acceptance of subjectivity and an awareness that one is attempting to explore a world that exists beyond their perceptions.

I am conscious of the Marxist heritage of this epistemology, where social scientific investigation can have moral implications beyond its findings because of its ability to question normative assumptions and highlight systemic inequalities (see Bhaskar and Collier, 1998; Wright, 2013). It is because of this, and the results of the analysis presented in subsequent chapters, that I adopt a feminist outlook in these pages. Much of the data explored in this monograph highlights not only the structural inequality that exists for women within the CofE but also the prejudicial attitudes that male clergy can hold towards them. This monograph will thus offer a series of solutions for more effectively addressing prejudice towards women within the CofE.[16]

However, feminism has no single definition, and many have considered the different understandings of it that exist (e.g., see Page, 2010). I largely share Page's approach to feminism, which recognises the utility of a plurality of feminist approaches whilst resisting essentialism, but with one caveat. I agree with the poststructuralist critiques of positivist (and therefore essentialist) attitudes towards gender that Page and many others discuss, and I recognise the emancipatory possibilities of poststructuralist approaches to gender. I would nonetheless emphasise a biological component of bodies given my critical realist stance. That is, whilst I accept with Page and others that gender is indeed constructed, I would emphasise that there is nevertheless a physical body that exists beyond perception, even though: (i) the labels often used to describe this—such as 'man' and 'woman'—are constructed and need not always refer to categories of sex; (ii) gender and

Introduction 13

sex can be erroneously conflated, as I understand Page to imply (see also Cornwall, 2015); and (iii) our understanding of biology is shaped by cultural factors. My critical realism therefore means that when I discuss 'men' and 'women' in reference to adult males and females, I am not precluding other uses of these terms. To put it another way, the language of 'men' and 'women' though—and because they are—socially constructed, is intended to signpost beyond the language itself, to the referent—in this case to sex rather than to gender.

My own feminism led me to assume that some participants would hold views that preclude gender equality. To reduce the risk of projecting my own assumptions onto my participants, I asked them to clarify tradition-specific language and asked them questions related to their tradition, including when I believed I would know the answer. The feminist underpinning of this monograph is also informed by Storkey's (1985) approach, which seeks to identify sexism within the Church so that it may be challenged, to rid it of misogyny. Whilst some feminists do not believe that it is appropriate to provide airtime to sexist views as it risks legitimising them, I argue, in keeping with Storkey (1985), that if they are to be effectively addressed, it is important to understand them. Much research indicates that marginalising the beliefs of a social group risks fortifying such beliefs given that identities are regularly formed in opposition to other social groups (e.g., see Tajfel, 1974), making the complete silencing of problematic views counterproductive.

In keeping with the critical realist underpinning of this monograph, the stratification of reality is assumed. This is the idea that no single academic discipline has the efficacy to fully describe and explain the social (and natural) world, but that disciplines are inter-reliant (Seybold, 2007). Indeed, the social scientific methods employed in this monograph are not exhaustive and so it ought to be noted that the present research contributes to several of multiple segments that constitute the overall picture of social reality. The adoption of this model is appropriate for three reasons. Firstly, as Seybold demonstrates, it is necessary to draw on research in several areas to further understand a variety of phenomena. In this respect, the stratification of reality may be understood as a necessary description of academic research.

Secondly, it allows for the possibility of a theological segment because the model does not preclude the possibility of theological claims. This leaves open the possible validity of participants' worldview where God is present in human affairs. Therefore, the proceeding analysis does not simply reduce participants' beliefs into a series of predetermined attitudes, inevitably resulting from a series of social forces entirely beyond their control. Relatedly, as Hindess (1996) has argued, reductive approaches such as this do not inherently preclude agency even if—as Caldwell (2007) notes in relation to discourse analysis—it decentres the agent. Indeed, as has been noted in discussion of the sociologist Bourdieu, whilst one's environment undoubtedly influences one's behaviour, they nevertheless maintain a level of volition (Gallagher, 2003).

14 *Introduction*

This enables me to avoid an imbalance of power between myself and the participants because I do not claim that a reductive social scientific account of participants' attitudes possesses sole explanatory power. Rather, I employ methods and theories from the social sciences to highlight empirically observable phenomena as they relate to the gender attitudes of my participants, and in doing so produce knowledge in the social segment of their world that is rooted in the data they have provided. It is within these boundaries that this monograph's explanatory power will be evident.

Thirdly, by being honest about the intellectual limitations (as well as the intellectual efficacy) of this research, I am better placed to practice reflexivity and thus reduce my bias because I am more aware of the claims I can and cannot make from the analysis of the data.

Reflexivity

With respect to my religious identity, I identify as an Anglican in the 'liberal evangelical' tradition, the strand of evangelicalism that is more socially engaged, which has tended to reject traditionalist gender values, and which has engaged more thoroughly with historical-critical approaches to biblical texts (see Bebbington, 1989). I was originally raised in the Roman Catholic Church and as an undergraduate student in Theology and Religion, I became persuaded that the scholarly arguments in favour of a fully contextualised reading of scriptural passages that are often used to justify the prohibition of women ministers is the most appropriate (e.g., see Witherington III, 1987, 1990). I am therefore in support of women's ordination to any part of the CofE's hierarchy and have been a part of congregations with female clergy in addition to those whose clergy believe that women's ordination is inappropriate. These details are important because they present both opportunities and challenges with respect to undertaking social scientific research on religion and gender.

Concerning the opportunities, I came with an understanding of where many of the participants would locate themselves theologically with respect to the ordination of women. In most cases, this meant that I did not need to spend as much time acquainting myself with various points of view as I would otherwise have needed to. It also meant that I was able to relate to participants more effectively than would otherwise have been the case. This helped foster the apparent honesty present in participants' narratives.

With respect to the challenges, I was aware that I had expectations regarding what participants of each tradition would say, and so there was a risk that it would influence my interpretation of the data. This meant I needed to take care not to represent the narratives of those who hold more traditional views of gender in an inaccurate way, nor to conflate more liberal theologies with my own. However, the impact of these challenges was mitigated in a few ways. In addition to employing semi-structured interviews and asking participants about tradition-specific language, I read the transcripts four times and re-listened to the audio recordings, looking to find anything new or unexpected that could inform my analysis. I also utilised memos, tables, and diagrams to visualise the data and thus better identify the relationships between the narratives and a variety of possible theoretical lenses before selecting any.

Causality

The final methodological consideration pertains to causality. In this monograph, I explore the factors that shape theologically conservative male clergy attitudes towards gender. This requires an understanding of causation. As my approach is qualitative in design, I am unable to infer causes of participants' attitudes through quantitative analyses of correlations. Nevertheless, process theory is apposite to the task of exploring causation using qualitative data. Process theory deals with events and the processes that connect them; it analyses the causal processes by which an event influences another. It does so by focusing on the description of a series of events, allowing one to identify where an event flows into the next and is particularly suited to interview-based research (see Weiss, 1995). To identify causation in this regard, I sought continuities in attitudes and values within religious traditions over time. However, this approach ought to include identifying the social contexts and structures in which they are situated, paying attention to how these might foster the continuation of such attitudes and values. This would involve tracing historical attitudes and values that are also found within participants' narratives in addition to tracing the sequence of related events within their narratives.

It is worth explaining that the following analysis does not seek to identify every part of a sequence of events that leads to my participants' gender attitudes. Rather, I explore participants' narratives chronologically from defined points in their lives, specifically from their sense of call to CofE ministry to the present day. This is supplemented with background information relating to family and upbringing as these are typically formative contexts for what occurs later in life. I also explore the wider societal culture and the religious traditions that they were immersed in at formative times in their lives, usually since birth. These have precedents that are traceable historically to the present day. Discussion is limited to aspects of participants' lives, societal culture, and religious traditions that are most clearly related to their gender attitudes for the sake of relevance. Moreover, process theory need not imply that only isolated social factors shape gender attitudes. Multiple strands of inter-flowing events and experiences can converge in an individual's life to shape their attitudes.

One must avoid the possible pitfall of a post hoc ergo propter hoc claim, i.e., stating that because X preceded Y, X must have caused Y (Trzebiatowska, 2015). The approach taken in this monograph identifies continuities in events that show ongoing relationships between social phenomena rather than inferring causation from apparently discrete events. Nor does it preclude the

16 Introduction

presence of other shaping factors. In fact, the present approach also involves an exploration of the underlying psychological processes, as well as the social contexts and structures, that come to shape the relationship between related events and gender attitudes.

Therefore, the identification of causation is not a simplistic claim to have comprehensively uncovered cause and effect via straightforward correlations. Rather, it is the identification of multiple (perhaps non-exhaustive) factors that contribute to gender attitude formation. In this sense, it is the outworking of the stratification of reality model given that it recognises the multi-layered nature of the social world. Also, whereas quantitative studies assume that causation is perceived through regularities in associations of events—and in this respect are an outworking of positivism—qualitative approaches understand causation to be a matter of processes and causal mechanisms. These might well—but do not necessarily—produce regularities. This approach has its genesis in the insights of critical realism (Maxwell, 2004a). Hence, underlying all observable social phenomena are a series of processes and mechanisms that produce them.

It is because they produce observable behaviour that such processes and mechanisms can be identified (Maxwell, 2004a).[17] This understanding of causation highlights the importance of exploring specific manifestations of social phenomena as a window into understanding the factors that contribute to them. It has the advantage of understanding context as intrinsically involved in causal processes and recognises that mental events and processes can cause other observable social phenomena (Maxwell, 2004a) and so can be readily applied to an analysis of attitudes that include beliefs and where behavioural intention can produce behavioural outcomes. This outlook will also be helpful in addressing specific instances of sexism—by being able to identify its causes, one is better equipped to effectively challenge them.

Such an approach has been outlined and developed by Maxwell (2004a, 2004b). They identified several ways of utilising it. One such way is with rich data, data that comes from a range of different types of sources, and that offers a detailed, chronological description of social settings or events. In doing so it reveals "many of the causal processes taking place", including mental processes, which can be inferred from behaviour, including speech (Maxwell, 2004a, p. 254). This has been undertaken in the present research by utilising multiple methods for data collection and by focusing on participants' narratives chronologically in the analysis. Two significant advantages of this approach are that: (i) it makes it more difficult for the researcher to restrict their observations so that they only observe that which supports their assumptions; and (ii) it reduces the danger of respondent duplicity by making it more difficult to produce data that uniformly supports a mistaken conclusion (see Maxwell, 2004a).

A related approach, also adopted here, is narrative and connecting analysis. This involves looking for antecedents and consequences. It includes—what is sometimes called—ethnographic microanalysis, where one considers the entirely of an event, analytically breaks it down into smaller fragments and then recomposes it into a whole, returning it to a level of sequentially connected social actions (Maxwell, 2004a). I have done this by breaking data down into codes and then building them back up into themes to explore the development of participants' gender attitudes over time. This has involved identifying features that closely connect participants' experiences and gender attitudes. For instance, there are explicit statements that outline participants' engagement with the ideas of others from their traditions and the reported influence that these have had in the formation of their gender attitudes. I have also connected my participants' current attitudes with those found previously within their traditions.

Despite this, all claims of causation need to contend with validity threats and so I have incorporated three ways of doing so into my analysis (see Maxwell, 2004a). First, there is the modus operandi approach where alternative explanations are assessed. This was undertaken during the post-coding stage where I used memos, tables, and diagrams in assessing the most appropriate theoretical lenses. Second, there is searching for discrepant evidence and negative cases. Where relevant, I have noted when individual participants deviated from the group norm. When these deviations might be inconsistent with the theoretical lenses employed in discussions of causation, I have explored whether such lenses might provide an explanation for this that are also evinced in the data itself. This has ensured that they are able to account for all such instances. Third, there is triangulation, the collection of information from a variety of methods or diverse range of persons. Whilst each group did not have much in the way of diversity, they were representative of their traditions. Nevertheless, as aforementioned, semi-structured interviews were supplemented with structured observations and ethnographic observations. This facilitated increased opportunity to encounter and address any validity threats.

There is more to be stated regarding causation, as process theory does not deal with the question of human agency per se. As aforementioned, humans do possess a level of volition. There is a tension between social structures and social actors' own decisions. Swingewood (2000) draws on the thinking of Goffman to articulate his theory of tight coupling, where social structures narrow down the options of one's everyday interactions. This is not because human agents lack freedom, according to Swingewood, but because they opt into the social structures that bind groups together to serve their motives.

There are two significant advantages of this understanding. First, it foregrounds the role of human agency in an analysis that is primarily concerned with the social forces that shape human attitudes and which is therefore at risk of decentring social actors and their agency. By decentring human agency an important aspect of gender attitudes is neglected, namely, those that hold them. By keeping the human person more fully in the picture, tight coupling allows for a more complete analysis of the social world because it maintains the tension between the structures that shape human

18   *Introduction*

beliefs, behaviours, and emotions, and the agency that humans themselves have in relation to their attitudes. Second, it recognises that adopting religious belief systems, not least those that promote more conservative values and attitudes, whilst no doubt motivated by a variety of factors, can stem from their ability to meet multiple epistemic, existential, and relational needs (Fry, 2019; see also Jost et al., 2013; Kay et al., 2008). In this respect, it is an accurate explanation of why devotees occupy their religious spheres.

It is also relevant to tease something else out further. The presence of human agency does not necessarily imply that attitudes are entirely conscious. Much of the relevant literature in social psychology employed in the coming analysis understands gender attitudes to stem from unconscious processes. This means that, in addition to holding human agency in tension with the surrounding social structures that influence them, it is also necessary to hold it in tension with the fact that my participants' gender attitudes stem from processes that they will not necessarily be entirely aware of.

Throughout this monograph, I will unpack specific instances of participants' narratives, examining expressions of gender attitudes and the context within which they emerge. However, the analytical process described above enables me to identify where there exist clear commonalities within each group studied, allowing me to then discuss each group in a way that remains anchored in individuals' experiences whilst providing explanations for them that are identifiable amongst the group as a whole. This will include the influence of group membership. In doing so, the relevance that such explanations have beyond each individual participant will become apparent.

Additionally, the clear affinities that my participants' narratives have with bodies of knowledge based in large-scale quantitative studies will allow me to identify several contributory social psychological factors to their gender attitudes. This will be coupled with the ability to identify several historical and sociological factors that likewise shape these. Collectively, such an approach will develop understanding of the theories based on quantitative analysis by employing them qualitatively. The qualitative analysis will also help to explain some of the causal mechanisms identified by the quantitative literature by identifying factors that lead up to them. This will enable a fuller picture of the social world.

Chapter summaries

The next chapter will contain a historical overview of the main events in the twentieth and twenty-first centuries that have shaped the ordination of women debate within the CofE. This will have specific reference to the gender attitudes and values found within wider society and within various Christian traditions. It will enable me to draw out specific features of the three traditions being explored that come to bear upon the gender attitudes of current clergy in subsequent chapters. In the third chapter, I will explore the gender attitudes in terms of the beliefs articulated by my participants, which will be compared with the historical attitudes within evangelicalism and traditional Anglo-Catholicism. I will then interpret them in light of previous social psychological research on prejudice, particularly sexism, given that much of the data has significant parallels with these areas of knowledge.

In the fourth chapter, I shall build directly on the previous one as participants' beliefs about women priests will be further examined through an initial exploration of their emotions. I will also explore the psychological models of gender that participants possess before unpacking their intersecting identities. In the fifth chapter, I will build on the previous two by offering an analysis of the behaviours that participants report having with clergy outside of their own traditions. I will do this with reference to the theories of prejudice and sexism introduced in the third chapter.

I build on this in the sixth chapter as I explore my participants' gender attitudes through an assessment of the relationship between their behaviours and emotions. In particular, I will focus on the extent to which they engage with their wider institutional structures. This chapter shall contain a sociological analysis of social capital and spiritual capital to tease out the multi-layered nature of social interaction. This will lead to a further discussion on intersectionality, specifically the ways in which participants' interlocking identities relate to their attitudes. In the seventh chapter, I will contextualise the analysis of evangelicalism within the transatlantic context. I will also analyse traditional Anglo-Catholicism within the wider context of Roman Catholicism, to draw out the historical and current relationships that exist between the religious traditions of the CofE and their wider international expressions.

The penultimate chapter will contain a summary of the findings of the monograph so far. I will offer a theory of the social factors that shape clergy gender attitudes by reflecting on the theoretical frameworks that have been used to interpret the data. In doing so, I will integrate the different theoretical perspectives adopted throughout the monograph, reflecting upon how they complement each other, collectively providing greater explanatory power for understanding the factors that shape the participants' responses to the ordination of women as priests and their consecration as bishops within the CofE. It will also include a number of practical applications for the CofE so that it can more effectively tackle gender inequality. The final chapter will contain some directions for future research and provide some concluding sentiments alongside a more general theory on the process of gender attitude formation.

As many of the theories were born out of quantitative research, I will offer a methodological reflection on the implications of applying these qualitatively at the end of the relevant chapters (namely chapters 3–7) as well as weaving these strands together in the eighth chapter. As a number of these theories, though well established in other disciplines, are yet to find application in the social scientific study of religion, I shall outline the relevant aspects of each theory for the present purpose whenever they are introduced.

Notes

1 It is worth noting that the CofE/Anglicanism is only established in England and not in the remainder of the UK.
2 From the 1960s, 'second-wave' feminism furthered the rights of women by challenging the lack of opportunities for them outside of the domestic sphere, as well as their subservient place within the home, and it tended to take the binary understanding of the sexes as male or female for granted instead of questioning these categories (see Alsop, Fitzsimons and Lennon 2002; Fry, 2021a; Pilarski, 2011). I have noted the limits of adhering too strictly to the wave metaphor in discussions of feminism and signposted to other relevant work in this area elsewhere (see Fry, 2021a).
3 Confirmation is when an individual affirms the commitment to faith made at their baptism through a public declaration. A key part of the ceremony is when a bishop lays their hand on the person's head and prays for God to confirm the presence of the Holy Spirit within the individual.
4 Assistant curates are those who have ministerial responsibilities that support the role of a parish priest.
5 Incumbents are those priests with overall responsibility for a church or group of churches.
6 Also known as Communion, it is the receiving of bread and wine, commemorating the Last Supper before Jesus' crucifixion as portrayed in the New Testament gospels.
7 A diocese is a district with boundaries set by the Church.
8 Sacraments are sanctioned religious activities and, in Anglo-Catholic thought, provide God's grace for salvation.
9 A sacrament involving immersion in or sprinkling with water to symbolise entry into the Christian Church.
10 The General Synod consists of three houses, namely Bishops, Priests, and Laity.
11 Diocesan bishops are responsible for dioceses and are assisted by suffragan (i.e., assistant) bishops.
12 Martin and Lembo (2020) have argued that the concept of values ought to be replaced with that of interests. However, this idea does not yet benefit from the empirical weight provided by the concept of attitudes, which, as will be seen, is able to make good sense of the data explored in this monograph.
13 On the topic of definitions, it is also worth foregrounding the difference in my use of terms 'Church' and 'church'. The former refers to either the Church of England as an institution or to other types of Church institutions (e.g., the Lutheran Church). The latter refers to local churches—specific congregations. Participants regularly discussed both interchangeably.
14 I refer to 'sex' as the categories of male and female that are based on biological understandings of what constitutes these categories. However, this should not be taken as a denial of the fact that some persons are intersex. Rather, I focus on males and females because that is what participants discussed with me. Also for the reason of scope, I refer to 'gender' as socially constructed beliefs and assumptions about what it means to belong to a particular category of sex. However, the focus of my discussion does not to preclude the legitimacy of gender identities that do not conform to the binary model. Hence, these definitions are not intended to offer complete, universally applicable ontological statements but are selected as they map onto the data under analysis. See the section on epistemology for elaboration.
15 Since conducting this study, Reform has been amalgamated into the Church Society, which exists to provide a voice for conservative evangelicals within the CofE. I continue to refer to my participants as associated with Reform throughout this monograph, reflecting the context of the research and of participants' affiliations when it was conducted.

16 It is established ethical practice that research must be honest and avoid glossing the truth but also that negative depictions of participants ought only be included if they are relevant to research (Martin, 2017). Although noting that the presence of prejudicial attitudes means offering something of a negative depiction, this assessment is based on much empirical support (as will be seen in subsequent chapters) and is found in much of the data. Failure to report this would be a disingenuous omission of significant parts of the data gathered, particularly data that directly concerns the research topic.

17 Maxwell refers to the processes themselves as being observable rather than identifiable, but this needs nuancing when the primary method of data collection involves interviews where participants report events rather than the researcher being present for them.

References

Aldridge, A. (1987). In the absence of the minister: Structures of subordination in the role of deaconess in the Church of England. *Sociology*, *21*(3), 377–392.

Aldridge, A. (1989). Men, women, and clergymen: Opinion and authority in a sacred organization. *The Sociological Review*, *37*(1), 43–64.

Aldridge, A. (1992). Discourse on women in the clerical profession: The diaconate and language-games in the Church of England. *Sociology*, *26*(1), 45–57.

Aldridge, A. (1993). Negotiating status: Social scientists and Anglican clergy. *Journal of Contemporary Ethnography*, *22*(1), 97–112.

Alsop, R., Fitzsimons, A., & Lennon, K. (2002). *Theorizing gender: An introduction.* Cambridge: Polity.

Bagilhole, B. (2003). Prospects for change? Structural, cultural and action dimensions of the careers of pioneer women priests in the Church of England. *Gender, Work and Organization*, *10*(3), 361–377.

Bagilhole, B. (2006). Not a glass ceiling more a lead roof: Experiences of pioneer women priests in the Church of England. *Equal Opportunities International*, *25*(2), 109–125.

Barticioti, F. (2016, December 1). Archive for the movement of the ordination of women [Blog post]. *LSE History*. Retrieved from http://blogs.lse.ac.uk/lsehistory/2016/12/01/archive-of-the-movement-for-the-ordination-of-women/.

Bebbington, D.W. (1989). *Evangelicalism in modern Britain: A History from the 1730s to the 1980s*. London: Unwin Hyman.

Bhaskar, R., & Collier, A. (1998). Introduction: Explanatory critiques. In M. Archer, R. Bhaskar, A. Collier, T. Lawson, & A. Norrie (Eds.), *Critical realism: Essential readings* (pp. 385–394). London: Routledge.

Braun, V., & Clarke, V. (2006). Using thematic analysis in psychology. *Qualitative Research in Psychology*, *3*(2), 77–101.

Braun, V., & Clarke, V. (n.d.). Questions about thematic analysis. The University of Auckland. Retrieved from https://www.psych.auckland.ac.nz/en/about/our-research/research-groups/thematic-analysis/frequently-asked-questions-8.html.

Brierley, P.W. (2018). *UK Church statistics no. 3: 2018 edition*. London: Christian Research.

Brown, A. (2014, July 14). *Church of England General Synod approves female bishops*. The Guardian. Retrieved from https://www.theguardian.com/world/2014/jul/14/church-england-general-synod-approves-female-bishops.

22 Introduction

Brown, A., & Woodhead, L. (2016). *That was the Church that was: How the Church of England lost the English people*. London: Bloomsbury.

Bryan, J. (2016). *Human being: Insights from psychology and the Christian faith*. London: SCM Press.

Burman, E. (1994). Interviewing. In P. Banister, E. Burman, I. Parker, M. Taylor, & C. Tindall (Eds.), *Qualitative methods in psychology* (pp. 49–71). Buckingham: Open University Press.

Caldwell, R. (2007). Agency and change: Re-evaluating Foucault's legacy. *Organization, 14*(6), 769–791.

Carlson, N., Martin, G., & Buskist, W. (2000). *Psychology*. Harlow: Pearson Education Limited.

Chadwick, O. (1972). *The Victorian Church (Part II)*. London: Adam and Charles Black.

Church of England Glossary. (2018a). *Bishop*. Retrieved from https://www.churchofenglandglossary.co.uk/dictionary/definition/bishop.

Church of England Glossary (2018b). *Anglo-Catholic*. Retrieved from https://www.churchofenglandglossary.co.uk/dictionary/definition/anglo_catholic.

Clarke, V., Braun, V., & Hayfield, N. (2015). Thematic analysis. In J.A. Smith (Ed.), *Qualitative psychology: A practical guide to research methods*, 3rd edition (pp. 222–248). London: Sage.

Cornwall, S. (2015). Laws "Needefull in later to be abrogated": Intersex and the sources of Christian theology. In S. Cornwall (Ed.), *Intersex, theology and the Bible: Troubling bodies in Church, text, and society*. Hampshire: Palgrave Macmillan.

Day, A. (2017). *The religious lives of older laywomen: The last active Anglican generation*. Oxford University Press.

European Institute for Gender Equality (2020). *Gender Equality Index*. Retrieved from https://eige.europa.eu/gender-equality-index/compare-countries.

European Union (2006). *On establishing a European Institute for Gender Equality (Regulation (EC) No. 1922/2006)*. Retrieved from https://eur-lex.europa.eu/legal-content/EN/TXT/PDF/?uri=CELEX:32006R1922&from=EN.

Francis, L.J., & Robbins, M. (1999). *The long diaconate, 1987–1994: Women deacons and the delayed journey to priesthood*. Leominster: Gracewing Publishing.

Francis, L.J., Robbins, M., & Astley, J. (2005). *Fragmented faith: Exposing the fault lines in the Church of England*. Milton Keynes: Paternoster Press.

Fry, A.D.J. (2019). Justifying gender inequality in the church of England: An examination of theologically conservative male clergy attitudes towards women's ordination. *Fieldwork in Religion, 14*(1), 8–32.

Fry, A.D.J. (2021a). Postfeminist, engaged and resistant: Evangelical male clergy attitudes towards gender and women's ordination in the Church of England. *Critical Research on Religion, 9*(1), 65–83.

Fry, A.D.J. (2021b). Clergy, capital and gender inequality: An assessment of how social and spiritual capital are denied to women priests in the Church of England. *Gender, Work & Organization, 21*(6), 2091–2113.

Furlong, M. (2000). *The CofE: The state it's in*. London: Hodder & Stoughton.

Gallagher, S.K. (2003). *Evangelical identity and gendered family life*. New Brunswick, NJ: Rutgers University Press.

Goodchild, S. (2002, March 10). *Church pays millions to clergy who walked out over women priests*. The Independent. Retrieved from https://www.independent.co.uk/news/uk/home-news/church-pays-millions-clergy-who-walked-out-over-women-priests-9196207.html.

Grady, M.P. (1998). *Qualitative and action research: A practitioner handbook*. Arlington, VA: Phi Delta Kappa International.

Greene, A.M., & Robbins, M. (2015). The cost of a calling? Clergywomen and work in the Church of England. *Gender, Work and Organization, 22*(4), 405–420.

Guest, M., Olson, E., & Wolffe, J. (2012). Christianity: Loss of monopoly. In L. Woodhead & R. Catto (Eds.), *Religion and change in modern Britain* (pp. 57–78). Oxford: Routledge.

Hackett, C. et al. (2016). *The gender gap in religion around the world: Women are generally more religious than men, particularly among Christians*. Washington D.C.: Pew Research Center.

Hindess, B. (1996). *Discourses of power: From Hobbes to Foucault*. Oxford: Baker Academic Press.

Hitlin, S., & Piliavin, J.A. (2004). Values: Reviving a dormant concept. *Annual Review of Sociology, 30*, 359–393.

Hylson-Smith, K. (1993). *High churchmanship in the Church of England: From the sixteenth century to the late twentieth century*. Edinburgh: T&T Clark.

Jones, I. (2004). *Women and priesthood in the Church of England: Ten years on*. London: Church House Publishing.

Jost, J.T., Hawkins, C.B., Nosek, B.A., Hennes, E.P., Stern, C., Gosling, S.D., & Graham, J. (2013). Belief in a just God (and a just society): A system justification perspective on religious ideology. *Journal of Theoretical and Philosophical Psychology, 34*(1), 1–26.

Kay, A.C., Gaucher, D., Napier, J.L., Callan, M.J., & Laurin, K. (2008). God and the government: Testing a compensatory control mechanism for the support of external systems. *Journal of Personality and Social Psychology, 95*(1), 18–35.

Krosnick, J., & Petty, R. (1995). Attitude strength: An overview. In R. Petty and J. Krosnick (Eds.), *Attitude strength: Antecedents and consequences* (pp. 1–14). New York: Psychology Press.

Legislation. (2010). *Equality Act 2010*. Retrieved from http://www.legislation.gov.uk/ukpga/2010/15/contents.

Maiden, J. (2018, February 19). *The charismatic turn of the long 1960s: Contexts and characteristics* [Paper presentation]. Contemporary Religion in Historical Perspective: Publics and performances. Milton Keynes, United Kingdom.

Maltby, J. (1998). One Lord, one faith, one baptism, but two integrities? In M. Furlong (Ed.), *Act of Synod- act of folly? Episcopal Ministry Act of Synod 1993* (pp. 42–58). London: SCM Press.

Martin, J.L. (2017). *Thinking through methods: A social science primer*. Chicago and London: University of Chicago Press.

Martin, J., & Lembo, A. (2020). On the other side of values. *American Journal of Sociology, 126*(1), 52–98.

Maxwell, J.A. (2004a). Using qualitative methods for causal explanation. *Field Methods, 16*(3), 243–264.

Maxwell, J.A. (2004b). Causal explanation, qualitative research, and scientific inquiry in education. *Educational Researcher, 33*(2), 3–11.

24 Introduction

McGrath, A. (1993). *The renewal of Anglicanism.* London: SPCK.

Nason-Clark, N. (1984). *Clerical attitudes towards appropriate roles for women in church and society: An empirical investigation of Anglican, Methodist and Baptist clergy in Southern England* (Doctoral dissertation, The London School of Economics and Political Science).

Nason-Clark, N. (1987a). Ordaining women as priests: Religious vs. sexist explanations for clerical attitudes. *Sociological Analysis, 48*(3), 259–273.

Nason-Clark, N. (1987b). Are women changing the image of ministry? A comparison of British and American realities. *Review of Religious Research,* 330–340.

Office for National Statistics. (2013). *Full story: What does the Census tell us about religion in 2011?* Retrieved from https://www.ons.gov.uk/peoplepopulationandcommunity/culturalidentity/religion/articles/fullstorywhatdoesthecensustellusaboutreligionin2011/2013-05-16.

Page, S-J. (2010). *Femininities and Masculinities in the Church of England.* (Doctoral dissertation, University of Nottingham).

Page, S-J. (2014). The scrutinized priest: Women in the Church of England negotiating professional and sacred clothing regimes. *Gender, Work and Organization, 21*(4), 295–307.

Page, S-J. (2017). Anglican clergy husbands securing middle-class gendered privilege through religion. *Sociological Research Online, 22*(1), 1–13.

Pilarski, A.E. (2011). The past and future of feminist biblical hermeneutics. *Biblical Theology Bulletin, 41*(1), 16–23.

Research & Statistics. (2019). *Statistics for mission 2018.* The Church of England. Retrieved from https://www.churchofengland.org/sites/default/files/2019-10/2018 StatisticsForMission_0.pdf.

Research & Statistics (2020). Ministry *Statistics 2020.* The Church of England. Retrieved from https://www.churchofengland.org/sites/default/files/2021-07/Ministry %20Statistics%202020%20report%20FINAL.pdf.

Riessman, C.K. (2005). *Narrative analysis.* In N. Kelly, C. Horrocks, K. Milnes, B. Roberts, & S. Robinson (Eds.). *Narrative, memory and everyday life,* (pp. 1–7). Huddersfield: University of Huddersfield.

Robbins, M., & Greene, A.M. (2018). Clergywomen's experience of ministry in the Church of England. *Journal of Gender Studies, 27*(8), 890–900.

Saldaña, J. (2009). *The coding manual for qualitative researchers.* London: Sage.

Sani, F., & Reicher, S. (1999). Identity, argument and schism: Two longitudinal studies of the split in the Church of England over the ordination of women to the priesthood. *Group Processes and Intergroup Relations, 2*(3), 279–300.

Sani, F., & Reicher, S. (2000). Contested identities and schisms in groups: Opposing the ordination of women as priests in the Church of England. *British Journal of Social Psychology, 39*(1), 95–112.

Sayer, A. (2000). *Realism and social science.* London: Sage.

Seybold, K.S. (2007). *Explorations in neuroscience, psychology and religion.* London: Routledge.

Steensland, B., & Goff, P. (Eds.). (2014). *The new evangelical social engagement.* Oxford University Press.

Storkey, E. (1985). *What's right with feminism?* London: SPCK.

Swingewood, A. (2000). *A short history of sociological thought,* 3rd ed. Aldershot: Palgrave.

Tajfel, H. (1974). Social identity and intergroup behaviour. *Social Science Information*, *13*(2), 65–93.

Trzebiatowska, M. (2015). What theologians need to know: Contributions from sociology. In A. Thatcher (Ed.), *The Oxford handbook of theology, sexuality, and gender* (pp. 120–136). Oxford University Press.

Village, A. (2013). Traditions within the Church of England and psychological type: A study among the clergy. *Journal of Empirical Theology*, *26*(1), 22–44.

Weiss, R.S. (1995). *Learning from strangers: The art and method of qualitative interview studies*. New York: The Free Press.

Witherington III, B. (1987). *Women in the ministry of Jesus: A study of Jesus' attitudes to women and their roles as reflected in his earthly life*. Cambridge University Press.

Witherington III, B. (1990). *Women and the genesis of Christianity*. Cambridge University Press.

Wood, W. (2000). Attitude change: Persuasion and social influence. *Annual Review of Psychology*, *51*, 539–570.

Wright, A. (2013). *Christianity and critical realism: Ambiguity, truth and theological literacy*. Oxford: Routledge.

Young, F. (2015). *Inferior office? A history of deacons in the Church of England*. Cambridge: James Clarke and Co.

2 The Church of England and gender in historical perspective

Introduction

To understand the gender attitudes that currently exist within the CofE, it is necessary to analyse their historical development because all devotees have inherited their religious traditions (see Vasey-Saunders, 2015). This means that the history of each Anglican tradition comes to bear on their present expressions. In the present chapter, I will outline the developments in gender roles that have shaped those within the CofE at an institutional level since the Industrial Revolution until the present day, including those that have been especially impactful on the evangelical and Anglo-Catholic traditions. I will show that the development of the Established Church's gender attitudes has a complex history as does its responses to the gender attitudes of wider English society.

Despite the Church reflecting the values of wider society prior to the second half of the twentieth century, there was a distinct shift in those of the English people from the late 1950s, which put them at odds with those of the CofE. However, one later sees a general assimilation of wider social attitudes over time. However, this is caveated by the evidence from the evangelical and traditional Anglo-Catholic traditions. Whereas the former became more divided with an evident split in attitudes towards women's ordination by the end of the last century, the latter consistently resisted women's ordination. Conservative evangelicalism—as distinct from a new, liberal evangelicalism that was more affirming of women's ordination (see Bebbington, 1989)—and traditional Anglo-Catholicism simultaneously engaged with and resisted the Established Church as it came to affirm the validity of women's ordination as deacons and priests and their consecration as bishops.

Modernity and Victorian England

One of the most important historical developments that has shaped the gender attitudes of English society is the rise of modernity. This is an era that spans centuries and it will be unpacked in more detail in the seventh chapter. The present chapter is concerned with modernity from the rise of the

DOI: 10.4324/9781003081913-2

The Church of England and gender in historical perspective 27

Industrial Revolution. Although much of what is discussed is applicable beyond this context, the present chapter will focus on England. It was at this point when society became more segregated and compartmentalised than it had previously been (Bruce, 2008). Prior to the Industrial Revolution, society was agrarian and so men were more present in the home, but with the onset of urbanisation, they found employment in manufacturing, which meant working away from the family. This led to a more gendered division of labour than had previously existed, where the responsibility for caregiving and the religious instruction of children fell more specifically to women (Balmer, 1994) and where men particularly became seen as providers (Gallagher, 2003).

During the Victorian period, women's inferior social status was enshrined in law. They were subject to the authority of their husbands and married women could not exercise full autonomy in legal matters and instead needed permission from their husbands to engage in such affairs. Women thus had no legal status but were to live under coverture, the protection of their husbands who would subsume their legal rights and responsibilities (Perkin, 1989). It was in this period that the CofE was perceived to be a guardian of anti-feminism at a time when feminism first emerged (Heeney, 1988). In this respect, it reflected the gender attitudes of the society of which it was a part. However, at this time, women began to make up the largest share of churchgoers in England and were taking on positions of authority and lay leadership within the Church (Heeney, 1988).

Religion in the Victorian era has been understood as embodying a crisis of faith and, whilst this perspective can be over-emphasised amongst historians, a series of writings emerged confessing doubts over the Christian worldview (Larsen, 2006). Church attendance was also waning at this time, a trend that continued until the outbreak of the Second World War (McLeod, 1999). This was accompanied by an increase of those identifying as nonconformist (i.e., Protestant but not CofE) and Roman Catholic Christians, all of which made the CofE's disestablishment appear to be a real threat to CofE clergy (Reed, 1996). This, combined with the decrease in the social role of the Church—evidenced, for example, by an increase in state rather than Church-funded education (see Hollis, 1967)—led Anglican clergy to believe that England was losing its religious vigour (Chandler, 2003).

Associated tensions peaked when the British Government proposed reducing the number of Anglican bishops in Ireland (Chapman, 2006; Fairweather, 1964). This move was met with fierce opposition from a group of Oxford-based clergy, not least because the CofE is episcopal in nature and the authoritative office of the bishop was believed to be under attack (Fairweather, 1964). The result was the rise of the Oxford Movement, whose members were known as Tractarians because of their use of tracts to disseminate their ideas (Reed, 1996). This group of clergymen advocated the theology of apostolic succession—the belief that the Church's bishops have inherited their authority from the original apostles appointed by Christ

28 *The Church of England and gender in historical perspective*

(Knox, 1933). From this movement emerged a new tradition within the CofE, namely Anglo-Catholicism.

As Anglo-Catholicism's first adherents wrestled with social change that was—in their eyes—undesirable, they looked to the past for direction. In doing so they emphasised the CofE's historical lineage, leading them to articulate a theology of ecclesiological continuation with the Roman Catholic Church (Pickering, 1989) and thereby with St Peter, the first leader of the Christian Church. The Tractarians also appealed to the Church Fathers to support their theological claims (Faught, 2003), sought to revive religious orders that had disappeared during the Reformation (Ollard, 1963), and could be particularly hesitant towards religious innovation (Martin, 1976). An irony of the movement lay in the way that Anglo-Catholics selectively adhered to the authority of their own bishops. Relationships between Tractarians and their ecclesial superiors could be problematic, and disagreements appeared to have had personal overtones. As a case in point, the Bishop of Worcester refused to ordain the assistant curate of leading Tractarian Keble to the priesthood because of Keble's Anglo-Catholic theology (see Martin, 1976).

That the rise of Anglo-Catholicism began in Oxford testifies to its historically male-dominated and enclave-like culture. The first Tractarians were Fellows of the University, which was predominantly filled with clergymen and their sons, many of whom would later be ordained themselves (Martin, 1976). It is notable that this religious culture was juxtaposed alongside resistance to women's increased agency in the Church and a strong affirmation of episcopacy, particularly the Roman Catholic understanding of apostolic succession. Whilst this theology does not directly concern matters of gender, the apostolicity of the priesthood—and thus authority within the Church—was assumed to be male. Indeed, such theology emerged alongside resistance to changes in women's roles within the Church. Hence, an enclave-like culture, a high view of episcopacy, and resistance towards changes in gender roles were intertwined from Tractarian origins. As will become evident in due course, that such views were intrinsic to the identity of early Anglo-Catholicism helps explain the traditional Anglo-Catholic reaction towards women's ordination as priests and their consecration as bishops.

World war

The First and Second World Wars significantly shaped English gender values. In many ways, the First World War reinforced traditional gender roles. For example, much importance was placed on women's responsibility as the guardians of morality, and propaganda aimed at motivating men to join the armed forces depicted war as a defence of the home and thus of women, who occupied the domestic sphere (Grayzel, 2002). Even though women came to occupy jobs traditionally done by men, their domestic responsibilities were frequently reinforced through posters that encouraged women to aid the war effort in their domestic duties, for instance, by being thrifty (Grayzel, 2002).

The Church of England and gender in historical perspective 29

Indeed, despite women joining voluntary organisations as part of the war effort, assumptions about their feminine qualities remained (Grayzel, 1999). Whilst some women were enfranchised in 1918, this was limited to those over the age of 30 and of relative privilege. In fact, arguments for women's enfranchisement were often based on the merits of women's roles as mothers; unsurprisingly then, the overall picture shows that gender roles changed little as a result of this war (Grayzel, 1999).

During the interwar years, the religious sphere was yet more strongly associated with women because increased state provision of services historically provided by the Church led to the further marginalisation of religious beliefs to the domestic (and thus female) sphere (Aune, 2008a). The expectation that women rather than men were to pass faith on to children was thus reinforced (see Brown and Woodhead, 2016). Within evangelicalism, the sexes were seen as binary opposites, a belief that lasted throughout the twentieth century alongside the view that men were more naturally immoral but women, godly and virtuous (Brown, 2001). Nevertheless, the evangelical narrative in England adapted to reflect economic change, which included the professional woman, but this shift maintained traditional feminine ideals at its heart, which were frequently passed on to children and teenagers through the medium of storytelling (Brown, 2001).

Historians do not all agree on the extent to which the Second World War served as a catalyst for subsequent changes to England's gender attitudes. It is true, however, that women once more took up roles traditionally occupied by men. Nonetheless, this pattern appeared to be short-lived when women re-adopted more traditional roles after 1945 with the expectation that they would become mothers to help increase the population after the war (Brown, 2001). Indeed, during this era, the belief that the woman's place was in the domestic sphere prevailed (Summerfield, 1998). Nevertheless, it became more normal for working-class women to enter the workplace (Brown, 2001) and women's role in the workforce during the war set a precedent for the following generation of women who pursued paid employment in larger numbers than their mothers' generation (Summerfield, 1998). In fact, mass consumption after 1945 encouraged women into the workplace due to the demand for a larger workforce (Thorne, 2000).

Whilst support amongst the laity for women's ordination emerged in the aftermath of the First World War, the movement did not gain much traction until the 1930s when the idea became popular as a result of the suffragette movement (Thorne, 2000). However, by 1941 the CofE affirmed that the order of deaconess was the only appropriate licenced post for women (Thorne, 2000). In this respect, the attitudes towards women's ordination in the CofE again reflected that of wider society with modest increases in support of widening women's role outside of the domestic sphere, but with an overall conservatism. Similarly, gender ideals narrowed after 1945 because the family unit was perceived to have been weakened by war (Hunter, 1987). The traditional division of labour was not only seen as sociably functional in this context but was even

30 *The Church of England and gender in historical perspective*

considered God-ordained, and gender roles were understood hierarchically, with men at the top (Gallagher, 2003). In fact, the family unit remained intimately associated with Christian faith because it served as a plausibility structure for it where religious instruction could be handed down from one generation to another (Hunter, 1987). It was not until the latter half of the 1950s that this began to change on an unprecedented scale.

The 'long sixties'

Callum Brown's (2001) reference to the years 1956–1973 as "the long sixties" (p. 188) is well known amongst historians of the twentieth century. This is understood to be the most significant period of religious decline in England and is juxtaposed alongside the rise of secularisation. It was during this era that gender roles shifted rapidly as evinced, for instance, by the introduction of the contraceptive pill which enjoyed widespread use amongst young women (McLeod, 2007). Increased control over their sexuality dovetailed with women's increased presence in the labour market (Brown, 2001), which rose steadily but continuously during this period (McLeod, 2007). The 1967 Abortion Act also provided women with increased control over their bodies, leading to prolonged periods in the workplace, and thus to the reconceptualisation of the purpose of the female body (Brown, 2006).

The increased professionalisation of women led to their lack of involvement in church life, despite the fact that their historical commitment had been instrumental to its running (Brown and Woodhead, 2016). This led to the loss of generations of active laywomen in the Church who were both a financial and a labour resource for the institution (Day, 2017). At the same time, the authoritative role of men in marriage was diminishing with a partnership of equals replacing the traditional model (MacCulloch, 2009). Role swapping was also becoming more common between husband and wife (McLeod, 2007) and the new, more affluent family model led to lifestyle concerns that detracted from the activities of the Church, resulting in a decrease in children attending Sunday schools (MacCulloch, 2009).

However, the increased utilitarian expectations of marriage ultimately led to increased divorce rates when reality failed to live up to expectation, and extramarital births noticeably increased during this time and into the 1970s (MacCulloch, 2009). Many felt isolated from the Church with its traditional teachings on gender and sexuality as a result (McLeod, 2007). The "new-style family was not good news for Churches, whose rhetoric of support for the family had not envisaged that it might be a competitor for rather than a mainstay of Church life" (MacCulloch, 2009, p. 986). The Church's response was to reinforce its traditional values with an "angry conservativism", resulting from the threat of marginalisation experienced by men in positions of leadership that were apparently becoming less needed as well as by men who might have expected to inherit these positions in the future (MacCulloch, 2009, p. 990).

The Church of England and gender in historical perspective 31

Masculinity throughout the twentieth century

Despite such changes in wider society, the idea of muscular Christianity permeated throughout the different Anglican traditions during the twentieth century and evinced a continuous understanding of male Christian chivalry (Delap, 2013). An Anglican culture of men possessing inter-personal ties where concepts such as love were a part of this Christian discourse on masculinity emerged. However, it was accompanied by a conservative gender hierarchy and the preference for male breadwinners, especially amongst the middle class, for both clergy and laity (Delap, 2013). Nevertheless, much of the muscular Christian image was influenced by secular sporting imagery (McLeod, 2012) which provided a male-dominated sphere where the voices of women were rarely heard, a phenomenon paralleled in evangelical culture throughout this century (Balmer, 2016).

There has been a continuation of muscular Christian ideals through the belief that preaching is a masculine domain amongst contemporary evangelicals in England, which results from the Victorian belief that speech was a masculine enterprise (Stewart, 2012; see also Hall, 1994). This is perhaps unsurprising given that evangelical identity has historically incorporated middle-class notions of gender and continues to promote the ideology of gender differentiation—separate gender spheres—including that of male breadwinners (Aune, 2008b; see also Fry, 2021a). This involves an assimilation of wider cultural gender attitudes, including anti-feminist sentiments in addition to feminist ideals (Aune, 2006, 2008b; see also Aune and Guest, 2019). The rhetoric of male "headship" is a central component of this navigation of contemporary evangelical identity but British evangelical notions of exclusively male leadership in marriage can work itself out in more egalitarian ways in practice, paralleling marriages in wider society (Aune, 2006). Contemporary evangelicalism (as well as Anglicanism more broadly) has thus inherited gender attitudes from the previous century that are still alive today.

Feminism

I have already noted the support for increased women's ministry that emerged after the First World War, during the so-called first wave of feminism. Indeed, the development of women's ordination cannot be understood apart from the feminist movement. The rise of feminist biblical hermeneutics in the 'second wave' proved to be a further catalyst (see Pilarski, 2011). Given the importance of scripture in Anglican theology, feminist theology was influential when it successfully argued that women were heavily involved in the ministry of the Early Church (Thorne, 2000). Feminist theologians likewise had some success when they called for women to remain active within the life of the Church to transform its patriarchal structures (Thorne, 2000).

32   *The Church of England and gender in historical perspective*

Those in a position of leadership within the CofE have helped to further this cause. Margaret Thrall (1958) was initially a deaconess and then one of the first women priests. Whilst her work is not overtly feminist, it was written during the 'long sixties' when the second wave of feminism emerged. Importantly, she noted that women, who by this time were beginning to enjoy increased opportunities in the occupational sphere, were also asking why they could not become priests. In doing so Thrall captured an important historical development in the attitudes of those within the Church, not least of the sex most actively involved in its life outside of its formal hierarchy. She also offered a theological reflection that considered the possibility of women priests, providing a framework for thinking about this potential development. Elaine Storkey (1985) is a more recent example and is consciously feminist. She penned *What's Right with Feminism?* which highlighted the various ways in which sexism manifests in Church life, interpreting this as the result of humanity's sin. Storkey developed a uniquely Christian interpretation of feminism—which was not uncritical of aspects of the feminist movement—and called for change in the (often dismissive) way that Christians had understood this ideology.

Another branch of theology, which is akin to but distinct from feminist theology, is redemptive trajectory hermeneutics. Like feminist theology, it seeks to employ biblical texts to challenge oppression by searching for the underlying values of love, justice, and equality (Vanhoozer, 2004). This hermeneutic affirms the authority of scripture and is, therefore unsurprisingly, often used by evangelicals (Graham, 2002; Vanhoozer, 2004). One such example of this hermeneutic that advocates gender equality in ministry is W. J. Webb's (2001) *Slaves, Women and Homosexuals*, a text that has become highly influential in Christian thought, whilst also being received with caution by some (see Blomberg, 2011).

Whilst these examples of feminist (or para-feminist) theology have emerged from within Protestantism, Roman Catholicism has its own tradition of feminist engagement. As aforementioned, scholarship arguing that women were vital for the ministry of the Early Church has been influential on Anglican theology. One key example of such work is (the Roman Catholic) Elizabeth Schüssler Fiorenza's (1983) *In Memory of Her*. She argues that women were effectively written out of the pages of scripture because those texts emerged in cultures that were patriarchal and understands that the task of the feminist theologian is to write them back into history. Schüssler Fiorenza also drew attention to the fact that the Bible has been employed to justify patriarchy in the Church and society through the (supposedly) divinely ordained subservient place of women. Similarly, the Roman Catholic Elizabeth Johnson (1993) identifies a history of "hierarchical dualism" (p. 10) in Christian theology which divides reality into two gendered spheres, preferring one to the other. Within this paradigm masculine discourse alone is understood as spiritual, leading to the subordination of women to men.

The Church of England and gender in historical perspective 33

Much of this work, however, did not fully challenge gender essentialism—the idea that each sex has unique traits that are exclusive to them—and thus the assumed gendered spheres. Later feminist works, in what is sometimes referred to as the third feminist wave, have been diverse and it is important not to homogenise or oversimplify them. Nevertheless, some more fully challenged gender essentialism, for example, by arguing that gender is socially constructed (e.g., Butler, 1990; Fausto-Sterling, 2000). Gender and sex became seen by some as two distinct phenomena, with the former referring to social roles associated with each sex whereas sex referred to the physical body that was typically male or female. However, others argued that the body was likewise a social construction and sometimes cast doubt on whether one could even perceive the body beyond culturally mediated interpretations of it (e.g., Butler, 1993; see also Laqueur, 2012).

Christians responded to feminism in multiple ways. I have already noted some of the ways in which such values have been incorporated into Christian thinking. However, there were also clear attempts to reject feminism. Popular US evangelical authors Piper and Grudem (1991) responded to evangelical feminism—an expression of feminism within the evangelical tradition—by arguing for a complementarian (or headship) model of gender roles. They asserted that certain biblical texts demand that men are called by God to (lovingly and sacrificially) lead in marriage and in church, whereas women are to submit to their husbands' authority, ideas that they have re-affirmed in more recent writing (Piper and Grudem, 2016). However, they have incorporated ideals of equality into their thinking, breaking with historical evangelicalism (see e.g., Grudem, 1994; see also Fry, 2021a). Anglican clergy have similarly evinced their ambivalence towards feminism (Page, 2013).

The Roman Catholic Church's Congregation for the Doctrine of the Faith (CDF) responded to feminism with the claim that there is a continuous tradition of male priesthood and that because the priest stands in the place of the male Christ ("in persona propria") it would be difficult to envision a woman priest (Groppe, 2009, pp. 162–163). The CDF also declared in 2004 that it is permissible for women to seek fulfilment outside of the domestic sphere whilst still orienting women to the home and family as their primary calling (Beattie, 2004). The document issued by the CDF implicitly blamed feminism for enmity between the sexes and criticised a compounding of sex and gender through understanding the former as a historical and social construction rather than a biological reality (Beattie, 2004). It allowed for the distinction between gender and sex while also blaming feminism for a new desire in women to seek power (Beattie, 2004).

The charismatic movement and ecumenism

Nevertheless, the charismatic movement provided a platform for female leadership in Christian settings (Guest, Olson, and Wolffe, 2012). The

34   *The Church of England and gender in historical perspective*

movement has historically emphasised miraculous healing, baptism in the Holy Spirit, and the idea that each Christian has been given a set of unique gifts by God (Buchanan et al., 1981). Despite being Pentecostal in origin, it spread into the Established Church during the twentieth century, yet remained distinct from more conservative expressions of evangelicalism (MacCulloch, 2009). The charismatic movement was deeply ecumenical (Maiden, 2018) and the CofE formally engaged with it during the 1970s. For instance, in 1973 the Church of England Evangelical Council co-wrote the *Gospel and Spirit* report with the charismatically-oriented Fountain Trust, and many Anglican churches came to implement house groups that were modelled on the house church movement, relying on lay leadership (Buchanan et al., 1981). It was this context in particular that enabled women to enjoy more informal leadership roles within evangelical churches (Guest, Olson, and Wolffe, 2012).

A further factor that shaped the debate over women's ordination to the priesthood was the CofE's relationship with the Roman Catholic Church. In his memoirs, former Archbishop of Canterbury George Carey admits that when he was a bishop he genuinely believed, with others, that he would see the unification of the CofE with the Roman Catholic Church in his lifetime. He explains that from the 1970s there had been intentional dialogue between the CofE and the Roman Catholic Church to establish that there was a common Christian doctrine between them. At this time the major argument against priesting women from the Anglo-Catholic tradition was that it would worsen relationships between the two Churches, something which at least some in the CofE's hierarchy were keen to avoid (Carey, 2004).

Equally, the situation of the worldwide Anglican Communion—the worldwide federation of Anglican Churches—had its bearing on the debate over women's ordination. The Lambeth Conference is a ten-yearly meeting of all bishops within the Anglican Communion. When it met in 1968, it declared that deaconesses ought to be amalgamated into the diaconate and rejected historical assumptions about the biological inferiority of women that had previously been used to bar them from ordination. Hence, the only objection to women's ordination was the fact that there was no historical precedent for it (Fletcher, 2013). The Anglican Consultative Council was established so that different Anglican provinces could consult the same body on the matter of women's ordination; it encouraged provinces to consider ordaining women whilst also asking those that would not to remain in Communion with those that did (Fletcher, 2013). Nevertheless, this decision was met with some debate across the Communion (Mayland, 2007).

By the 1978 Lambeth Conference, four of the 27 Anglican provinces had ordained women (Hong Kong, New Zealand, Canada, and the USA), a development which strained relationships amongst different provinces, leading the 1978 conference to explore how the Communion may remain diverse yet united (Fletcher, 2013). Ten years later, however, having accepted the legitimacy of ordaining women as deacons and priests, the key question for several

The Church of England and gender in historical perspective   35

provinces was the consecration of women to the episcopate. This led the 1988 Lambeth Conference to affirm each province's autonomy on making decisions pertaining to women's ordination (Fletcher, 2013).

Within the CofE, the evangelical argument against women's ordination centred around biblical interpretation, particularly the theology of headship (Mayland, 2007). Moreover, whilst the CofE debated women's ordination with minimal reference to the developments in the Free Churches, the Methodist Church in England, which was in dialogue with the CofE over the possibility of greater unity between the two denominations, declared that full unity would only be permitted if women were permitted to all areas of licenced ministry (Mayland, 2007). Equally, the Lutheran Churches of Norway and Sweden—which entered into Communion with the CofE through the Porvoo Agreement—had women bishops during the CofE's debate about women priests (Mayland, 2007). The Established Church was therefore located within a diverse spectrum of Christian Churches, forced to navigate a deeply divisive concern that had been received differently by different Christian traditions.

Broader developments within the CofE

Other factors indicate that either individual Anglicans or the whole institution were incorporating some of the social changes in English society at the time. For example, younger Anglicans were regularly reconciling contemporary attitudes towards sexuality with their Christian faith, even though they were not as sexually liberal as their secular peers (McLeod, 2007). The salience of this development ought not to be underestimated given that, as aforementioned, changing attitudes towards sexuality allowed women a more visible presence in the English workforce, making women's employment more normative in society and thus challenging traditional patterns of gender.

The introduction of the 1980 Alternative Service Book provided an authorised alternative to the 1662 Book of Common Prayer, a break with centuries of tradition in Anglican worship (Guest, Olson, and Wolffe, 2012). That the Book of Common Prayer is an important source of Anglican theology means this historic development set a precedent for other theological developments and legitimated theological diversity. Moreover, the emergence of different Bible translations fostered an awareness of theological pluralism amongst evangelicals at this time, whilst the public evangelical Anglican figure John Stott sought to encourage awareness of the biases that readers bring to the Bible and promote a contextualised reading of scripture as a remedy (Perrin, 2016). Advocating such ideas would also have increased awareness of theological pluralism. Also, after this period, evangelical writings emerged that adopted a contextualised reading of biblical passages concerning gender, concluding that no universal prohibition of women ministers could be found therein (e.g., Witherington, 1987, 1990). Whilst some of these changes do not

36   *The Church of England and gender in historical perspective*

directly concern gender, the above evidences that the CofE was becoming increasingly open to theological pluralism in areas that were either related to gender roles or in matters pertaining to the sources of authority that inevitably influenced gender attitudes within the CofE.

Not only did evangelicals within the Established Church become more aware of theological diversity but to some extent they even embraced it. In 1966, Westminster Chapel preacher Martin Lloyd-Jones, concerned about the apparent liberalism found within mainline denominations, called on all evangelicals to leave their churches and create a unified evangelical free Church, a move that was immediately rebutted by John Stott who encouraged evangelical Anglicans to remain in the CofE (Bebbington, 1989). Then, at the 1967 National Evangelical Anglican Congress in Keele, evangelical Anglicans affirmed their commitment to the CofE and agreed to play a more active role within it than they had previously, to enhance evangelical influence from within (Bebbington, 1995). Whilst this did not amount to approval of women's ordination within the evangelical wing of the Church, it suggests that this group was not entirely resistant to the changes happening within it.

The momentum for (and response to) women priests

This view is buttressed by the fact that the year prior to Keele saw the publication of the *Women in Holy Orders* report. It stated that the ordination of women had not yet occurred because of practical rather than theological concerns (Thorne, 2000). Clearly, evangelical Anglicans were willing to work within a Church where women's ordination was not only deemed theologically acceptable but also a possible future reality.

In 1975, the CofE passed a measure that officially stated that there was no theological objection to women's ordination, although the motion to enable it was rejected when brought to the General Synod in 1978, spurring the formation of the Movement for the Ordination of Women (MOW), which generated much support (Thorne, 2000). Evangelicals within the CofE responded to these developments. For example, leading evangelical figure J. I. Packer (1973) wrote that whilst women could be ordained to the priesthood in theory, they should stay under the authority of a male priest as they do so, making it preferable not to ordain women to the priesthood because the difficulties those structural restrictions would impose in pragmatic terms. To justify this position, he alluded to a (largely unspecified) physiological difference between men and women as well as to the creation narratives in Genesis, understanding them to mean that men are created to lead whereas women are created to help men rather than lead them. Nevertheless, other evangelicals became more affirming of women's ordination. Colin Craston (1988) promoted an alternative understanding of New Testament passages that are used to promote male headship and female submission. For example, he affirmed F.F. Bruce's view that the Greek word κεφαλή is best

The Church of England and gender in historical perspective 37

understood as 'source' rather than 'head', meaning that men are not the authoritative head of women as complementarians suppose.

The 1981 report entitled *The Deaconess Order and the Diaconate* suggested to the General Synod that both men and women be made eligible for the ordained diaconate, which was approved in 1986; this allowed the laity to become accustomed to the idea of women priests through their experience of women deacons (Thorne, 2000). The first women deacons were ordained the following year, but to the permanent diaconate as there were no provisions in place for ordaining women as priests (Francis and Robbins, 1999).

Despite these developments being justified theologically, there is evidence that indicates that pragmatism played a more decisive role than theology in ordaining women. Robert Runcie was the Archbishop of Canterbury at the time. When he addressed the General Synod in 1984, he said:

> It is clearer now that the ordination of women to the priesthood—like it or like it not—is almost certainly a permanent development in the ministry of at least some Anglican [C]hurches [...] There can hardly be a way back as long as there are women priests in the Communion. They are here to stay.
>
> (Mantle, 1991, pp. 188–189)

In other words, because other provinces had already ordained women as priests, their inclusion in holy orders within the CofE is simply inevitable. Such was Runcie's own rational for supporting it (Mantle, 1991). The Bishop of Birmingham, Hugh Montefiore (1978), expressed similar views in his edited collection entitled *Yes to Women Priests*. George Carey similarly recalls that, when he was Archbishop of Canterbury, his reluctance about bringing the ordination of women as priests to the General Synod in 1992 was reversed when he came to believe that the CofE's relationship with the Roman Catholic Church was so strained that ordaining women could not make it any worse. He subsequently decided to table the motion (Carey, 2004). Reluctance to push too forcefully for women's ordination was also reflected in the chapter that Michael Perry, the Archdeacon of Durham, contributed to Montefiore's book, in which he advocated for a slow progression towards women's priesthood. Such responses highlight that tensions over the role of women in the Church's hierarchy ran high. Greater evangelical commitment towards the CofE, therefore, was insufficient for fully curtailing opposition to ordaining women as priests.

The level of tension is best explained by the fact that clergy across the CofE were split relatively evenly on their opinions of women's ordination (see Nason-Clark, 1987a). Indeed, the fact that the CofE has been more accommodating of those who object to the ordination of women than other provinces shows that this remained a thorny issue in the latter part of the twentieth century (Avis, 2004). In his memoirs, Carey recalls opposition to women's priesting coming from prominent traditional Anglo-Catholic voices in particular; although his recollection of events may well have been skewed

38   The Church of England and gender in historical perspective

by the backlash he received after publically labelling the Anglo-Catholic view of priesthood as heretical (see Carey, 2004).

Nonetheless, Carey (2004) claimed that most bishops were in favour of women's ordination, a fact born out in the voting results of the 1992 Synod. Within the House of Bishops, 39 voted in favour of ordaining women to the priesthood with only 13 against, whereas in the House of Clergy, 176 voted in favour with 74 against, and in the House of Laity, 169 voted in favour with 82 against. The motion was carried and the way for the ordination of women to the priesthood was made with the first women priests being ordained in 1994. On hearing the vote, traditionalist clergy removed their clerical collars as a sign of protest and some reported feelings of isolation and confusion, and congregants reported seeing their priests in tears in the weeks that followed (Jones, 2004). By August 1994, 300 clergy had left the CofE for the Roman Catholic Church, and the traditional Anglo-Catholic group Forward in Faith was established the month after the Synod's vote, in opposition to it, a move some saw as creating a space for developing alternative ecclesial structures in the event of greater schism (Jones, 2004). Members of this new group became active in protesting the ordination of women, advocating their own position through a rally and use of printed and audio-visual media (Sani and Reicher, 2000).

Opposition was also found in evangelical quarters. Reform emerged in 1993 to save the CofE from—what was seen as—a more general and pervasive theological liberalism (Jones, 2004), which evinced a clear divide in evangelical responses to women's ordination (see also Bebbington, 1989). Conservative evangelicals, as they had come to be called, opted for a programme of reformation. Such objections were pre-empted by the wider Church, however. In 1988 a House of Bishops report entitled *The Ordination of Women to the Priesthood* outlined the key disagreements on women's ordination. It stated that for some gender traditionalists, the ordination of women would beg the question of the efficacy of the sacraments if they were performed by anyone other than a man because it was believed by some that Jesus' maleness is integral to the priesthood, as with traditional Anglo-Catholics. It also recognised that others would object to it on the basis that the Bible is believed to teach male headship and female subordination, making it inappropriate for a woman to lead a church, as with conservative evangelicals (General Synod of the Church of England, 1988).

Not all evangelicals were opposed to ordaining women to the priesthood, however. Carey recalls how the Evangelical Group of the General Synod was the biggest evangelical group in Synod at the time and mostly voted in favour of ordaining women as priests. However, he also notes that a number were reluctant to do so in case it led to the ordination of practising homosexuals at a later date. Carey's solution was to promise that this would never happen under his leadership and that women's ordination and that of practising homosexuals were entirely separate debates, leading to a further 25 votes in favour of women's priesthood, by Carey's own estimation (Carey, 2004).

The Church of England and gender in historical perspective 39

Nevertheless, the 1992 Measure for Priesting women stipulated that it would not consider it unlawful for women to be discriminated against on the grounds of their sex regarding: (i) their ordination as priests; (ii) their licensing as such; or (iii) their appointment beyond something more senior than an assistant curate (Furlong, 2000). This set a precedent for the 1993 Act of Synod that provided greater protection for those opposed to the ordination of women as priests, which introduced the notion of the two integrities, the idea that the CofE would accommodate gender traditionalists and those with more egalitarian gender values (Maltby, 1998). There were two main provisions made within the spirit of accommodation (Maltby, 1998). Firstly, there was the introduction of Provincial Episcopal Visitors (or flying bishops), which provided clergy opposed to women's ordination with an alternative, theologically sympathetic bishop in the stead of their diocesan bishop, if the latter was more egalitarian. Secondly, gender traditionalist bishops could call on other bishops to conduct the ordinations of women and modernist bishops could call on their traditionalist colleagues to conduct the ordinations of men who were against women's ordination.

Additional discriminatory protections were passed as part of the Measure approved by the General Synod in 1992. For example, women clergy were exempt from the 1975 Sex Discrimination Act and Parochial Church Councils[1] could pass either Resolution A or B so that women could be prevented from presiding at the altar (the former resolution) as well as from receiving any appointment in a parish (the latter resolution), despite the fact that parishes could not express preference for a woman priest (Maltby, 1998). The clergy who left the CofE over the introduction of women priests received £30,000 in compensation and those who later returned to the Church were not required to pay it back (Maltby, 1998). Moreover, the Measure stated explicitly that there was no provision for women to become bishops and that no bishop could be required to ordain women if he objected to it on theological grounds (Maltby, 1998).

The impact this had on women was evident. Most women deacons waiting to be priested found the protections for gender traditionalists discriminatory, although deacons in the catholic tradition were more likely to feel that the CofE did not value their ministry than did those within the evangelical tradition (Francis and Robbins, 1999), reflecting a general evangelical affirmation of women's priesting. However, those female deacons who felt undervalued were more likely to be under the age of 40 (Francis and Robbins, 1999), suggesting that the cultural changes that younger generations experienced growing up impacted their expectations concerning gender equality.

Women's frustration with inequality persisted once they were ordained. For example, the first generation of women priests experienced an imbalance of responsibilities when compared with their male colleagues, with women being given a disproportionate number of ministerial activities involving children, and subsequently feeling that their work was seen as less important

40 *The Church of England and gender in historical perspective*

than that of male clergy (Bagilhole, 2003). These women also felt silenced by the male-dominated structures of the CofE, feeling pressured to conform to a male model of priesthood and thus forced to jettison elements of their female identity (Bagilhole, 2003).

Even once women were ordained as priests, they still faced discrimination in the selection process for ordained ministry. Women with children were often required to train on different pathways from men, and those women who were over the age of 45 were expected to train as non-stipendary (i.e., unpaid) ministers (Greene and Robbins, 2015). Women priests were also subject to physical abuse, such as being spat on in public, abusive e-mails and telephone calls, and even verbal abuse in the professional setting. It was also common for lay and ordained men to refuse to take Communion from women priests. Unsurprisingly, these experiences led some women to feel threatened and—in some cases—fearing for their lives (Greene and Robbins, 2015). Moreover, female clergy married to male clergy have felt forced into supporting roles, including in part-time or unpaid capacities (Peyton and Gatrell, 2013). In fact, in recent years, the sacrificial role that the clergy are expected to play has been gendered with women entering a male-dominated culture where women's authority is not always accepted. Hence, ordained women face a "stained glass ceiling" in the CofE (Peyton and Gatrell, 2013, p. 16; see also Gatrell and Peyton, 2019).

Changing attitudes: Ten years on

By 2002 the vast majority of clergy came to support women's ordination, indicating a clear rise in support for women's ordination from the clergy over the ten-year period, although this is partially because most gender traditionalists either left the CofE or took early retirement in protest (Jones, 2004). Those clergy who opposed women's ordination in 1992 yet stayed in the CofE were very unlikely to change their mind (Jones, 2004).

In 2000, the General Synod passed a motion calling for a theological enquiry into the appropriateness of consecrating women to the episcopate, leading to the report *Women Bishops in the Church of England?* in 2004. The report mostly summarised the variety of views on the matter. It stated that the experience of women priests has led to a new way of understanding scripture for some, whilst rejecting the notion that this is itself a new source of authority for making theological claims. It explained that, for many, because the Bible strongly supports women's priesting, the pertinent question is: when does the CofE proceed to comply more fully with the Bible and consecrate women as bishops? Furthermore, it recognised the belief that there is a scriptural trajectory that indicates the full inclusion of women in the life of the Church and that restrictions within the New Testament are best understood as time-conditioned rather than reflecting the universality of God's will. Relatedly, the report described the accompanying preference for a contextual reading of scripture. Nevertheless, it also recognised the

The Church of England and gender in historical perspective   41

presence of the theology of male headship/female submission within the CofE as well as the belief that the extensive role played by women in the Early Church is a reason for consecrating them to the episcopate (The Archbishops' Council, 2004).

Women Bishops in the Church of England? additionally recognised that others believed that Church tradition had departed from the biblical witness of equality between the sexes. It therefore argued that, for tradition to be considered essential to the Christian faith, the Church must have "considered a particular question in a decisive fashion at some point in its history, as in the case of the Nicene doctrine of the Trinity" (p. 171). It also acknowledged the belief, held by some, that both sexes are needed to represent Christ because both "are incorporated into Christ" (p. 172). The report insisted that the CofE has a right to develop its own order independently from other denominations not least because this was the basis of Anglicanism during the English Reformation. It also acknowledged the belief amongst some Anglicans that women were eligible to become bishops by virtue of being priests because priests have always been able to become bishops and that the introduction of women bishops is necessary "to give credibility to the Church's proclamation of the gospel in today's society" (p. 175).

The developments of thought on women's episcopacy outlined in the report demonstrate the assimilation of thinking within academic theology into the CofE. There are echoes of redemptive-trajectory hermeneutics in the discussion of the trajectory of women's increased inclusion into the life of the Church, for example. There are also echoes of the claim that women were actively involved in the life of the Early Church, as claimed by feminist theologians during the so-called second wave. The above also demonstrates that the CofE had made headway on how it could affirm women's ordination whilst simultaneously locating itself within the universal Church by affirming its historic precedent of making unilateral decisions by virtue of its break with Roman Catholicism at the Reformation.

The fact that the report acknowledges an openness to new ways of reading the Bible is in continuation with the recognition and embrace of alternative theologies evinced by evangelical Anglicans from the 1960s. Moreover, an important feature of the report ought not to be overlooked. It was chaired by the then Bishop of Rochester, Michael Nazir-Ali, an evangelical at the time. In fact, he wrote an article in *The Guardian* in 2001 outlining some of the main arguments for and against women's consecration as bishops without clearly coming down on one side, summarising arguments by Schüssler Fiorenza as he did so (see Nazir-Ali, 2001). Although, he later became involved in the schismatic group GAFCON (Raven, 2019), discussed in the fifth chapter and has since joined the Roman Catholic Church (Caldwell, 2021). The combination of these facts shows just how precarious the relationship between evangelicalism and the wider CofE has sometimes been. Equally, however, the report was co-written by several other evangelicals. One such example is Christina Baxter, the then Principal of the evangelical St John's

42 *The Church of England and gender in historical perspective*

College, Nottingham, which trained men and women for the CofE's ordained ministry. Hence, in some evangelical circles, women's authority within the Church had been growing. That the report was co-written by other women is indicative of the fact that their voice had also been growing within the CofE.

The advent of women bishops

It was not until 2012 when the CofE first voted on whether to consecrate women. The Motion gained an insufficient number of votes to pass. Despite receiving the necessary two-thirds majority in support from the House of Bishops and the House of Clergy, it was rejected in the House of Laity seemingly because many, despite being in favour of women bishops, did not believe that there was adequate provision for those who rejected the move to consecrate women as bishops on theological grounds (The Faith and Order Commission, 2018). Indeed, in the following days, this is what members of the House of Laity themselves claimed (Leafe, 2012). During this time, Christopher Hill, the then Bishop of Guildford, suggested three ways in which unity may be achieved within the CofE with the introduction of women bishops (Jenkins, 2005). In particular, he put forward: the possibility of implementing a single-clause measure within the legislation that would see the consecration of women, accompanied by a code of practice, a number of legislative safeguards for gender traditionalists, or the implementation of a third province where those opposed to women bishops could continue under a male bishop of the same theological persuasion.

However, the ensuing debate was criticised by Affirming Catholicism, a movement that was set up to promote the ordination of women and that was in favour of women joining the episcopate (Jenkins, 2005). Richard Jenkins, its leader, wrote a letter to Christopher Hill explaining that the focus on providing for gender traditionalists could lead to a lack of catholicity (i.e., unity) within the CofE by undermining the status of women bishops (Jenkins, 2005). Instead, it was suggested that a single clause enabling women to become bishops that is accompanied by "a robust mechanism to ensure consistent appliance" (p. 138) be introduced. During this time, the question of ecumenism was also pertinent in some quarters of the CofE. Jonathan Baker (2004) edited a collection on women's consecration from a traditional Anglo-Catholic perspective, with Aidan Nichols contributing a chapter from a Roman Catholic perspective.

In November 2014, the General Synod voted in favour of consecrating women as bishops. In the House of Laity, 152 voted in favour of the motion, with only 45 against; there were larger majorities in the Houses of Bishops and Clergy (Brown, 2014). This time the Five Guiding Principles accompanied the motion and outlined a way forward for a Church with both egalitarians and gender traditionalists within it (The Faith and Order Commission, 2018): firstly, clergy are to recognise that all orders within the

The Church of England and gender in historical perspective   43

CofE are open to both men and women and so both "deserve due respect and canonical obedience" (p. 18); secondly, all who are licensed in the CofE are to recognise that the Church has reached a clear and decided opinion on this matter; thirdly, the CofE recognises that this development is set within a wider ecumenical context of discernment amongst the Anglican Communion and the rest of the Christian Church; fourthly, the CofE is committed to continue to allow diversity on this matter for all clergy whose theology is within the CofE's "spectrum of teaching and tradition" (p. 27); and finally, there will be "pastoral and sacramental provision for the minority" who reject women's priesthood in order to enable "mutual flourishing", allowing gender traditionalists to continue to minister within the CofE on equal terms with those in favour of women bishops and thereby maximising unity (p. 32). As a result, the provision of 'flying bishops' was maintained.

In January 2015, the first woman bishop—Libby Lane—was consecrated, followed by the consecration of Philip North and Rod Thomas, to represent gender traditionalists in the Anglo-Catholic and evangelical traditions respectively (The Faith and Order Commission, 2018). These consecrations added to the number of flying bishops already in post, despite less than three per cent of parishes previously requesting such oversight (Butt, 2011), indicating a disproportionate representation of gender traditionalists in the Church's hierarchy. Lee Gatiss edited a collection for the Church Society with three chapters dedicated to discussions of episcopacy and gender. These chapters promoted a traditional evangelical view of gender (see Benn, 2016; Ruddick, 2016, and Tooher, 2016). Thus, by the time that the first woman became a bishop, one notes that the CofE had remained committed to maintaining unity.

Nevertheless, this is juxtaposed alongside the development of a clear resolve to affirm women's ministry in all layers of the Church's hierarchy. In fact, when Philip North was later announced as the next Bishop of Sheffield in 2017—a post that would make him bishop of an entire diocese, not just the traditional Anglo-Catholics within it—protest abounded, so much so that he felt compelled to reject the post (Handley, 2017). Clearly, the tides have begun to change, despite the ongoing presence of gender inequality.

Resistance and engagement

The way in which the CofE has responded to developments in the gender values and attitudes of English society has been complex, exhibiting neither total resistance nor total assimilation. Prior to the second half of the twentieth century the Church—on the whole—was in step with the gender values of wider society, exhibiting some modest changes within a broader framework of conservativism. The Anglo-Catholics were the exception, being less trusting of any change in this domain. The main disjunction between Church and society occurred during the 'long sixties'. It was at this point that the CofE underscored its traditionalist gender attitudes in opposition to the developments taking place in wider society at that time. However, the assimilation of some

44 *The Church of England and gender in historical perspective*

sporting ideals throughout the twentieth century is indicative of the fact that, as the Established Church rather than a partisan institution, the CofE incorporated gender values that existed externally to itself. Nevertheless, these values were still conservative overall and not entirely reflective of wider society.

In the nineteenth and first half of the twentieth centuries, this conservativism reflected that of wider society, whereas from the late 1950s, it was a reaction against the social changes happening in England. The Roman Catholic Church was similarly mixed in its response to feminism from the latter half of the twentieth century, exhibiting mostly resistance and a limited amount of assimilation. Nevertheless, the seeds of change were sown in the CofE during this time which came to bear some fruit in favour of women's ordination as priests and then their consecration as bishops. This was not a quick journey, however.

The charismatics in the CofE tended to embrace the emerging gender values more readily than conservative evangelicals, evidencing that gender attitudes within the CofE have been shaped not only by wider society but by other Christian traditions also. Moreover, the above has shown that the Established Church both resisted and incorporated the perspectives of other Christian churches and traditions just as it had done with English society. By the end of the second millennium, it had become cautiously accepting of the gender values that had been emerging over the previous 50 years, incorporating them at a much slower rate than wider society and remained internally divided over the appropriate roles for women in the Church.

Regarding internal division, (tradtional) Anglo-Catholics tended to resist these developments through retreat and protest whereas conservative evangelicals did so via a programme of reform. Resistance from both groups, however, was exhibited towards the CofE rather than to society more broadly. This is a significant shift. By the time that women were priested, the tension between engagement and resistance was not simply exhibited by the CofE towards English society but from some wings of the Church towards the wider institution. Whilst this was not entirely new, it was the first time that resistance was exhibited primarily over the matter of gender roles. Other evangelicals, however, were more accepting of women's ordination, albeit with a level of caution, mirroring the attitudes of the wider Church. That the ordination of women as priests or their consecration as bishops cannot be seen as the full embrace of wider societal ideas of equality is evident from the provisions made for gender traditionalists that preclude women from holding offices within the Church on the same basis as men.

Notwithstanding, by the time that the Five Guiding Principles were published, the CofE had made clear headway in the direction of gender equality. Indeed, the gender values that emerged from the so-called second wave onwards found broad acceptance. Equally, the concern for maintaining unity within a broad Church prevailed (see Furlong, 2000) and so neither feminism nor traditionalism can be seen as overall representative of the institution's gender values (see also Percy, 2017).

The Church of England and gender in historical perspective 45

Hunter (1987) has argued that, in the US context, evangelicalism has exhibited both resistance towards and accommodation of wider society, meaning that a persistent tension between these two forces exists. He elaborates that the general movement is accommodation over time, eroding the symbolic boundaries[2] of evangelicalism, which is facilitated by exposure to modernity. However, this happens somewhat selectively (see Penning and Smidt, 2002). Whilst this interpretation is contested with respect to evangelicalism, the above discussion evidences that much of this has been true of the CofE as a whole with respect to its gender attitudes since the second half of the twentieth century, despite initial protest. In this instance, it is the symbolic boundaries of traditional Anglicanism that showed signs of erosion as the CofE slowly assimilated the gender values of wider English society that have been developing since modernity. Given the gradual increase of such values into the present time, alongside a conscious move away from traditional gender values, it is possible that such an erosion of traditional Anglican boundaries is still underway.[3]

However, this is not without important exception as conservative evangelicalism and traditional Anglo-Catholicism have exhibited the behaviours that Smith et al. (1998) identify as engaged orthodoxy. This is where conservative Protestants simultaneously engage with wider society and resist it, adhering to their traditional beliefs, which can lead to a softer expression of such beliefs (e.g., see Aune, 2006). Evangelical Anglicans have evinced this model with respect to their engagement with wider society (see Guest, 2007a) but the above analysis shows that it also applies specifically to conservative evangelicalism and to traditional Anglo-Catholicism with respect to how they interact with the wider CofE. However, the former tradition evinces this more than the latter. Nonetheless, whilst the latter tradition has shown resistance towards the wider Church, many of its adherents have remained within the CofE and make use of the alternative ecclesial structures introduced by the Act of Synod.

Conclusion

Having charted the historical development of gender values and attitudes throughout the eighteenth, nineteenth, and twentieth centuries and into the present one with specific relation to the CofE, I have identified several attitudes within the Established Church. However, it is worth emphasising the paradoxical nature of accommodation and resistance on developing gender roles and associated attitudes within evangelicalism and traditional Anglo-Catholicism. This evidences that the identities of these traditions are (in part) based on opposition and engagement with the wider CofE. It is also worth highlighting that, alongside the rise of the charismatic movement, evangelical attitudes towards gender became more diversified and some evangelicals became affirming of women's ordination. Such developments will enable a better understanding of the gender attitudes of my participants, to which I shall now turn.

46 *The Church of England and gender in historical perspective*

Notes

1 Otherwise known as a PCC, it is the executive committee of a CofE parish. They support parish governance.
2 Symbolic boundaries are social markers that distinguish a group from others.
3 That is not to suggest that the symbolic boundaries of charismatic evangelicalism are being eroded. True to its evangelicalism, there are indications of resistance to wider societal trends as is apparent in some of my participants' gender attitudes, discussed in later chapters.

References

Aune, K. (2006). Marriage in a British evangelical congregation: Practising post-feminist partnership? *The Sociological Review*, 54(4), 638–657.

Aune, K. (2008a). Evangelical Christianity and women's changing lives. *European Journal of Women's Studies*, 15(3), 277–294.

Aune, K. (2008b). Making men men: Masculinity and contemporary evangelical identity. In M. Smith (Ed.), *British evangelical identities past and present, vol. 1.: Aspects of the history and sociology of evangelicalism in Britain and Ireland* (pp. 153–166). Milton Keynes: Paternoster Press.

Aune, K., & Guest, M. (2019). Christian university students' attitudes towards gender: Constructing everyday theologies in a post-feminist climate. *Religions*, 10(2), 133–154.

Avis, P. (2004). The Episcopal Ministry Act of Synod: A "bearable anomaly"? In P. Avis (Ed.), *Seeking the truth of change in the Church: Reception, communication and the ordination of women* (pp. 152–170). London: T&T Clark.

Bagilhole, B. (2003). Prospects for change? Structural, cultural and action dimensions of the careers of pioneer women priests in the Church of England. *Gender, Work and Organization*, 10(3), 361–377.

Baker, J. (Ed.). (2004). Consecrated women? *A contribution to the women bishops debate*. Norwich: Canterbury Press.

Balmer, R. (1994). American fundamentalism: The ideal of femininity. In J. Hawley (Ed.), *Fundamentalism and gender* (pp. 47–62). Oxford University Press.

Balmer, R. (2016). *Evangelicalism in America*. Waco, TX: Baylor University Press.

Beattie, T. (2004). *The new Catholic feminism: Theology, gender theory and dialogue*. London: Routledge.

Bebbington, D.W. (1989). *Evangelicalism in modern Britain: A History from the 1730s to the 1980s*. London: Unwin Hyman.

Bebbington, D.W. (1995). The decline and resurgence of evangelical social concern 1918–1980. In J. Wolffe (Ed.), *Evangelical faith and public zeal: Evangelicals and society in Britain 1780–1980* (pp. 175–197). London: SPCK.

Benn, W. (2016). Evangelical episcopacy. In L. Gatiss (Ed.), *Positively Anglican: Building on the foundations and transforming the church* (pp. 43–54). Watford: Church Society.

Blomberg, C. (2011). The New Testament in North America. In A. Köstenberger & R. Yarbrough (Eds.), *New Testament studies in the 21st century: Essays in honor of DA Carson on the occasion of his 65th birthday* (pp. 277–299). Wheaton, IL: Crossway.

The Church of England and gender in historical perspective 47

Brown, A. (2014, July 14). *Church of England General Synod approves female bishops.* The Guardian. Retrieved from https://www.theguardian.com/world/2014/jul/14/church-england-general-synod-approves-female-bishops.

Brown, C.G. (2001). *The death of Christian Britain: Understanding secularisation, 1800–2000.* London: Routledge.

Brown, C.G. (2006). *Religion and society in twentieth-century Britain.* Harlow: Pearson Longman.

Brown, A., & Woodhead, L. (2016). *That was the Church that was: How the Church of England lost the English people.* London: Bloomsbury.

Bruce, S. (2008). *Fundamentalism.* Cambridge: Polity.

Buchanan, C., Craston, C., Gregg, D., Gunstone, J., Howard, C., & Pattison, D. (1981). *The charismatic movement in the Church of England.* London: The Central Board of Finance of the Church of England.

Butler, J. (1990). *Gender trouble: Feminism and the subversion of identity.* London: Routledge.

Butler, J. (1993). *Bodies that matter: On the discursive limits of sex.* London: Routledge.

Butt, R. (2011, May 5). *Archbishop of Canterbury appoints flying bishops.* The Guardian. Retrieved from https://www.theguardian.com/world/2011/may/05/archbishop-canterbury-flying-bishops.

Caldwell, S. (2021, October 14). *Dr Michael Ali-Nazir, former Anglican Bishop of Rochester, joins the Catholic Church.* Catholic Herald. Retrieved from https://catholicherald.co.uk/dr-michael-nazir-ali-former-anglican-bishop-of-rochester-joins-the-catholic-church/.

Carey, G. (2004). *Know the truth: A memoir.* London: HarperCollins.

Chandler, M. (2003). *An introduction to the Oxford Movement.* New York: Church Publishing Incorporated.

Chapman, R. (Ed.). (2006). *Firmly I believe: An Oxford Movement reader.* Norwich: Canterbury Press.

Craston, C. (1988). *Biblical headship and the ordination of women.* Bramcote: Grove Books.

Day, A. (2017). *The religious lives of older laywomen: The last active Anglican generation.* Oxford University Press.

Delap, L. (2013). "Be strong and play the man": Anglican masculinities in the twentieth century. In L. Delap & S. Morgan (Eds.), *Men, masculinities and religious change in twentieth century Britain* (pp. 119–154). Basingstoke: Palgrave Macmillan.

Fairweather, E.R. (Ed.). (1964). *The Oxford Movement.* Oxford University Press.

Faught, C.B. (2003). *Oxford Movement: A thematic history of the Tractarians and their times.* University Park, PA: Pennsylvania State University Press.

Fausto-Sterling, A. (2000). *Sexing the body: Gender politics and the construction of sexuality.* New York: Basic Books.

Fletcher, W. (2013). There for the burials; there for the births: Women in leadership in the Anglican Communion. In K. Pui-lan, J. Berling, & J. Plane Te Paa (Eds.), *Anglican women on Church and mission* (pp. 55–75). Norwich: Canterbury Press.

Francis, L.J., & Robbins, M. (1999). *The long diaconate, 1987–1994: Women deacons and the delayed journey to priesthood.* Leominster: Gracewing Publishing.

48 *The Church of England and gender in historical perspective*

Fry, A.D.J. (2021a). Postfeminist, engaged and resistant: Evangelical male clergy attitudes towards gender and women's ordination in the Church of England. *Critical Research on Religion, 9*(1), 65–83.

Furlong, M. (2000). *The CofE: The state it's in.* London: Hodder & Stoughton.

Gallagher, S.K. (2003). *Evangelical identity and gendered family life.* New Brunswick, NJ: Rutgers University Press.

Gatrell, C., & Peyton, N. (2019). Shattering the stained glass ceiling: Women leaders in the Church of England. In A-S. Antoniou, C. Cooper, & C. Gatrell (Eds.), *Women, business and leadership* (pp. 299–315). Cheltenham: Edward Elgar Publishing.

General Synod of the Church of England. (1988). *The ordination of women to the priesthood: A second report by the House of Bishops.* London: The Central Board of Finance of the Church of England.

Graham, J.M. (2002, December). Review of *Slaves, women and homosexuals: Exploring the hermeneutics of cultural analysis,* by W. J. Webb. *Journal of the Evangelical Theological society, 45*(4): 678–679.

Grayzel, S.R. (1999). *Women's identities at war: Gender, motherhood, and politics in Britain and France during the First World War.* Chapel Hill, NC: University of North Carolina Press.

Grayzel, S.R. (2002). *Women and the First World War.* London: Pearson Education.

Greene, A.M., & Robbins, M. (2015). The cost of a calling? Clergywomen and work in the Church of England. *Gender, Work and Organization, 22*(4), 405–420.

Groppe, E. (2009). Women and the persona of Christ: Ordination in the Roman Catholic Church. In S. Abraham & E. Procario-Foley (Eds.), *Frontiers in Catholic feminist theology: Shoulder to shoulder* (pp. 153–171). Minneapolis, MN: Fortress Press.

Grudem, W.A. (1994). *Systematic theology: An introduction to biblical doctrine.* Nottingham: InterVarsity Press.

Guest, M. (2007a). *Evangelical identity and contemporary culture: A congregational study in innovation.* Eugene, OR: Wipf and Stock Publishers.

Guest, M., Olson, E., & Wolffe, J. (2012). Christianity: Loss of monopoly. In L. Woodhead & R. Catto (Eds.), *Religion and change in modern Britain* (pp. 57–78). Oxford: Routledge.

Hall, D. (1994). Muscular Christianity: Reading and writing the male social body. In D. Hall (Ed.), *Muscular Christianity: Embodying the Victorian age* (pp. 3–15). Cambridge University Press.

Handley, P. (2017, September 15). *The Philip North Sheffield fiasco—and the question that simply wasn't asked.* The Church Times. Retrieved from https://www.churchtimes.co.uk/articles/2017/15-september/news/uk/the-sheffield-fiasco-and-the-question-that-simply-wasn-t-asked.

Heeney, B. (1988). *The women's movement in the Church of England 1850s–1930.* Oxford: Clarendon Press.

Hollis, C. (1967). *Newman and the modern world.* London and Aylesbury: Compton Printing Ltd.

Hunter, J.D. (1987). *Evangelicalism: The coming generation.* New York: Barron's Educational Series.

Jenkins, D. (2005). "Letter from Richard Jenkins, director of affirming Catholicism to the Rt Revd Christopher Hill on the provision for those to the admission of women to the Episcopate." Received by Rt Revd Christopher Hill. In Rigney, J with

The Church of England and gender in historical perspective 49

M. Chapman (Eds.), *Women as bishops* (pp. 131–138). London and New York: Mowbray, 3 Nov. 2008.

Johnson, E.A. (1993). *Women, earth, and creator spirit*. Mahwah, NJ: Paulist Press.

Jones, I. (2004). *Women and priesthood in the Church of England: Ten years on*. London: Church House Publishing.

Knox, E.A. (1933). *The Tractarian Movement, 1833–1845: A study of the Oxford Movement as a phase of the religious revival in Western Europe in the second quarter of the nineteenth century*. London: Putnam.

Laqueur, T.W. (2012). The rise of sex in the eighteenth century: Historical context and historiographical implications. *Signs: Journal of Women in Culture and Society, 37*(4), 802–813.

Larsen, T. (2006). *Crisis of doubt: Honest faith in nineteenth-century England*. Oxford University Press.

Leafe, S. (2012, November 21). *Why I voted no to women bishops*. The Independent. Retrieved from https://www.independent.co.uk/voices/comment/why-i-voted-no-to-women-bishops-8340833.html.

MacCulloch, D. (2009). *A history of Christianity: The first three thousand years*. London: Penguin.

Maiden, J. (2018, February 19). The charismatic turn of the long 1960s: Contexts and characteristics [Paper presentation]. Contemporary Religion in Historical Perspective: Publics and performances. Milton Keynes, United Kingdom.

Maltby, J. (1998). One Lord, one faith, one baptism, but two integrities? In M. Furlong (Ed.), *Act of Synod – Act of folly? Episcopal Ministry Act of Synod 1993* (pp. 42–58). London: SCM Press.

Mantle, G. (1991). *Archbishop: The life and times of Robert Runcie*. London: Sinclair-Stevenson Ltd.

Martin, B., (1976). *John Keble: Priest, professor and poet*. London: Croom Helm Ltd.

Mayland, J. (2007). The ordination of women and the ecumenical movement. In J. Wootton (Ed.), *This is our story: Free Church women's ministry* (pp. 105–128). Peterborough: Epworth.

McLeod, H. (1999). Protestantism and British national identity, 1815–1945. In P. Van der Veer and H. Lehmann (Eds.), *Nation and religion: Perspectives on Europe and Asia* (pp. 44–70). Princeton, NJ: Princeton University Press.

McLeod, H. (2007). *The religious crisis of the 1960s*. Oxford University Press.

McLeod, H. (2012). The "Sportsman" and the "Muscular Christian": Rival ideals in nineteenth century England. In P. Pasture, J. Art, & T. Buerman (Eds.), *Beyond the feminisation thesis: Gender and Christianity in modern Europe* (pp. 85–96). Leuven: Leuven University Press.

Montefiore, H. (1978). *Yes to women priests*. Great Wakering: Mayhew-McCrimmon.

Nason-Clark, N. (1987a). Ordaining women as priests: Religious vs. sexist explanations for clerical attitudes. *Sociological Analysis, 48*(3), 259–273.

Nazir-Ali, M. (2001). *Can women be bishops?* The Guardian. Retrieved from https://www.theguardian.com/world/2001/mar/31/religion.uk.

Ollard, S.L. (1963). *A short history of the Oxford Movement*. London: Mowbray.

Packer, J.I. (1973). Thoughts on the role and function of women in the Church. In C. Craston (Ed.), *Evangelicals and the ordination of women*. Bramcote: Grove Books.

50 The Church of England and gender in historical perspective

Page, S-J. (2013). Feminist faith lives? Exploring perceptions of feminism among two Anglican cohorts. In N. Slee, F. Porter, & A. Phillips (Eds.), *The faith lives of women and girls: Qualitative research perspectives* (pp. 51–63). Farnham: Ashgate.

Penning, J.M. & Smidt, C.E. (2002). *Evangelicalism: The next generation.* Ada, MI: Baker Academic.

Percy, E. (2017). Women, ordination and the Church of England: An ambiguous welcome. *Feminist Theology, 26*(1), 90–100.

Perkin, J. (1989). *Women and marriage in nineteenth-century England.* London: Routledge.

Perrin, R. (2016). *The Bible reading of young evangelicals: An exploration of the ordinary hermeneutics and faith of Generation Y.* Eugene, OR: Pickwick Publications.

Peyton, N., & Gatrell, C. (2013). *Managing clergy lives: Obedience, sacrifice, intimacy.* London: A&C Black.

Pickering, W.S.F. (1989). *Anglo-Catholicism: A study in religious ambiguity.* London: Routledge.

Pilarski, A.E. (2011). The past and future of feminist biblical hermeneutics. *Biblical Theology Bulletin, 41*(1), 16–23.

Piper, J., & Grudem, W. (Eds.). (1991). *Recovering biblical manhood and womanhood: A response to evangelical feminism.* Wheaton, IL: Crossway.

Piper, J., & Grudem, W. (2016). *50 crucial questions: An overview of central concerns about manhood and womanhood.* Wheaton, IL: Crossway.

Raven, C. (2009, March 30). *Bishop Michael Nazir-Ali—"Enough is enough".* Virtue Online. Retrieved from https://virtueonline.org/bishop-michael-nazir-ali-enough-enough-charles-raven.

Reed, J.S. (1996). *Glorious battle: The cultural politics of Victorian Anglo-Catholicism.* Nashville, TN: Vanderbilt University Press.

Ruddick, A. (2016). Complementarian ministry in the local parish church. In A. Gatiss (Ed.), *Positively Anglican: Building on the foundations and transforming the church* (pp. 55, 66). Watford: Church Society.

Sani, F., & Reicher, S. (2000). Contested identities and schisms in groups: Opposing the ordination of women as priests in the Church of England. *British Journal of Social Psychology, 39*(1), 95–112.

Schüssler Fiorenza, E. (1983). *In memory of her: A feminist theological reconstruction of Christian origins.* London: SCM Press.

Smith, C. with Emerson, M., Gallagher, S., Kennedy, P., & Sikkink, D. (1998). *American evangelicalism: Embattled and thriving.* Chicago, IL: University of Chicago Press.

Stewart, A.R. (2012). Gender, faith, and storytelling: An ethnography of the charismatic internet (Doctoral dissertation, University of Sussex).

Storkey, E. (1985). *What's right with feminism?* London: SPCK.

Summerfield, P. (1998). *Reconstructing women's wartime lives: Discourse and subjectivity in oral histories of the Second World War.* Manchester: Manchester University Press.

The Archbishops' Council. (2004). *Women Bishops in the Church of England? A report of the House of Bishops' Working Party on Women in the Episcopate.* London: Church House Publishing.

The Faith and Order Commission. (2018). *The five guiding principles: A resource for study.* London: Church House Publishing.

The Church of England and gender in historical perspective   51

Thrall, M.E. (1958). *The ordination of women to the priesthood: A study of the biblical evidence.* London: SCM Press.

Thorne, H. (2000). *Journey to the priesthood: An in-depth study of the first women priests in the Church of England.* Bristol: Centre for Comparative Studies in Religion and Gender.

Tooher, J. (2016). Overflowing with ministry opportunities! In L. Gatiss (Ed.), *Positively Anglican: Building on the foundations and transforming the church* (pp. 67–72). Watford: Church Society.

Vanhoozer, K. (2004). Into the "Great Beyond": A theologian's response to the Marshall plan. In I.H. Marshall (Ed.), *Beyond the Bible: Moving from scripture to theology* (pp. 81–95). Ada, MI: Baker Academic Press.

Vasey-Saunders, M. (2015). *The scandal of evangelicals and homosexuality: English Evangelical Texts, 1960–2010.* London: Routledge.

Webb, W.J. (2001). *Slaves, women and homosexuals: Exploring the hermeneutics of cultural analysis.* Nottingham: InterVarsity Press.

Witherington III, B. (1987). *Women in the ministry of Jesus: A study of Jesus' attitudes to women and their roles as reflected in his earthly life.* Cambridge University Press.

Witherington III, B. (1990). *Women and the genesis of Christianity.* Cambridge University Press.

3 Clerical sexism

Introduction

In the previous chapter, I outlined the historical developments within the CofE on gender, particularly the various understandings of women's ordination as deacons and priests, and their consecration as bishops, that existed within it. These processes set the scene for understanding current gender attitudes amongst Anglican clergy. In this chapter, I will explore the gender attitudes—specifically, beliefs about women—articulated by my participants. As I do so, my analysis will tease out the continuities in thought that may be traced historically to the current day. As engagement with participants' data reveals a clear relationship with existing research on prejudice more broadly and sexism in particular, this will be used as an interpretive lens for further understanding the narratives of the clergy interviewed. In doing so, I shall argue that evangelical gender attitudes continue to evince the simultaneous rejection and embrace of wider social values that were noted in the previous chapter, whereas the traditional Anglo-Catholic gender attitudes continue to evince resistance towards gender norms that have developed over the last century.

These attitudes are often articulated in such a way that are, in social psychological terms, sexist. However, previous research on gender within conservative Protestantism has neglected to employ social psychological research on sexism and so does not offer as full a picture of gender-based prejudice as it might. As my analysis develops in subsequent chapters, using this lens will provide a greater depth of understanding of the phenomena that shape clergy gender attitudes.

The focus of this and subsequent chapters will be on how my participants' gender attitudes manifest within the CofE, although parish life is an immersive context for them, not entirely separable from other aspects of their life, including their family/personal lives. I will unpack this further in the next chapter. Their attitudes towards women beyond this context will also be explored because factors beyond the Church are formative for participants' gender attitudes within it. Indeed, their gender attitudes entail beliefs about women that are found beyond the CofE.

DOI: 10.4324/9781003081913-3

Clerical sexism 53

In what follows, I shall explore the themes from the conservative evangelical narratives that are most appropriate for understanding their gender attitudes before doing likewise with the charismatic evangelical, and then the Anglo-Catholic, narratives. As I do so, I will explore how these traditions evince continuity with their respective histories and with the expressions of these traditions that exist outside of the CofE. After this, I shall outline the relevant theories pertaining to sexism before analysing the themes in light of them. I will also provide a methodological reflection before I offer my conclusions to more fully appreciate the depth of analysis that utilising a combination of historical, sociological, and social psychological research provides, and the extent to which this fusion illuminates the factors that shape participants' gender attitudes.

The Reform narratives

Two themes will be the focus of discussion on the Reform participants in this chapter. These are: (i) Created order of male headship and female submission; and (ii) Ambivalent attitudes towards feminism. The latter has two sub-themes, namely Positives of feminism and Negatives of feminism. To understand what social factors contribute to the formation of the gender attitudes held by theologically conservative male clergy, it is necessary to understand their theologies of gender roles and it was this discussion during the interviews that led to the emergence of the first theme. It was conversations around wider societal gender norms that led to the emergence of the second theme.

Created order of male headship and female submission

The first theme was discerned from the strand of questions concerning participants' theology of women and men's roles in the Church, in the family unit, and in the occupational sphere. Thirteen of the 14 participants believed that, according to the Bible, God has designed men to lead in the Church and family, whereas women are designed to follow male leadership. For example, Greg said, "We [complementarians] want to model male responsibility in leadership in the church family with the conviction that that will encourage the same in the home." When discussing the creation narrative in Genesis 2, Greg elaborated, "[The Bible is] saying that Adam is created first .... Eve was created to be a complement to Adam .... I think that the two are to work together as equals with those different roles that are given to us." Similarly, Callum stated, "I'm ... a complementarian. Men and women are made differently, and I think there is a natural headship that men have over women .... It's ... ingrained into us."

Greg and Callum identified as complementarians. Participants explained that this is someone who believes that men are created by God to be the head of (i.e., lead) churches and the family unit, whereas women are created to

54 *Clerical sexism*

help men but also to be subservient to them. Greg's rationale for this was the fact that, in the Genesis 2 creation narrative, Adam (the man) was made before Eve (the woman), indicating a belief in causal priority, the idea that the one who comes first has greater authority (see Thiselton, 2000). Participants also offered other justifications for this belief. For instance, Callum's rationale stemmed from an internal sense that men are natural leaders. More importantly, however, participants (with one exception) agreed that God has created men to lead and women to submit in the Church and familial spheres.

Nevertheless, there is an important caveat to this. Participants held mixed views about whether it was acceptable, according to biblical mandate, for women to lead in the workplace. When asked whether the principle of male leadership and female submission ought to apply in the workplace, Adam stated, "I think inevitably if ... there is a subordination ... in the Trinity ... [and] if we're made in God's likeness then that surely should be mirrored in society and in cultural and political [and other] ... areas of life." Adam is alluding to 1 Corinthians 11 in the New Testament, where Paul states that God the Father is the 'head' (κεφαλὴ) of Christ. Following conservative evangelical interpretation of this passage (e.g., see Grudem, 1994), Adam reported using this as a rationale for male leadership and female submission in all areas of life, including those beyond the Church and familial spheres. However, this belief was only found in three of the narratives, and none of the participants were adamant that this is something they expected to see adhered to. Adam continued, "While I would be complementarian within a Church framework and within the home, I do not think that that is the right thing to tell society to be, because ... it's a secular society." Likewise, Joshua said, "I see the role of men and women as equally valuable but different [only] at home and Church."

Adam explained that whilst, in theory, he believes that the gender patterns he thinks ought to be exhibited in the Church and family should also be exhibited in all areas of life, he accepts that wider society has different values. Those who theoretically disagreed with women's leadership in all areas of society did not hold tightly to this belief, and 11 of the participants did not share this belief at all: Joshua, for instance, did not think it was appropriate to prescribe a complementarian pattern to wider society (see also Fry, 2019). Nevertheless, other participants stated that women occupying professional roles should do so in a "feminine way", to use Justin's words.

Participants' gender attitudes are essentialist, seeing certain characteristics and social roles as intrinsic and unique to each sex. The relationship between such theology and violence (physical and symbolic) has been documented (e.g., see Westenberg, 2017 and Jagger, 2021, respectively), but such attitudes are also problematic in an indirect way. The pay disparity between men and women in comparable—and even identical—professional positions is well documented. This is the result of several factors. Of relevance for this study, the gendering of skills is a cause of employment inequality. More specifically, women are often in lower-paid jobs due to the gendering of skills, where those traditionally associated with women are undervalued. This is because such skills are thought to be 'natural' to women and thus not as worthy of merit, which contributes to the underrepresentation of women in higher-status jobs (Redfern and Aune, 2010). The fact that the Reform participants believe that women are created to be followers rather than leaders demonstrates that they hold an attitude that exists beyond the Church and that contributes to gender inequality in the occupational sphere. Indeed, it is such beliefs that they advocated during the debates on the ordination of women that led to restrictions on women's professional ministry to maintain unity within the Church.

Given that evangelical opposition to women's ordination centred on theological articulations of headship from the previous century, it is unsurprising to see this objection manifest in the Reform narratives. Moreover, that Greg tries to mirror male leadership in the Church as in the family strongly resonates with the inseparable nature of family and religious life that was apparent in evangelicalism more widely throughout the twentieth century. Indeed, the fact that most Reform participants expressed that they wish to distinguish between the home and church spheres as the arena of Christian living against the occupational sphere is in keeping with previous findings that the family can serve as a plausibility structure for faith (Guest and Aune, 2017; see also Fry, 2019). The discussion around this theme also highlights the continuation that Reform share with historical evangelicalism as they believe that much of the traditional division of labour is God-ordained.

Ambivalent attitudes towards feminism: Positives of feminism and Negatives of feminism

Participants expressed negative and positive understandings of feminism. For example, Stephen said:

> I think there are branches within [feminism—] one of seeking to affirm women and be constructive and creative, and one that can become over militant and become denigrating of men .... I've seen ... a movement that can become denigrating, over-asserting women over men.

There is evidently an anxiety about the nature of feminism to (supposedly) subvert men and place women higher in the social hierarchy. This was seen in half of the Reform participants' answers to a question that asked them to give their response to the feminist movement. Joshua reported:

> Radical feminism that moves beyond ... trying to raise up the rights of women ... to promoting a ... feminine alternative as being stronger than the prevailing masculine reality ... and thinking 'actually we'd be better off if this package of feminine ideals ... had the upper hand' ... is something I take real issue with.

56 *Clerical sexism*

The other seven narratives, however, contained similar sentiments which were less pronounced, entertaining the idea that feminists could be "angry" or "militant", for example. Nevertheless, the critique of feminism was extended to the fact it denied distinct spheres for the sexes in 13 of the narratives. Alistair said of feminism that it "seeks to eradicate difference in order to reach equality and therefore sees difference as undermining equality. [However], I don't think that the fact that a husband and a wife have different roles in marriage in any way undermines their status."

These comments reflect something of a postfeminist[1] outlook. They demonstrate an appreciation for the value of equality promoted by feminism in addition to a critique of it, which is accompanied by the assumption that men and women (ought to) occupy distinct spheres (see Aune, 2006; see also Fry, 2021a). Participants thus mirrored Aune's findings that evangelical gender attitudes are not always that distinct from those of non-religious members of society. This reflects what Guest et al. (2013) found in their study of student Christians, indicating that such beliefs are cross-generational.

There are several links between participants' attitudes towards feminism and findings in other studies. In particular, the appreciation for certain aspects of feminism highlights their appreciation for a relatively new movement and that participants have incorporated an element of wider societal gender norms into their own thinking. However, the negative assessments of feminism that they exhibited are symptomatic of the fact that their incorporation of feminist values into their own is limited (see also Fry, 2021a). Participants, therefore, exhibited a mixture of rejection and incorporation of wider (feminist) societal values. It is true, though, that a mixed response to feminism is evinced in wider society (see Press, 2011). In this respect, the Reform narratives indicate a fuller incorporation of gender values that exist outside of the Church beyond those who consciously identify as feminists. Equally, participants' understanding of feminism is accompanied by traditional theological beliefs, which are not held by wider society. In other words, the Reform narratives reflect the model of engaged orthodoxy. In this case, engaged orthodoxy is not exhibited towards the wider CofE, as was the case with conservative evangelicals from the 1990s (as discussed in the previous chapter), but towards wider society, leading to a selective incorporation of its gender values that allows them to retain a conservative stance on women's ordination.

The charismatic evangelical narratives

A larger number of themes will be discussed as I engage with the charismatic evangelical data, because these narratives are less homogenous. These are: (i) Affirmation of women's ordination; (ii) Rejection of the theology of headship; (iii) Gender differences as observable; (iv) Belief in the flexibility of gender roles; and (v) Ambivalent attitudes towards feminism, which also has two sub-themes: Positives of feminism and Negatives of feminism. These

Clerical sexism 57

themes provide insight into participant's theology or their understanding of gender within society.

Affirmation of women's ordination and Rejection of the theology of headship

All participants in this group reported believing that it is entirely appropriate for women to be ordained, and all but two reported believing that this could be to any part of the CofE's hierarchy. For instance, Ken said:

> I am fully supportive of women being deacons, priests, and bishops and I think ... that there's a good biblical case for that .... I think that if you look behind at what was actually going on ... culturally/historically [in the communities the biblical texts were written to, they're] talking about a cultural situation rather than a timeless truth.

The more permissive gender attitude expressed by Ken shows that the clear articulations of restrictive roles found in the Reform narratives are largely absent in the charismatic evangelical ones. In fact, eight of the participants directly rejected the theology of male headship and female subordination. Richard remarked:

> I definitely don't believe in headship and submission. I believe in equal partnership in marriage ... I believe in equal submission ... in [Ephesians 5] before it goes on about 'wives submit to your husbands' [it is] preceded by 'husbands and wives submit to each other.'

He explained that he understands the biblical texts employed in support of male headship/female submission to be misinterpreted. Instead, Richard believes that both sexes ought to be equally submissive. However, four participants, whilst affirming women's ordained ministry, neglected to mention headship at all. Another two participants, on the other hand, expressed a similar interpretation to members of Reform: they claimed that there is a created pattern of male headship/female submission and that this makes it inappropriate for women to lead churches. However, this would not bar them from ordination per se, nor from taking any leadership responsibilities in a congregation so long as they do not have overall responsibility of a church as incumbents. For instance, these participants believed that it would be entirely appropriate for a woman to preach to a mixed-sex congregation. This is one of the main distinctions between these two narratives and those in Reform. Oscar said that male headship "seems to be argued from creation, not from culture and ... there is a difference in ... role[s] between men and women .... I do think there is something going on with headship that is valid for all time."

Oscar articulated his belief that the Bible suggests women may teach in different settings, but that there is nonetheless a universal, created pattern of

58 *Clerical sexism*

male leadership. However, he does not believe that it is inappropriate for a woman to be a bishop, whereas the other complementarian in this group does. Nevertheless, neither of these participants were comfortable articulating this in a decisive manner. As a case in point, Michael stated:

> Our theology is formed by the church that we're a part of .... I was in ... a ... church .... [that] had nominated ... that [we] would like a male incumbent. So that was the tradition of HTB and we were a HTB plant ... and [so that is] my understanding.

Michael deflected the question concerning his gender attitudes, to some extent, by asserting that he has simply inherited a pre-existing view, a behaviour that Oscar similarly exhibited. Both were leading churches that had been planted by Holy Trinity Brompton (HTB), a large charismatic evangelical church in London that has planted (i.e., created) new churches and supported the growth of existing ones across England. However, the deflection of questions in this area was accompanied by a lack of detailed elaboration on their understanding of the social and biological implications of belief in a created order, despite mirroring something of the complementarian theology found in the Reform narratives.

Participants' theology of women's ordination somewhat reflects the context of the late 1950s where Christians were beginning to question why women couldn't hold the same roles in the Church as men. Their beliefs concerning the functional equality of the sexes mirrors much of the aims of 'second-wave' feminism more broadly. However, those interviewed did not typically evince an understanding of existing patriarchal structures within the CofE (although a minority did). Hence, the majority of this group do not reflect the theology found in work such as Storkey (1985). These narratives also reveal a level of rejection of the gendered dualism that has permeated Christian thought for centuries, a clear break with tradition and a further distinction from the Reform narratives. All of this indicates that participants' engagement with wider social ideas is selective, incorporating only certain aspects of others' gender ideals into their own. Participants in this group also reflect Guest et al.'s (2013) finding that most evangelicals believe in gender equality regarding women's role in church.

It is also worth mentioning that the ideas articulated by participants are in continuity with the Evangelical Group of the General Synod who, in 1992, were mostly in favour of ordaining women as priests. The charismatic evangelical participants' rejection of complementarian theology parallels the CofE's official position that theologies of subordination are a non-contextualised misreading of scripture and therefore inappropriate. There is also evidently a continuation of thought and practice that was a key component to the charismatic movement historically, namely the space for women to exercise leadership roles in church. In fact, several participants expressed the importance of spiritual gifts, rather than gender, as the basis for their theology of women's ordination. That is, the history of participants' tradition impacts their current gender attitudes.

Gender differences as observable and Belief in the flexibility of gender roles

Despite the comparative levels of support for women's leadership in the Church in participants' narratives, generalisations about gender are present in most of them. Matt said:

> It's very difficult to generalise about characteristics of male or female leadership. However, female leadership can be more emotionally intelligent …. I think a more—quote—female leadership approach could be one of very few rays of light [for the CofE].

Participants regularly articulated that there is evidence for gender differences. Matt's comment here is one of the clearest examples, despite being very broad and lacking in detail. Others were yet more vague and didn't specify any differences but suggested that subtle ones existed. They also explained that they are open to the concept of flexible gender roles when it comes to the roles that men and women may fulfil in church, home, and wider society. Richard said, "I don't think there should be prescribed [gender] roles …. I think, as a general rule, there are differences between men and women. …. There are undoubtedly exceptions to those rules." Similarly, Michael said, "You can't caricature [gender roles]. For example, I am a better cook [than my wife], so I do the cooking." Participants do not think that men or women should always conform to traditional roles.

In many cases, participants have professional wives and see no theological, practical, or social problem with this. Furthermore, whilst ten interviewees in the charismatic evangelical group suggested that there are gender differences, all 14 agreed that female and male roles are flexible across a range of domains. Participants did not usually ascribe a biological or God-ordained origin to gender differences or gender roles (other than with respect to reproductive biology). Overall, participants appeared rather agnostic on the matter. Nevertheless, one participant reported believing that motherhood and fatherhood are distinct roles, each with its own characteristics. However, another participant explained that male clergy are often keen to develop their "feminine side" for pastoral reasons, implying that observable gender differences are not understood to be biologically exclusive.

The fact that participants are happy with some gender flexibility reflects their upbringing that included a childhood and/or young adulthood in the wake of the social developments from the mid-to-late twentieth century, where contraception allowed women more workplace opportunities. My participants demonstrated a belief that there is a definitive quality (or set of qualities) that is/ are intrinsic to being female or male. However, despite lacking knowledge of academic literature in this area, their avoidance of describing how this might

60 Clerical sexism

manifest in detail, and their rejection of fixed gender roles, indicates something of a non-gender essentialist position. In fact, at times participants outright rejected gender essentialist ideas. The above indicates that, whilst participants have rejected "hierarchical dualism" (Johnson, 1993, p. 10) to some extent, evidence of this thinking remains, highlighting further the fact that their tradition's history impacts devotees' attitudes in the present.

A further example of this mixed approach to gender was highlighted during one interview with someone who rejected a theology of male headship and reported being comfortable with women in a variety of roles. However, on arriving at their home, I was offered a cup of tea before our interview. The participant then gave the tea order to his wife (herself a theology graduate) and ushered me into the living room to begin. The woman in question could be heard walking up the stairs as the kettle (also audible) was boiling. After several minutes, the participant got out of his seat, opened the living room door, and shouted up the stairs to his wife, asking where the tea was. As I had explained to the participant in advance of our meeting that I would be asking about his own gender attitudes, I noted the lack of awareness of the apparent discord between his espoused beliefs and this specific instance, even though this does suggest a level of openness on his part during the interview as he was not trying to conceal behaviour that could be interpreted as evidence of traditionalist gender attitudes.

Ambivalent attitudes towards feminism: Positives of feminism and Negatives of feminism

As with Reform, participants hold Ambivalent attitudes towards feminism, which has likewise been separated into two sub-themes. Matt said:

> Most of [feminism] I'm really happy with. When it gets shrill and demonising men, I get stroppy about it and disagree .... I don't agree with that, and I feel there's an imbalance in [that] view, which actually is very similar to the way that some men—in a chauvinistic way—talk about women.

Ten participants expressed a belief that feminism could overreach itself by attacking men and/or minimising differences between the sexes, conflating the two. This is similar to the Reform narratives, other than the fact that four charismatic evangelical participants did not evince such beliefs, whereas all of the Reform narratives did. It also reflects gender-related beliefs found outside of the CofE, providing further evidence that the wider evangelicalism of the CofE (as well as wider society) has shaped this tradition.

The Anglo-Catholic narratives

As with the previous group of participants, a larger number of themes will be discussed as these narratives are less ubiquitous. However, there are not as many themes as there were for the charismatic evangelical narratives, because the traditional Anglo-Catholics were less heterogeneous than them. The themes I will discuss in this chapter are: (i) Ecumenical objection to the ordination of women; (ii) Sacramental objection to the ordination of women; (iii) Apostolic objection to the ordination of women; and (iv) Ambivalent attitudes towards feminism, which is likewise divided into Negatives of feminism and Positives of feminism.

Ecumenical objection to the ordination of women

All but two of the participants in this group expressed various reasons for their objection to the ordination of women to the priesthood and, by extension, their consecration as bishops. All the Anglo-Catholic priests interviewed who object to the ordination of women to the priesthood articulated that it deviates from the teaching of the Roman Catholic and Orthodox Churches. For example, Ashley said emphatically and with frustration in his voice:

> The Church of England has no authority to [ordain women] .... It is not the place of a province in the universal Church to make a unilateral change to order and so therefore until such time as the Catholic and Orthodox Church embrace this change, it's a change we have no authority to do.

These 11 participants explained that they believe it is important to emphasise the CofE's continuity with the rest of the worldwide Church, particularly the Roman Catholic Church, which they believe the CofE descended from. For them, if other Churches have not agreed to ordain women, then, as an expression of catholicity (i.e., Christian unity), neither should the CofE. This is not necessarily an argument against the validity of women's ordination per se, but for many of the interviewees, it does "cast doubt" on whether women's holy orders are sacramentally effective. Some participants repeated the language of doubt when asked about their theology of gender, couching their opposition in softer terms, rather than being as forthright as Ashley. It is also worth explaining that participants rarely objected to the ordination of women to the diaconate with the justification that deacons do not preside at the altar during Communion. (The two Anglo-Catholics who do not object to women's ordination to the priesthood had previously held more traditionalist views when they were younger but had gradually re-evaluated their theological position).

Sacramental objection to the ordination of women

Ten of my participants elaborated on their objection to women's ordination in terms of sacramental uncertainty. They are unconvinced that women's

62   *Clerical sexism*

holy orders have the efficacy to allow them to stand in the place of Christ at the altar or administer other sacraments. Malcolm explained:

> The main role of priesthood is to represent the people to God and God and Christ to the people ... within a sacramental nature of priesthood ... [so] you're not happy with women priests because you're not sure about the validity of [the] sacraments.

Malcolm was referring to the Mass, where the priest presides at Communion to act in the place of Christ (a man) and in doing so is God's agent in changing the bread into the body of Christ, and the wine into his blood,[2] a key tenet of Anglo-Catholicism. For Anglo-Catholics, the bread and wine used for Communion becomes the body and blood of Christ as a means of attaining God's grace for salvation, a Roman Catholic belief. If there is doubt over the ability of a female priest to consecrate the bread and wine, there is doubt over the ability for a person to obtain grace by receiving them.

Apostolic objection to the ordination of women

All participants who oppose women's ordination to the priesthood also explained that their objection is based on the belief that it breaks the historic chain of male apostles appointed by Jesus. Oliver, for instance, said (in a matter-of-fact way):

> [Priesthood] has always been exclusively male .... Jesus' own deliberate choice of 12 [men as apostles] ... was a very specific calling .... The Early Church decided that bishop, priest, and deacon ... descended from the 12 ... it was apostolic in that sense and ... therefore excluded women.

He believes that the early tradition of the Christian Church was that all ordained ministers were succeeding the 12 men appointed by Jesus, even though scholarship that has employed historical-critical methods has recognised the presence of female apostles and deacons (e.g., see discussion in Dunn, 1998). Whilst most of the Anglo-Catholic participants disagree with Oliver on the ordination of women as deacons, the other point made in the above quote reflects all 11 Anglo-Catholic participants who object to women's ordination otherwise. It also mirrors Aldridge's (1992) findings in the run up to the debate about women's priesthood in the early 1990s. He argued that Jesus was used as a charismatic leader figure to assert the theology of male-only apostolic succession and that this is an example of a social group employing sacred imagery to legitimate group objectives.

Only one participant entertained the notion that it was inappropriate for women to work if they are mothers. The rest of the Anglo-Catholic participants have no objection to women having other roles in society. Whilst participants do believe that each sex possesses distinct characteristics, and that one's sex can make someone ineligible for priesthood, for almost all of them, this does not reflect what women may (not) do outside of the Church's ordained hierarchy. Thus, participants do not hold a gender essentialist position, nor do they hold a fully non-essentialist position given their belief that sex does have some implications for gender roles in the Church; they are partially gender essentialist.

One can discern the presence of theological ideas often challenged by feminist scholarship in these narratives. For example, the division of the sexes for the suitability of the priesthood reflects historical Christian dualism. However, it is discernible in participants' thinking only with respect to clergy roles, indicating that the dualism is limited in scope. Johnson (1993) has argued that patriarchal theological language implies that men are in some sense more like God than women. This is suitably applied to the traditional Anglo-Catholic conviction that only men may represent Christ at the altar, suggesting that men are more like Jesus than are women.

Participants' rejection of the legitimacy of women bishops, despite believing in apostolic succession, demonstrates continuity with the selective nature of submission to ecclesial authority evidenced in Anglo-Catholicism historically. In fact, on several occasions, participants recalled times when they directly opposed their bishop because they saw him as holding to inaccurate theology. The appeal to the tradition of the Early Church is also in keeping with the Tractarians' appeal to the Church Fathers for support of their theological claims. The prominence of ordaining women to the priesthood and consecrating them to the episcopate is evidently linked to the apostolic hierarchy participants believe was established amongst the first generations of Christians. In this respect, their concern with gender and episcopacy reflects a more general concern for protecting (what they perceive to be) the integrity of episcopacy, as was the case during the nineteenth century.

Furthermore, in the years leading up to the 1992 vote in the General Synod, there was widespread belief amongst Anglicans that unity with the Roman Catholic Church would be possible, and that ordaining women would damage this possibility (Brown and Woodhead, 2016). It is within this context that Forward in Faith organised rallies protesting the ordination of women (Sani and Reicher, 2000). Given that those interviewed expressed the importance of unity with Rome, this recent historical context sheds light on why they continue to resist women's ordained ministry.

Ambivalent attitudes towards feminism: Negatives of feminism and Positives of feminism

In contrast to the other groups, 50% more Anglo-Catholics evinced an appreciation of feminism than criticised it, whereas in both evangelical groups those who criticised feminism were almost always those who articulated some appreciation for it also. Regarding Negatives of feminism, Peter claimed:

64 *Clerical sexism*

> I'm not really sure what feminism is all about ... because it strikes me that [women are] desperately trying to do away with what it is to be feminine. They're trying to equate themselves [with men].... And that is really an outpouring of the spirit of the present age, which will evaporate.

Peter, like many of the evangelical participants, understands feminism to involve a conflation of the sexes. His reference to feminism as part of "the present age" appears to be an allusion to Paul's New Testament letter to the Galatians (1:4) where he wrote that believers are to be rescued from the evil of the present age. Indeed, this passage has an eschatological significance, meaning that it concerns the future coming of God's kingdom (Stanton, 2001). It could well be that when Peter claimed that feminism will "evaporate" he was drawing on such theological resources when he criticised the feminist movement. This statement reflects a gender essentialist sentiment that was also articulated by those who did not speak of feminism in negative terms.

When Adrian was asked about his reaction to feminism, he explained that, as a gay man (who also grew up in a lower socio-economic stratum of society), he feels that his own experience of inequality has been ignored within CofE teaching, which still requires that clergy abstain from same-sex sexual activity. He concluded his answer by trailing off with the words "Fuck feminism. Fuck everybody". In response to the same question, Oliver (through the auspices of a joking manner) said, "Well [feminists should] get a life, basically." He seemed slightly surprised when he paused for laughter but there was none, suggesting that he had not fully considered the need for feminist discourse.

Nonetheless, more participants in this group expressed positive attitudes towards feminism than negative. Edward said the following of feminism: "It's a good thing in so much as it's about where women have been downtrodden in society or denied access to vocation and jobs and where they're particularly held down in poverty and so on." Participants regularly demonstrated appreciation for the contribution that feminism has made to creating greater equality, indicating a shift in thinking from around the mid-twentieth century. However, this was with some inconsistency. Edward's comment above indicates an approval that women can more fully explore their vocations because of the achievements of the feminist movement. However, for him—as for many others in this group—this does not include their ordination as priests in the CofE. Malcolm's comment is also relevant in this respect:

> I think some feminists do take the view that it means women: good, men: bad. Perhaps that's a bit of an exaggeration, but if the feminist movement meant—I don't know how to phrase this. No, I think I'll just stick with what I said [previously], that if feminism simply means that men and women are equal in society ... within the constraints of things like strength and so on, then I have no problem with it.

Clerical sexism   65

Malcolm stopped himself from elaborating on the negatives of feminism and then closed his statement by asserting something positive about the movement. It is apparent from the second sentence in this statement that Malcolm was about to express a caricature. Mirroring the findings of Guest et al. (2013)—but there amongst university students—participants claimed that feminism could overreach itself. They also claimed that it could seek to denigrate men.

During the interview, Adrian showed me several pictures he has around his house. This included a painting hanging in the room next to his study, which he described as feminist. He explained that it was painted by a female friend of his who is a feminist and that the yellow flowers in the painting symbolise female orgasm. When I asked him why yellow flowers symbolise female orgasm, Adrian was hesitant to answer before merely stating that this is what the artist had told him. This indicates that his engagement with feminist ideas lacks depth of understanding. This is paralleled in Oliver's narrative. He reported personal relationships with two feminist intellectuals, one of which is well-known in Church circles and the other is a media personality. As his comment above shows, though, this does not lead to much appreciation for feminist causes.

Prejudice, sexism, and prejudice suppression

Much of the above data has historical precedents and/or reflects wider evangelicalism within and without the Established Church and within Roman Catholicism. The above narratives also have strong affinities with social psychological research on prejudice which is yet to be utilised in research on English Anglicanism. It is to an exploration of these affinities that I will now turn.

Recent research on prejudice has intellectual roots in Gordon Allport's (1979) *The Nature of Prejudice*. Whilst his work was primarily concerned with ethnic prejudice, Allport's theory has been widely utilised in numerous areas of cognate research, not least gender discrimination (e.g., Rudman, 2005). It has also been employed in research on occupational spheres (e.g., Green, 2007) and religious diversity (e.g., Merino, 2010), making it a useful interpretive lens for understanding my participants. In fact, Allport's theory, stemming from quantitative research, has been tested and affirmed cross-nationally over a 60-year time frame, indicating its robustness for application in the present study (see Pettigrew and Tropp, 2008).

Prejudice has three components (Allport, 1979). Firstly, there is hostility towards (and the rejection of) individuals, particularly those who are believed to belong to different social groups (i.e., outgroups), a phenomenon that is frequently drawn along the lines of gender or sex (see Vonk and Olde-Monnikhof, 1998). Secondly, there are faulty and unfounded generalisations about outgroups. Thirdly, persons who hold prejudicial beliefs about others reject evidence that would undermine that prejudice. However, prejudice may

66 Clerical sexism

be lessened when members of different social groups exhibit four criteria. Firstly, they must possess equal status. Secondly, they must seek common goals. Thirdly, they need to be co-operatively dependent on one another. Finally, they need to interact with each other with the support of mitigating authorities or structures (Pettigrew, 1971). This will be explored in more detail in later chapters. For now, it is important to recognise that the absence of these factors is more likely to be present when prejudice is discerned.

A separate strand of quantitative research has developed in dialogue with Allport's theory, to produce a psychological theory of sexism that is a sub-set of prejudice. Glick and Fiske (1996) have drawn on ambivalence psychology and formulated the theory of ambivalent sexism, where women specifically are the targets of gender prejudice. There are two strands in this theory, namely hostile sexism and so-called benevolent sexism. Hostile sexism describes attitudes towards women that are in keeping with the above definition of prejudice. 'Benevolent' sexism designates an attitude towards women that may initially appear subjectively positive, but that actually undermines conceptions of women's competence. For example, a man may be all too happy to help a woman because he believes that she requires protection as the (allegedly) weaker sex. A biological determinism often underlies 'benevolent' sexism. Sexism is thus ambivalent because it incorporates these two different aspects of gender-related prejudice, but also because an individual can harbour both kinds of sexism but in different contexts.

The theory of ambivalent sexism has been developed since its conception. Initially, hostile sexism was associated with the justification of male power, traditional gender roles, and men's exploitation of women as sex objects, achieved through demeaning caricatures of women. However, it is now associated with a hostile response to women when they are perceived by men to be threatening their power or status in some way, such as through endorsing feminist ideals (Masser and Abrams, 2004).

Both hostile and 'benevolent' sexism can be further sub-categorised into three distinct parts (Glick and Fiske, 1997). Firstly, "power differences between the sexes [...] are rationalized through ideologies of *paternalism*" (p. 121, emphasis original). Paternalism may be further sub-categorised. Dominative determinism is a sub-set of hostile sexism and is the idea that men should control women. Protective paternalism, by contrast, is a subset of 'benevolent' sexism and asserts that men ought to protect women because of their (supposedly) superior strength and power.

Secondly, there is gender differentiation. On the one hand, there is competitive gender differentiation, a sub-set of hostile sexism that relies on negative stereotyping of women by men so that the latter maintain a sense of gender-related superiority. On the other hand, there is complementary gender differentiation, a sub-set of 'benevolent' sexism which is made up of traditional stereotypes about women that are more positive and are theorised to be the result of men's dyadic relationships with women. In this respect, women are seen to complement characteristics typically associated with men and (supposedly) male roles. Complementary gender differentiation thus relies on the perception that women have virtuous traits that complement men's traits. Thirdly, there is heterosexuality. Heterosexual hostility (a subset of hostile sexism) describes an inclination to view women as sex objects and a male fear that women will use their sexuality to gain mastery over men, whereas intimate heterosexuality (a sub-set of 'benevolent' sexism) describes men idealising women as sexual objects.

Both forms of sexism (hostile and 'benevolent') may be labelled as such because they consist of prejudicial attitudes that evoke traditional gender stereotypes, including a patriarchal status quo, which limit the role of women in society (Glick and Fiske, 1996, 1997). Again, the reliability of the ambivalent sexism theory has been well attested from its origins with large-scale testing in numerous contexts and with a diverse range of participants and large effect sizes. It is therefore an understanding of sexism that is widely agreed upon. However, a limitation of much of the work to date has been that it has not focused on sexism in real-life situations. A descriptive analysis of how those with sexist outlooks present their beliefs will therefore shed much-needed light on how sexism can manifest in everyday life.

A further methodological note ought to be made. Glick and Fiske (1996) understand sexism, whether hostile or 'benevolent', with respect to the above definitions they have provided. This enables one to employ the theory in a qualitative context because the researcher is not reliant upon a fixed questionnaire to determine whether one has sexist attitudes. Thus, in the present study, whether or not a person's gender attitudes are deemed sexist is dependent upon whether or not their statements reflect the aforementioned definitions. However, any statement being analysed for sexism must meet all aspects of any one of the definitions of sexism or its sub-categories to be considered sexist.[3] Whilst the above understandings of prejudice and sexism are designed to capture attitudes more broadly, their definitions are especially useful for assessing beliefs and so are employed in this chapter. Later chapters, that focus on behaviours and emotions, will utilise complementary approaches to prejudice to assess these dimensions of participants' gender attitudes.

It is apparent that Glick and Fiske's model assumes a binary understanding of sex. Their theory of sexism was designed to capture attitudes towards women at a time when the assumed binary nature of the sexes was more widespread in society than it is in the present. However, it remains useful in capturing the gender attitudes of those who currently possess binary assumptions about sex, such as this study's participants. Given the scope and critical realist underpinning of this research, this is done without seeking to offer a full, universally applicable ontology of sex and gender.[4]

It is also worth noting that the term 'benevolent sexism' is problematic. Glick and Fiske (1996) appear to pre-empt objection to the term. They explain that it is intended to explain the *subjective appearance* of 'benevolent'

68   *Clerical sexism*

sexism rather than communicate their value judgement on it. Nevertheless, partly because of the insights gained through the theory of ambivalent sexism, there is now greater awareness of the extent to which women still face discrimination in relatively subtle ways, making the appropriateness of benevolence as a descriptor questionable. Therefore, I argue that 'indirect sexism' is a preferable term because it denotes that this expression of prejudice is not *necessarily* as obvious as its more overtly hostile counterpart, given that such beliefs can be thought to give the appearance of a positive attitude towards women.

Finally on the theoretical front, it is important to understand that the lack of social desirability surrounding prejudice can lead those with such attitudes to hide it. The justification-suppression model explains that suppressed prejudice manifests when a person perceives that it is legitimated by their circumstances (Crandall and Eshleman, 2003). The theory posits that several factors encourage the suppression of such prejudice. These include: (i) value systems; (ii) social norms; (iii) playing for an audience by displaying less prejudice publically than privately; and (iv) the concern to appear unprejudiced to oneself.

There are also three main effects of prejudice suppression (Crandall and Eshleman, 2003). First, there is suppression as justification, the denial of prejudice leading to the failure to acknowledge its manifestations. Second, there is reactance, backlash against challenges to unfavourable outlooks towards a group. Third, there is the release of suppressed prejudice as a means of reward, meaning that expressing prejudice can alleviate the build-up of anxiety gained by the failure to previously express emotional (prejudicial) states. These insights will provide a helpful framework for interpreting aspects of participants' narratives.

Sexism and Reform

Created order of male headship and female submission

Returning to the first theme from Reform, Greg said:

> We [complementarians] want to model male responsibility in leadership in the church family with the conviction that that will encourage the same in the home .... Eve was created to be a complement to Adam ... the two are to work together as equals with those different roles ...

Similarly, Joshua said:

> Men and women are not created identical. That basic principle for me comes across very strongly [in the Bible] ... what happens [in Genesis 3] as far as I see it is you have an abdication of responsibility. The man hands it over to the woman ... amongst the many things that goes wrong, there is a reversal of roles that have been God ordained.

Clerical sexism 69

Such a belief is indicative of complementary gender differentiation; it is an example of indirect sexism for several reasons. Firstly, subjectively positive attitudes are present with the concept of women being a *complement to* men. Secondly, this complement indicates distinct roles between *all* men and women, which suggests the presence of stereotyped roles. Thirdly, a biological determinism underlies this belief with men and women being created by God to be different, indicating that the distinct roles are underpinned by inherent differences (i.e., traits) between the sexes. These are seen to be in some way virtuous in so far as they are a part of the created order and are understood to be the antithesis of "the many things that [go] wrong". There is also recognition of men's dependence on women as co-workers and complements. Paradoxically, however, for most participants, this belief is not to be universally upheld but applied only in the Church and family spheres. Thus, in keeping with previous research, the sexism is ambivalent in that any one type would not manifest in all the contexts discussed.

This was highlighted during one interview when I was greeted by a participant's wife, a part-time academic at a prestigious university. She took me into the living room and voluntarily spoke to me about her own work whilst the participant made us tea. This included showing me a book that she had co-authored that affirmed traditional gender roles in church and family spheres. This is likely playing for an audience to challenge any overly simplistic, pre-conceived notions I or my readers may have about those with traditionalist gender attitudes. Regardless, this event demonstrates the contextual nature of participants' beliefs. However, it also offers a further nuance. To fulfil her role as mother to her and her husband's children, she works on a part-time basis. That is, the domestic sphere is prioritised above the professional sphere and so any aspirations that women may have beyond home and church risk being curtailed in practice, despite affirmations that male leadership does not typically apply in the (non-confessional) work sphere.

Only one participant deviated from the above discourse. Karl has no theological objection to women taking on any level of leadership in any religious context. He said, "I feel like I'm a bit of a liberal because I will let women teach .... Have you got women leaders in scripture? Yes ... God does raise up women who lead." Karl does not believe that women should be prevented from leadership positions based on their sex. Instead, he believes that one's suitability for leadership—and associated activities such as teaching—ultimately depends on whether God has called a person to that role, regardless of sex. However, there is a lack of awareness that Karl's position as an incumbent means that he wields power over women as permission to preach is given by him (see also Fry, 2021b).

Ambivalent attitudes towards feminism: Positives of feminism and Negatives of feminism

Stephen and Joshua's statements evince hostile sexism. Stephen said:

70 *Clerical sexism*

I think there are branches within [feminism—] one of seeking to affirm women and be constructive and creative, and one that can become over militant and become denigrating of men .... I've seen ... a movement that can become denigrating, over-asserting women over men.

Equally, Joshua claimed:

Radical feminism that moves beyond ... trying to raise up the rights of women ... to promoting a ... feminine alternative as being stronger than the prevailing masculine reality ... and thinking 'actually we'd be better off if this package of feminine ideals ... had the upper hand' ... is something I take real issue with.

Participants were assuming feminists would be women at this stage. The attitude expressed in Stephen and Joshua's comments shows that hostile sexism is present in the Reform narratives for several reasons. First, it is a hostile response to a caricature of some women that, according to Stephen, involves female attempts to assert women over men. Second, it is accompanied by an advocation of traditional gender roles. This includes a theological justification for male authority over women. This latter point indicates that such a belief is accompanied by a dominative paternalism as this inevitably includes an element of control.

Moreover, participants evidently believe that the 'militant' feminism was a representative and hence highly visible strand of feminism given that they spoke of its perceived negative characteristics as if they are self-evident rather than requiring explanation or justification. In other words, they feel that such feminism is sufficiently widespread and apparent that they assumed I would recognise the phenomenon they were describing and recognise the validity of their interpretation of it. This is tantamount to the rejection of evidence that would undermine their caricatured assumptions about feminism as evidence of this phenomenon being widespread or representative is lacking, something that is made clear by the more nuanced approach to feminism contained within the popular and academic feminist literature drawn on in previous and later chapters of this monograph.

In addition to this, there is a clear indication of competitive gender differentiation given that: (i) there is a strong presence of negative stereotyping; and (ii) each narrative that asserts such caricatures also reinforces the theological necessity of male leadership and female submission, thus indicating a sense of male superiority. Nevertheless, this assessment applies only to half of the Reform participants; those narratives that are less pronounced fall short of the hostile sexism and associated criteria. However, the fact that the other seven narratives include language such as "angry" or "militant" indicates that all the Reform clergy interviewed are operating in a sphere where attitudes associated with sexism are regularly present even if they manifest with different degrees of intensity. This attitude towards feminism is most clearly directed within the Church context, given that it is this sphere where—participants believe—gender differences are required to be enacted.

Sexism and the charismatic evangelicals

Gender differences as observable and Belief in the flexibility of gender roles

I have already stated that Matt's narrative contains clear evidence for the belief in differences between the sexes: "It's very difficult to generalise about characteristics of male or female leadership. However, female leadership can be more emotionally intelligent ...." Nevertheless, I also explained that participants in this group remained vague about how this is expressed in actuality. Interviewees' reluctance to extrapolate avoids the possibility of identifying sexist attitudes. It may be that participants were suppressing attitudes that they think would be perceived as prejudicial, as the result of social desirability. Equally, they may genuinely reject certain gendered stereotypes.

It is helpful to note that this group articulated an engagement with wider society with more intensity and consistency than those in the other groups. It is thus conceivable that wider societal norms contributed to the possible prejudice suppression here. Likewise, given that contact can lead to the reduction of prejudice (Allport, 1979), it is entirely possible that such contact reduces the likelihood of prejudice from this group of clergy. Participants are also at ease with their wives' employment statuses. Whilst this does not give much information to help one decide whether participants were suppressing prejudicial attitudes, it is notable that this group of participants evinced greater flexibility on the matter than those in Reform.

Ambivalent attitudes towards feminism: Positives of feminism and Negatives of feminism

Once more Matt's statement will be of use:

> When [feminism] gets shrill and demonising men, I get stroppy about it and disagree .... I don't agree with that, and I feel there's an imbalance in [that] view, which actually is very similar to the way that some men, in a chauvinistic way, talk about women.

This statement is indicative of an attribute of hostile sexism because a caricaturing generalisation is made about feminists—understood to be women at this point—that accuses them of unduly attacking men. It also indicates the rejection of evidence that would undermine their caricatured assumptions about feminism as with Reform. Importantly, however, this statement does lack the other elements that collectively make up hostile sexism and its related categories, and so one must conclude that the charismatic evangelical participants do not in fact possess hostile sexism per se. However, they did exhibit aspects of attitudes that are associated with it.

72   *Clerical sexism*

Sexism and the Anglo-Catholics

The first three themes for this group do not contain any evidence of either hostile or indirect sexism. It is important to note that heterosexuals are more likely than homosexuals to display certain forms of ambivalent sexism, hence heterosexuality is a subset of ambivalent sexism (Glick and Fiske, 1997). Seven of the participants indicated that they were homosexual. Some are in civil partnerships whereas others have remained single. Whilst this does not rule out the presence of sexism (and thus prejudice suppression) it nevertheless helps explain the apparent lack of it in the narratives so far. However, hostile sexism is present.

Ambivalent attitudes towards feminism: Negatives of feminism and Positives of feminism

When discussing feminism, Adrian said, "Fuck feminism" and Oliver commented, "Well [feminists should] get a life, basically." Clearly, these are hostile responses, and participants were also assuming that feminists in this instance were women. Participants elaborated. Akin to the evangelical narratives, other traditional Anglo-Catholic participants claimed that the feminist movement could be unduly aggressive towards men. For example, Edward remarked, "I think there are feminist writers who go far too extreme, and ... derid[e] men ... and see men as unnecessary .... We ... fail to realise where women had power ... [such as in] matriarchies." Edward believes that feminists can attack men and that women have wielded power that has gone unnoticed. He also believes that feminism can be a vehicle for asserting women over men. As in the Reform narratives, the presence of hostile sexism—particularly dominative paternalism—is clear: (i) Edward's narrative contains a hostile response and a caricature of feminist women that is contrary to beliefs found within popular and academic feminism, likewise indicating the rejection of evidence that undermines prejudicial belief; and (ii) it is accompanied by an advocation of traditional gender roles amongst the clergy in the form of a theological justification for men to be in the higher positions of authority within the Church.

However, there is an important nuance that is unique to the Anglo-Catholic narratives. Traditional roles do not have to be adhered to in the family unit for all but one of the participants. Although generalisations are made about feminists more broadly, hostile sexism amongst this group was focused within the Church sphere where the perceived aims of feminism were deemed to be most inappropriate, indicating that sexism is primarily ambivalent/context dependent for them.

Turning again to Malcolm's statement: "I don't know how to phrase this. No, I think I'll just stick with what I said [previously], that if feminism simply means that men and women are equal in society ... then I have no problem with it." The fact that he then prevented himself from elaborating on a caricature is indicative of prejudice suppression. Indeed, the somewhat abrupt decision to switch from a negative evaluation of feminism to a positive one after deciding not to expand on his caricature indicates that Malcolm was trying to deflect attention away from some of his beliefs about the feminist movement. The source of such suppression has multiple origins. For instance, participants were aware that their comments were being recorded and could be cited in this study, which will have a wider audience. When this occurs, therefore, I argue that participants were playing for an audience.

Also, Malcolm responded in a context where women's consecration as bishops is relatively new, in a diocese that is largely less conservative than the traditional Anglo-Catholic and evangelical wings of the CofE. The interview took place after the Church had issued a clear statement expressing the necessity for all members of the CofE to accept the decision concerning women bishops (see Ferns, 2014). In fact, participants in this group reported a sense of pressure and exclusion from the diocese because of their more traditional beliefs. For example, Ashley claimed that "the liberal catholics in [this diocese] have predominantly been hostile and unwilling to engage in any discussion whatsoever; they have gone out of their way to marginalise people like myself." Social norms (particularly those of the wider CofE) were thus likely also a factor influencing prejudice suppression.

Initial reflections

Reform

Thus far, both accommodation and resistance towards the gender attitudes found in wider society and within the CofE have been identified within the Reform narratives. Given Reform's commitment to promote traditional theology within the CofE, the level of engagement found therein can be understood as being reinforced by the commitment evangelicals made to transform the CofE from within at Keele in 1967. Additionally, the fact that indirect and hostile sexism have been found provides evidence from people's everyday lives for the claim that sexism can be ambivalent. The fact that it is restricted to the Church and family spheres likewise provides evidence from everyday life that its expression is context dependent.

The charismatic evangelicals

Thus far, the charismatic evangelical participants have demonstrated a level of engaged orthodoxy, just as is present in the Reform narratives. That is, there is evidently an assimilation of more contemporary gender ideals in addition to a continuation with the evangelical tradition. However, with respect to gender values, the present group evinced a greater incorporation of contemporary gender ideals than did the Reform participants. Nevertheless, the type of engagement that each of these groups has with the wider Christian tradition is qualitatively different, given that the present group—with

74 *Clerical sexism*

minimal exceptions—demonstrates no resistance towards the CofE's settled theology on female clergy.

The Anglo-Catholics

The Anglo-Catholic narratives evidently have some similarities when compared with the evangelical—particularly conservative evangelical—narratives. For example, the restrictions made on women are context dependent. There is also the presence of engaged orthodoxy as they have incorporated some feminist ideals whilst advocating traditional gender roles within the Church. In this instance, though, it is exhibited towards wider society. However, a key difference here is that the emphasis on the family unit is significantly more pronounced amongst the conservative evangelicals than it is amongst the Anglo-Catholics. The above is testament to the continuing distinct impact that each tradition's history continues to have on them given that evangelicals have historically given more attention to familial concerns than Anglo-Catholics have.

Methodological reflection

The discussion of the Reform narratives juxtaposed insights from sociological approaches to gender alongside social psychological approaches to sexism. It presents obvious links between ambivalent sexism and the sociology of gender: the social psychological theory provides the appropriate tools for identifying problematic attitudes in individuals; both types of literature help contextualise these identifications by offering a panoramic view of how such attitudes impact women; and the sociological literature allows one to trace the maintenance of such views at a societal level over time. This provides a fuller understanding of the impact that various social phenomena have on participants' views in addition to highlighting the impact that these views can have on women. In keeping with the critical realist underpinning of this research, it therefore foregrounds the ethical dimension of the present enquiry given the detrimental consequences of prejudicial beliefs.

The examination of the data gained from the charismatic evangelicals provides further justification for the methodological fusion of sociological and historical enquiry in the endeavour to understand clergy gender attitudes. It demonstrates how historical views on gender continue to be (re)articulated in the present but in such a way that evidences the impact of more contemporary social influences. The fact of re-articulation is also true of the traditional Anglo-Catholic narratives, which demonstrate the continuation of reaction to modernity noted in the previous chapter, alongside an integration of some more modern ideals into the Anglo-Catholics' present gender attitudes.

Conclusion

In this chapter, I have explored the gender attitudes of all three groups of participants. It has become apparent that the evangelical groups articulated a

Clerical sexism 75

very different source of primary authority for their beliefs compared with the Anglo-Catholic contingent. Whilst the Bible was key for the former (see also Fry, 2019, 2021a), tradition and Roman Catholic teaching was of great importance for the latter, reflecting the multiplicity of authorities within the Anglican Church (see Sykes, 1987). As I have argued elsewhere (Fry, 2019, 2021a), biblical texts contribute to the formation of the conservative evangelicals gender attitudes, even though later meanings are anachronistically projected onto them. The charismatic evangelicals also reflected on biblical passages as they articulated their gender attitudes, but as a group they have a more heterogenous approach with most interpreting them in contrast to their conservative counterparts, although a minority perceived universal truths in them that led to a more traditional view.

In addition to this, there are evidently other sources of authority for the participants that are largely unrecognised by them, namely their various social contexts. In this case, one has begun to observe the impact of the traditions that participants have inherited, just as Vasey-Saunders (2015) found in his study of evangelical attitudes towards homosexuality. Indeed, the discussion on justification suppression has indicated that the values of wider society are, in a sense, a source of authority for some participants in that they have shaped how they present their beliefs to an external audience. This mirrors previous research that has demonstrated how wider social values have informed the ways in which conservative Protestants articulate their beliefs (e.g., Gallagher and Smith, 1999; Smith et al., 1998) whilst identifying more of the process that contributes to this phenomenon.

Moreover, it is important to explain that, as these traditions engage with their wider social context, the sexism discerned from participants' narratives must also be understood in this light. Whilst gender inequality has been a part of the historical development of the Anglo-Catholic and evangelical traditions, the sexism of wider society cannot be ruled out as a source of such prejudice. Indeed, just as Vasey-Saunders (2015) noted that evangelical homophobia cannot be historically separated from the homophobia of wider society, so neither can historical Christian sexism be separated from the society in which it has been a part.

However, I wish to develop this claim further by adding that it is not just the historical sexism of wider society that undoubtedly influences contemporary Christian sexism. Given the evidence of interaction between conservative Protestants and their wider social context, contemporary sexism that exists beyond the Church informs the gender prejudice of this study's participants. Indeed, hostile and indirect sexism are empirically widespread and manifest in divergent parts of society (Glick and Fiske, 2011). In this sense, participants' sexism is not uniquely 'Christian', but rather finds particular expression in their various Christian contexts. This does not mean that sexism is simply a non-religious import that is later given religious garb by the Church. It is also well-established that Christianity has a long history of sexism (e.g., Radford Ruether, 1974). In this instance, one must note that

76 *Clerical sexism*

the CofE, being an Established Church rather than a partisan institution, does not have particularly clear boundaries with the society in which it is situated, and so sexist ideas found beyond the Church have been more readily incorporated into pre-existing attitudes.

Indeed, the discussion in the previous chapter, on the limitations imposed upon women's ministry in the 1993 Act of Synod, indicates that the CofE stands within the historical Christian legacy of gender discrimination. It is therefore important to remember that, in addition to wider society and the historical and contemporary influence of participants' specific traditions, the wider denomination of which they have been a part has also influenced the formation of their gender attitudes. I have thus begun to identify the sources of participants' prejudice, noting the multiple contexts that contribute to its formation. Having identified participants' attitudes towards women, it is appropriate to continue the examination of each of the three Anglican traditions through a still deeper exploration of how participants respond to women and how they conceptualise gender.

Notes

1 Although this term has different meanings (as discussed in Fry (2021a)), I use the term in the way that Aune (2006) does, referring to a nostalgic 'look back' to feminism with a mixture of endorsement and rejection.
2 This is not necessarily understood to be a literal change but a matter of transubstantiation where there is a change in 'substance' rather than in the outward characteristics of the bread and wine.
3 It should be noted that 'sexism' is being used to refer to sex-based prejudice (i.e., sexism that is attitudinal as defined in the social psychological literature) rather than precluding other understandings of sexism (e.g., that which is highlighted by discourse analysis). See the Introduction for elaboration on the stratification of reality.
4 See the Introduction for elaboration on this.

References

Aldridge, A. (1992). Discourse on women in the clerical profession: The diaconate and language-games in the Church of England. *Sociology*, 26(1), 45–57.
Allport, G. (1954/1979). *The nature of prejudice*. Cambridge, MA: Perseus Books.
Aune, K. (2006). Marriage in a British evangelical congregation: Practising postfeminist partnership? *The Sociological Review*, 54(4), 638–657.
Brown, A., & Woodhead, L. (2016). *That was the Church that was: How the Church of England lost the English people*. London: Bloomsbury.
Crandall, C.S., & Eshleman, A. (2003). A justification-suppression model of the expression and experience of prejudice. *Psychological Bulletin*, 129(3), 414–446.
Dunn, J. (1998). *The theology of Paul the apostle*. Grand Rapids, MI: William B. Eerdmans Publishing Company.
Ferns, S. (2014). *The five guiding principles: Guidance for candidates for ordination in the Church of England*. Ministry Division. Retrieved from https://www.churchofengland.org/sites/default/files/2017-10/the_five_guiding_principles.pdf.

Fry, A.D.J. (2019). Justifying gender inequality in the Church of England: An examination of theologically conservative male clergy attitudes towards women's ordination. *Fieldwork in Religion, 14*(1), 8–32.

Fry, A.D.J. (2021a). Postfeminist, engaged and resistant: Evangelical male clergy attitudes towards gender and women's ordination in the Church of England. *Critical Research on Religion, 9*(1), 65–83.

Fry, A.D.J. (2021b). Clergy, capital and gender inequality: An assessment of how social and spiritual capital are denied to women priests in the Church of England. *Gender, Work & Organization, 21*(6), 2091–2113.

Gallagher, S.K., & Smith, C. (1999). Symbolic traditionalism and pragmatic egalitarianism: Contemporary evangelicals, families, and gender. *Gender and Society, 13*(2), 211–233.

Glick, P., & Fiske, S.T. (1996). The ambivalent sexism inventory: Differentiating hostile and benevolent sexism. *Journal of Personality and Social Psychology, 70*(3), 491–512.

Glick, P., & Fiske, S.T. (1997). Hostile and benevolent sexism: Measuring ambivalent sexist attitudes toward women. *Psychology of Women Quarterly, 21*(1), 119–135.

Glick, P., & Fiske, S.T. (2011). Ambivalent sexism revisited. *Psychology of Women Quarterly, 35*(3), 530–535.

Green, T.K. (2007). Discomfort at work: Workplace assimilation demands and the contact hypothesis. *North Carolina Law Review, 86*(2), 379–440.

Grudem, W.A. (1994). *Systematic theology: An introduction to biblical doctrine.* Nottingham: InterVarsity Press.

Guest, M., & Aune, K. (2017). Students' constructions of a Christian future: Faith, class and aspiration in university contexts. *Sociological Research Online, 22*(1), 1–13.

Guest, M., Aune, K., Sharma, S., & Warner, R. (2013). *Christianity and the university experience: Understanding student faith.* London: Bloomsbury.

Jagger, S. (2021). Mutual flourishing?: Women priests and symbolic violence in the Church of England. *Religion and Gender, 11*(2), 192–217.

Johnson, E.A. (1993). *Women, earth, and creator spirit.* Mahwah, NJ: Paulist Press.

Masser, B.M., & Abrams, D. (2004). Reinforcing the glass ceiling: The consequences of hostile sexism for female managerial candidates. *Sex Roles, 51*(9–10), 609–615.

Merino, S.M. (2010). Religious diversity in a "Christian nation": The effects of theological exclusivity and interreligious contact on the acceptance of religious diversity. *Journal for the Scientific Study of Religion, 49*(2), 231–246.

Pettigrew, T.F. (1971). *Racially separate or together?* New York: McGraw-Hill.

Pettigrew, T.F., & Tropp, L.R. (2008). How does intergroup contact reduce prejudice? Meta-analytic tests of three mediators. *European Journal of Social Psychology, 38*(6), 922–934.

Press, A.L. (2011). 'Feminism? That's so seventies': Girls and young women discuss femininity and feminism in America's Next Top Model. In R. Gill & C. Scharff (Eds.), *New femininities: Postfeminism, neoliberalism and subjectivity* (pp. 117–133). Basingstoke: Palgrave Macmillan.

Radford Ruether, R. (1974). Misogynism and virginal feminism in the Fathers of the Church. In R. Radford Ruether (Ed.), *Religion and sexism: Images of woman in the Jewish and Christian traditions* (pp. 150–183). New York: Simon and Schuster.

78 *Clerical sexism*

Redfern, C., & Aune, K. (2010). *Reclaiming the F word: The new feminist movement*. London: Zed.

Rudman, L.A. (2005). Rejection of women: Beyond prejudice as antipathy. In J.F. Dovidio, P.E. Glick, & L.A. Rudman (Eds.), *On the nature of prejudice: Fifty years after Allport* (pp. 106–120). Hoboken, NJ: Blackwell Publishing.

Sani, F., & Reicher, S. (2000). Contested identities and schisms in groups: Opposing the ordination of women as priests in the Church of England. *British Journal of Social Psychology, 39*(1), 95–112.

Smith, C. with Emerson, M., Gallagher, S., Kennedy, P., & Sikkink, D. (1998). *American evangelicalism: Embattled and thriving*. Chicago, IL: University of Chicago Press.

Stanton, G.N. (2001). Galatians. In J. Muddiman & J. Barton (Eds.), *The Oxford Bible commentary: The Pauline epistles* (pp. 151–169). Oxford University Press.

Storkey, E. (1985). *What's right with feminism?* London: SPCK.

Sykes, S.W. (1987). Introduction: Why authority? In S. Sykes (Ed.), *Authority in the Anglican Communion: Essays presented to Bishop John Howe* (pp. 11–23). Toronto: Anglican Book Centre.

Thiselton, A.C. (2000). *The first Epistle to the Corinthians: A commentary on the Greek text*. Grand Rapids, MI: William. B. Eerdmans Publishing.

Vasey-Saunders, M. (2015). *The scandal of evangelicals and homosexuality: English Evangelical Texts, 1960–2010*. London: Routledge.

Vonk, R., & Olde-Monnikhof, M. (1998). Gender subgroups: Intergroup bias within the sexes. *European Journal of Social Psychology, 28*(1), 37–47.

Westenberg, L. (2017). "When she calls for help"—domestic violence in Christian families. *Social Sciences, 6*(3), 71.

4 Empathy, intersectionality, and gender schemata

Introduction

In the previous chapter, I outlined the specific gender attitudes held by my participants. In this chapter, I will extend that discussion in four ways. First, I will explore an important facet of the prejudice literature, namely empathy, and unpack its relevance for understanding my participants' gender attitudes by focusing on an emotion component of them. Second, I will explore the cognitive framework for interpreting gender-related information evinced by the clergy interviewed (i.e., their gender schemata) and their relationship to participants' prejudice or lack thereof. Third, I shall explore the identities held by my participants that are also fundamental for the formation of their gender attitudes, as will become apparent in subsequent chapters. Finally, I will continue to reflect methodologically on the approach I have taken to data interpretation.

I will establish the extent of participants' empathy towards women priests and the role that this aspect of emotional intelligence plays in the shaping of gender attitudes. I will then explore the gender schemata held by those interviewed. This is because these schemata enable one to more clearly identify the impact that the variety of historical, sociological, and social psychological phenomena discussed have on the way that my participants think about gender. I will then briefly outline participants' (multiple) social identities because the insights gained from an analysis of their intersectionality will enable greater understanding of the impact that various social phenomena have on their gender attitudes. This flows from a discussion on gender schemata as both help one understand the relevance of early life and one's social context for shaping gender attitudes.

This will also be a useful discussion to refer back to in subsequent chapters given that participants' identities are critical for understanding their gender attitudes. In the methodological reflection, I will take some of the implications of the previous chapter in tandem with those of the present one to further tease out the depth of detail that a qualitative study of individuals and groups can provide. As I will be utilising theories born out of quantitative studies in a qualitative way, reflecting on the insight into social processes that is

DOI: 10.4324/9781003081913-4

80 *Empathy, intersectionality, and gender schemata*

gained by such an approach will allow for a greater appreciation of the depth of knowledge that may be produced when it is adopted.

Empathy and prejudice

A discussion on empathy is relevant for the present study because it is an important mediator of prejudice; persons with more empathy tend to be less prejudicial whereas those with less empathy tend to exhibit greater levels of prejudice (see Brown, 2011). With respect to sexism from males, this is true in relation to hostile sexism but not with indirect sexism, which has no direct relationship with empathy (e.g., see Garaigordobil, 2014). Empathy is also related to co-operation (Eisenberg and Miller, 1987). This is relevant for the present study because co-operation between distinct social groups can lead to prejudice reduction (e.g., see Stephan and Finlay, 1999). In other words, empathy bears an important relationship to prejudice by enabling co-operation, which can then mediate prejudice. I will explore co-operation in more detail in the fifth and sixth chapters. It is also important to note that empathy is context dependent rather than being a quality that most people either do or do not possess (Batson and Powell, 2003). Individuals are more likely to be empathetic towards those whom they identify with, i.e., those within their social groups, than to those beyond them (see Turner and Reynolds, 2012).

Assessing the extent of participants' empathy can enhance understanding of their attitudes towards women. More specifically, if those with hostile sexism also display a lack of empathy (and vice versa), then the appropriateness of prejudice and intergroup contact for interpreting participants' narratives holds further weight. However, given that empathy can be altruistic or derive from the need to alleviate one's own distress (Toi and Batson, 1982), it is important to discern which type of empathy is being exhibited, if and when it is present. This can be achieved through a simple test: participants are presented with a hypothetical situation where an individual is in a distressing situation. Those taking part in the experiment are then asked to imagine themselves in that scenario and explain how they would respond. Those who decided to help the imaginary victim, despite having the opportunity to exit the situation, are understood to possess altruistic empathy. Those who would only help when there was no indication that they could exit the scenario are understood to display empathetic behaviour to reduce their own sense of distress at the suffering of others (see Dovidio, Allen and Schroeder, 1990).

I assessed participants' empathy towards women priests by asking participants to imagine a scenario where they were discriminated against because of their sex and were either barred from priesthood or had the validity of their vocation called into question. This has been the experience of many female clergy, whose vocation most participants call into question, making it a suitable imagine-based scenario for the present research. Participants were

Empathy and Reform

aware that they could steer the questions as deemed relevant, including being under no obligation to answer any question; this was made clear to them prior to interview as a matter of research ethics. As this provides my participants with opportunities to avoid engaging with imagining a potentially distressing situation, empathetic answers can be considered altruistic.

Empathy and Reform

Only one theme is relevant for discussion here: Lack of empathy towards women priests.

Lack of empathy towards women priests

In addition to determining the presence of empathy on the basis of the above, participants' answers to other questions were also relevant. No participants in this group replied in a way that demonstrated empathy. For example, in response to a question on the role of feminism and gender inequality, Callum responded, "[In] countries where women are married off when they're twelve, and there's female genital mutilation ... [is] where there's gender injustice .... In liberal, middle-class England, I don't personally have much [time for] 'We're under the cosh of patriarchy'."

Greg was asked how he would respond to his sense of priestly vocation being called into question in a Church historically run by women. He said, "If that's what scripture is saying, that's what I will be committed to doing, I hope whole heartedly and joyfully .... I'm sure it would be a positive joy." Three participants did begin to empathise but did not do so fully. When asked how he would feel if his sense of calling to the priesthood was rejected based on his sex, Stanley replied, "I wouldn't want to get too caught up in your call ... so hopefully I wouldn't be that bothered .... But I do understand when women find it very difficult." Ron responded, "I wouldn't like it initially ... but hopefully I would want to be [asking] ... 'What does the Bible say on this issue?' and then seeking to submit to that." Stanley and Ron demonstrated the potential for empathy but were unable to imagine a scenario that directly placed themselves in the same situation as women priests who had their sense of call denied. Therefore, they did not meet the criteria required for an empathetic response.

However, as expected from the literature, participants were empathetic towards each other and their families. To recruit participants, the Chair of Reform in the diocese being explored allowed me to come to a Reform meeting to invite other clergy to interview, on the proviso that I didn't use the meeting as data for my research. This is because it provided a forum to strategise Reform's impact on the wider CofE. En route to the meeting, the Chair picked up another one of the participants in his car (I was a passenger for this journey). When the Chair asked this other participant about his family, he explained that his wife was unwell, to which his colleague

82 *Empathy, intersectionality, and gender schemata*

responded with an empathetic sigh which communicated a sense of care for the person in question.

Empathy and the charismatic evangelicals

As with the Reform narratives, only one theme is relevant for discussion here: Empathy towards women priests.

Empathy towards women priests

A clear contrast to the Reform narratives was the level of empathy that the charismatic evangelical participants exhibited. In total, nine of the 14 were able to clearly demonstrate that they could understand, to at least some extent, the challenge of having the validity of one's vocation challenged or denied on the basis of their sex. There were two types of answers that displayed empathy. Firstly, in relation to the imagine-based question, Patrick said, "I would probably have felt a very deep sense of frustration, possibly anger. I would have probably gone on the marches and protest and done the things that those for the ordination of women were doing." Secondly, after seeing an ordained woman argue with a preacher for not using, what she understood to be, gender-inclusive language, Nick said:

> It gives me more grace to remember that it was a struggle, and it must have been hard, and it must have hurt, and it must have caused deep scars .... I have seen the evidence of the scars and I know that it hurt other people ... and I don't like being told I can't do something, so I imagine it would hurt me too, but I wouldn't know until I was there.

In Patrick's case, there was a clear engagement with the empathy question. He readily imagined what he would have felt if he was in the same situation as women sensing a priestly vocation during the 1980s–1990s. Nick's narrative was more detached from the situation, drawing on someone else's response. Nevertheless, despite his assertion that he cannot know his response for certain (a fair answer in itself), he nevertheless employed his imagination in trying to understand what it must have felt like for the women he described.

Those participants who did not display any indications of empathy had mixed responses to the question. These ranged from being uncertain of how they would respond, to accepting the situation and finding alternative ways to serve God and the Church, and—for one of the participants who espoused a belief in headship—to trusting in the authority of the Bible. For instance, Richard replied, "It's hard to know isn't it?" Graham said, "I wonder whether actually I would just have ended up doing something else ...." Michael explained, "I think I would have to approach it in the way of ... looking at scripture." Some of these views mirror Reform, whereas others are notably distinct. The level of empathy amongst this group of participants is therefore typically affirming whilst also being mixed.

Empathy and the Anglo-Catholics

As with the other two groups, only one theme is relevant for discussion here: Lack of empathy towards women priests.

Lack of empathy towards women priests

More than half of the participants in this group did not express empathy towards women priests. The same imagine-based question was asked of the Anglo-Catholic participants as it was for the evangelical groups. Peter remarked, "It's difficult to imagine because one would assume then that the whole apostolic tradition was completely different .... It's difficult because, fundamentally, I don't believe women can be priests." Peter was unable to place himself in the position of those whose sense of vocation he rejected. In fact, his thinking is so strongly tied to the concept of male apostleship that my question led him to believe that he would have to imagine an entirely different history (and New Testament) to try and empathise. That he ended his answer by reaffirming his belief in the impossibility of a genuine vocation to the priesthood for women further highlights this. Out of the five participants who did display empathy, two of them were the same two who are decisively in favour of women's ordination to the priesthood. However, given the hostile sexism already evinced, the lack of empathy is unsurprising considering the findings of previous research on the interface of prejudice and empathy.

Initial reflection on empathy

The lack of empathy displayed by most participants (taking all three traditions together) is related to their hostile sexism as empathy accompanies lower levels of this form of prejudice (or its total absence). Although, in the case of the charismatic evangelicals, it is more accurate to state that the lack of empathy, where present, is most appropriately linked with the components of hostile sexism that participants evinced, as discussed in the previous chapter. That the lack of empathy applies to a minority of charismatics is related to the fact that the presence of hostile sexism within this group is weak, as only elements of prejudice are found within it. There is also consistency between previous studies and the present; those who display hostile sexism towards an outgroup also neglect to display empathy towards that same group.

The causal relationship between empathy and prejudice amongst my participants is difficult to determine. Are those with prejudicial attitudes lacking in empathy because of pre-existing prejudice, or does their lack of empathy preclude favourable attitudes towards women? Given the complexity of the social world, this is not a straightforward matter. Nevertheless, it remains

84 *Empathy, intersectionality, and gender schemata*

instructive to understand empathy as a mediator whereby its presence is likely to reduce prejudice and its absence, reduce the likelihood that prejudice will be challenged. This means that its utility in the present study is in providing greater evidence for employing research on prejudice as an interpretive lens for understanding participants' narratives, given the consistency with which they reflect what one would expect from psychological research.

Gender schemata

Gender schemata, according to Bem (1981a), are mental frameworks formed in childhood that individuals possess for interpreting gender-related information. Future gendered information is then interpreted within this framework, which further shapes how people think about gender and how they behave in light of this. These schemata are not merely culturally transmitted but transmuted, albeit apparently with a stable core, and often result in psychologically ingrained stereotypes about gender whereby to be male is associated with traditional masculine roles and attributes and to be female is associated with traditional feminine roles and attributes.[1] This serves to encourage thinking and behaviour that conforms to traditional expectations associated with gender. However, individuals vary in the extent that they uphold these schemata, of which there are four types (Bem, 1981a).

First, there are sex-typed individuals who process and integrate gender-related information in line with existing cultural assumptions about gender that have been—in societies such as England—predominantly binary. They therefore exhibit behaviour and thinking that reflect traditional assumptions about gender. In such instances, men would conform to stereotypically male behaviour, women would conform to stereotypically female behaviour, and both view the opposite sex through traditional lenses. Second, there are cross-sex-typed persons who exhibit the opposite pattern to sex-typed individuals. They are more likely to exhibit behaviour and thinking that reflect traditional assumptions about the opposite sex. Third, there are androgynous people who process and integrate gender-related information in line with the cultural assumptions about both sexes and would think and behave in ways that reflect this. Fourth, there are undifferentiated individuals who do not strongly process sex-typed information.

The stronger one's gender schema, the more that gender-related information will be recalled if it is consistent with the schema. Equally, information that is inconsistent with it is less likely to be recalled because it cannot be readily interpreted with the existing schema. These facts lead to the reinforcement of any gendered stereotypes that have been culturally transmuted. This is particularly the case for sex-typed individuals. Gender schemata thus influence gender attitudes so that (especially sex-typed) individuals uphold inherited beliefs concerning what it means to be male and female, something that is bolstered by historical assumptions where men and women are understood to be inherently different (Bem, 1981a).

Empathy, intersectionality, and gender schemata 85

That gender schemata significantly shape how one understands gender makes those of my participants worthy of study. The previous two chapters have already provided evidence that historical cultural (including religious) gender values and attitudes have shaped the attitudes of my participants and that these have been transmuted given that they have not been entirely static over time. However, there remains the question of what schemata the clergy interviewed possess. In other words, how (more specifically) have wider cultural assumptions shaped the way they think about gender? This may be answered by asking the question of how these schemata relate to the attitudes participants have articulated thus far.

First though, it is important to attend to some methodological considerations. It was argued that an individual's gender schema can be discerned from the extent to which they adopt gendered stereotypes (Bem, 1981a), meaning that the measure utilised in the formulation of the theory was not employed to assess gender schematic processing but to identify those who process information in this way (Bem, 1981b). However, the theory has been criticised on the grounds that the measures employed assume too binary a distinction between genders that do not readily account for the more multifaceted understandings of gender held by many (Spence, 1993). For example, according to the theory, even persons with androgynous gender schemata process gender-related information in ways that assume differences between the sexes, despite their processing and integrating information about both. The theory is also based on the assumption that one who stereotypes based on sex therefore also processes information in line with a gender schema, a claim which some consider to be a questionable leap (Starr and Zurbriggen, 2016).

Nevertheless, there are a few things to be stated in favour of the theory. Gender schema theory recognises the importance of early life for the transmission of gender attitudes, something akin to the repeated findings in the sociological literature that understands the influential role of the family unit for passing down gendered religious beliefs. It also recognises the relevance of wider social context for shaping an individual's gender attitudes. Moreover, whilst some later studies have failed to support Bem's initial conclusions (e.g., Lobel, 1994), other studies have succeeded in doing so (e.g., Frable and Bem, 1985). The theory also recognises that schemata increase the likelihood of assimilating information that readily fits into pre-existing schemata than that which does not, an idea that is supported by schema research in other areas (e.g., see Brewer and Treyens, 1981).

Gender schema theory has also been successfully utilised in divergent areas of scholarship in providing an explanation of why stereotypical understandings of gender exist (see Starr and Zurbriggen, 2016). In fact, research into programmes aimed at reducing stereotypes, predicated on the insights of the theory, has had successful outcomes (Nathanson et al., 2002). On balance, this collectively attests to its explanatory power and to its relevance for research on prejudice, a phenomenon which depends on stereotypes. The above particularly highlights its applicability to research on prejudice within

86 *Empathy, intersectionality, and gender schemata*

a religious context, especially given the salience of the family unit for many of my participants, as will be further evidenced below.

In addition to this, the conservative evangelicals and traditional Anglo-Catholics have shown that they possess binary gender attitudes within the context of the CofE, with all of the former and most of the latter evincing the belief that these naturally occur in all areas of life. They also conflate gender and sex. Equally, despite the absence of gendered stereotypes in their narratives, the charismatic evangelicals spoke of there being general differences between the sexes indicating that they still think of the sexes as distinct categories, even though they may well have some shared characteristics and share professional/vocational space. The binary and essentialist aspects of my participants' gender attitudes thus further suggests that gender schema theory is an appropriate fit in the context of this study. Indeed, the categories provided by gender schema theory neatly map on to the data provided by my participants, further supporting its potential to offer explanatory power in the present study.

As has been the case with previous research on prejudice, existing knowledge on gender schemata is largely based on quantitative measures where participants rate themselves according to a list of pre-selected gendered characteristics. This provides insight into participants more general understanding of gender because one's self-concept (beliefs about oneself) is assimilated into the gender schema (Bem, 1981a). This means that one can deduce a person's belief about gender by looking at how that individual understands their own gender identity. In keeping with the qualitative approach of this monograph, I explore my participants' schemata by analysing material that they provide on gender roles thereby capturing their own subjective understanding of what it means to be male or female. It is in doing so that the natural overlap between the data and Bem's theory becomes apparent. Whilst I did not directly ask participants how they understood their own characteristics and their relationship to their sex, it is clear from the data discussed in this and the previous chapter (and in keeping with gender schema theory) that participants' gender ideals were consistent with their self-understanding, particularly among the evangelicals.

I have thus determined what schemata participants possess by comparing their own assumptions about gender with traditional stereotypes. However, I have not limited my evaluation to the characteristics identified by Bem because, as much research has since shown, there are many more gendered stereotypes than she identified. My analysis is thus in keeping with the direction of travel established by Bem, but not limited by it. If participants consistently understand what it is to be male and female in light of traditional stereotypes about gender, then I consider them to have sex-typed schemata. Participants would have been considered to possess cross-sex typed schemata if they processed information in line with traditional assumptions about women. Equally, if they understood each sex to incorporate traditional stereotypes from both sexes then they would possess androgynous gender schemata. They would have been considered to possess undifferentiated gender schemata if they did not evince much in the way of conformity to any traditional expectations pertaining to gender.

Gender schemata and Reform

The theme and sub-theme relevant for discussion here are: (i) Created order of male headship and female submission; and (ii) Negatives of feminism. I will analyse these (sub)themes together because of the overlap in information relevant for an analysis of gender schemata.

Created order of male headship and female submission and Negatives of feminism

Callum's statement "I'm ... a complementarian. Men and women are made differently, and I think there is a natural headship that men have over women .... It's ... ingrained into us"[2] is telling. Just like Greg believes in "male responsibility in leadership in the church family", Callum believes that men are natural leaders and included himself in this category with use of the word "us", indicating that his self-concept has been assimilated into his understanding of gender. In other words, there are certain characteristics that are innate to being male and these are distinct from the characteristics that are innate to being female, which are reflected in his thinking and behaviour. Similarly, Alistair commented that feminism "seeks to eradicate difference [between the sexes] in order to reach equality .... I don't think that the fact that a husband and a wife have different roles in marriage in any way undermines their status." Comments such as this evince participants' belief that differences between the sexes should lead to differences in gender roles. I have already explained that this is a gender essentialist belief which has found expression in historical evangelicalism. Nevertheless, there is more to be discussed on this matter.

The fact that such beliefs are binary, essentialist, and accompanied by the belief that men should undertake distinct roles to women indicates that the conservative evangelical participants hold sex-typed schemata. Whilst most of the participants in this group do not take issue with professional women, this group believe that there are biologically ingrained characteristics for each sex—stemming from creation—which have implications for their own roles in marriage (as husbands) and church (as clergy). These characteristics reflect traditional gender stereotypes that men are natural leaders and women are naturally more submissive.

These beliefs reflect the development of gender values charted in the second chapter, and analysis in the third chapter has established that these have developed in dialogue with wider societal values and attitudes. Hence, participants possess beliefs that have been transmuted over time. Therefore, a greater understanding of the gender stereotypes within wider society will

88   *Empathy, intersectionality, and gender schemata*

offer insight into the factors contributing to participants' gender attitudes. To do this, I shall highlight examples from widely-read literature that articulate beliefs—or make assertions based on beliefs—commonly found within wider society.

Richard Dawkins, whilst antagonistic to religious faith, has been influential in wider society and his understanding of differences between the sexes, as articulated in *The Selfish Gene,* have affinities with the Reform participants'. Dawkins (1989) recognises the presence of sexual inequality but insists that the differences between men and women that lead to inequality are a matter of biology. He argues that females are naturally more committed to their offspring from the moment of conception than are males because the former carry their young during pregnancy (because the female gamete—the egg—is larger than the male gamete—the sperm), and so the mother rather than the father is usually left caring more fully for the off-spring. Dawkins writes:

> Each individual wants as many surviving children as possible. The less he or she is obliged to invest in any one of those children, the more children he or she can have. The obvious way to achieve this desirable state of affairs is to induce your sexual partner to invest more than his or her fair share of resources in each child, leaving you free to have other children with other partners. This [...] is more difficult for the female to achieve. Since she starts by investing more than the male, in the form of her large, food-rich egg, a mother is already at the moment of conception 'committed' to each child more deeply than the father is [....] The female sex is exploited, and the fundamental evolutionary basis for the exploitation is the fact that eggs are larger than sperm (p. 146).

To put this another way, men and women are biologically pre-dispositioned to enact distinct social roles. Whilst Dawkins believes that this inevitably leads to inequality, however, the Reform participants do not. Nevertheless, the affinities that their biological determinism has with ideas found within wider society are apparent. Another distinction is that Dawkins does not see this outcome as inevitable at all times, whereas my participants hold to biological determination in a purest way, believing that it reflects a God-ordained (and thus universal) design. In this respect, what one finds in their narratives is an incorporation of popular beliefs about the sexes into a theological framework; whilst biological beliefs inform theological ones here, theological convictions likewise shape understandings of human biology.

John Gray wrote the well-known *Men Are from Mars, Women Are from Venus* and later penned *Men Are from Mars, Women and from Venus, and Children Are from Heaven.* In his books, Gray (1992, 2011) asserts that men and women have distinct communicative preferences and understands these to be predetermined by "psychological differences" (1992 p. 4) meaning that, supposedly, "Even today we still need translators. Men and women seldom mean the same things even when they use the same words" (1992, p. 26). Whilst these examples are anecdotal, they highlight common beliefs in society that have often been noted by feminist and gender theorists (e.g., Greer, 1970; Tannen, 1990; see also Gilligan, 1993 to a lesser extent) and likewise evince the gender essentialism and binary conceptualisations of gender articulated by my participants.

Such views have also made their way into popular evangelical literature. In addition to the popularisation of complementarianism by figures such as Wayne Grudem and John Piper, discussed in the second chapter, John Eldredge wrote *Wild at Heart*. According to Eldredge (2001), men are designed by God to behave and think in particular ways, chiefly as (metaphorically) sword-yielding warriors. He writes, "A man needs a battle to fight; he needs a place in him for the warrior to come alive [....] If we can reawaken that fierce quality in a man [...] then the boy can grow up and become truly masculine" (p. 141). This masculinity is predicated on the fact that humankind is, for Eldredge, made in the image of God, who likewise "has a battle to fight" (p. 27). Hence, there is a created design serving as a blueprint for a man's nature.

John Eldredge co-authored *Captivating* with Stasi Eldredge. They claim that women need to be secure in their own sense of femininity and in so doing reflect how God has created them to be: "God wanted to reveal something about himself, so he gave us Eve", who they treat as a blueprint for womanhood that reveals that "God is relational to his core [...] he has a heart for romance [....] God has a beauty to unveil" (Eldredge and Eldredge, 2005, p. 27). The Reform participants articulated sex-typed gender attitudes that have close affinities with these beliefs. This idea, that men and women naturally operate in divergent cultural spheres, has evidently shaped how their theology of gender is articulated.

Participants reported reading such Christian literature and recognised that it has been impactful in informing their own gender attitudes. Some participants pulled this Christian literature off their shelves or pointed out where in their study it was placed. Equally, conservative evangelical engagement with wider society has shaped the way that this tradition articulates their gender values (see Fry, 2021a). This means that the ideas found within this Christian literature, to some extent, reflect those found within wider society, indicating a dual influence on participants' gender attitudes. I will return to this point in the seventh chapter.

There is a nuance to be added here. Nearly all the conservative evangelicals interviewed were raised in this tradition. I have already explained that the family unit has been an important sphere in historical evangelicalism where religious values—not least those relating to gender—can be passed down from one generation to another. Given that gender schemata are formed in childhood, the family is an influential context for the formation of participants' gender attitudes. The gender attitudes instilled in participants in

90 *Empathy, intersectionality, and gender schemata*

the home, though, will have been buttressed by their socialisation at church, where their parents' gender values will most likely have been shared. In the second chapter, I discussed at length the development of gender attitudes within conservative evangelicalism and explained how a traditional outlook remained despite the emergence of comparatively egalitarian ideals in wider society and the CofE. In the previous chapter, I also highlighted the continuation in thought that is evident within my participants' narratives. Hence, the religious tradition that participants were raised and socialised in has also shaped the cognitive structures that participants have for interpreting gender-related information.

This means that the impact of wider societal gender values and attitudes will have been mediated through the family context and the church communities that participants grew up in. Their gender schemata would thus more readily assimilate information that is consistent with these conceptions of gender and likely 'filter out', in effect, any information that is not congruous with it. In this respect, later engagement with one's tradition and society serves to reinforce ways of understanding gender that have their roots early on in life. Whilst not all participants grew up in this tradition, their traditional gender schemata are not entirely unique to conservative evangelicalism, as I have evinced through the discussion of non-religious popular literature. The implication of this being that the minority who did not grow up within conservative evangelicalism may well have already possessed gender schemata that are nonetheless sex-typed and so dovetail with conservative evangelical assumptions about gender.

Gender schemata and the charismatic evangelicals

The relevant themes for discussion here are: (i) Gender differences as observable; and (ii) Belief in the flexibility of gender roles. I will also analyse these themes together.

Gender differences as observable and Belief in the flexibility of gender roles

Matt stated that:

> It's very difficult to generalise about characteristics of male or female leadership. However, female leadership can be more emotionally intelligent .... I think a more—quote—female leadership approach could be one of very few rays of light [for the CofE].

Richard said, "I don't think there should be prescribed [gender] roles .... I think, as a general rule, there are differences between men and women .... There are undoubtedly exceptions to those rules." In a similar fashion, Michael reported, "You can't caricature [gender roles]. For example, I am a better cook [than my wife], so I do the cooking."

Empathy, intersectionality, and gender schemata 91

Participants in this group evinced androgynous gender schemata. That they incorporate some sex-typed thinking into their cognitive structures for processing gender-related information was apparent from their identification of particular characteristics (such as emotional intelligence) with women. It was also apparent from the assertion that "as a general rule" men and women display distinct characteristics. Nevertheless, the fact that my participants also believe that such general rules are not hard and fast, and explained that they possess characteristics traditionally associated with women, indicates that they also have the ability to process and integrate gender-related information culturally associated with the opposite sex.

In the previous chapter, I explained that the charismatic evangelicals grew up during (or after) the changing social patterns from the mid-twentieth century. However, there is more to be stated regarding the cultural factors that shape my participants' gender schemata. The androgynous sex typing has affinities with wider assumptions about the sexes, particularly as exemplified in *The Essential Difference*. Here, Baron-Cohen (2003) argues that there not only exist observable differences between the sexes but that such differences are rooted in biological—in addition to social—factors. Whilst acknowledging that socialisation impacts behaviour in a gendered way, he argues that men's and women's brains develop in different ways. Within this paradigm, males tend to think in a more systematised fashion, using more of the right hemisphere of their brains and thus are often better technologists, whereas females use more of the left hemisphere of their brains and are thus better empathisers and so are more communicative. Baron-Cohen writes, "*The female brain is predominantly hard-wired for empathy. The male brain is predominantly hard-wired for understanding and building systems*" (p. 1, emphasis original). This is followed by: "I am only talking about statistical averages, and we can learn from exceptions to this rule" (p. 4).

The thesis of *The Essential Difference* captures a combination of traditional assumptions about gender as biologically rooted and therefore leading to distinct behaviours and the belief that these differences ought not be overestimated. This combination is found in the charismatic evangelical narratives. The idea that the sexes use their brains differently is a common belief in society and owes its prevalence to popular psychology (see Joel, 2011). This group's gender schemata are thus related to the fact that they inhabit a society where traditionalist assumptions as well as comparatively recent beliefs about gender are simultaneously present.

Their schemata are not simply a hybrid of (sometimes) competing societal narratives, however, but are mediated by their religious tradition. It is worth noting here the parallel in the present narratives to the reinterpretation of traditional gender assumptions within Anglicanism in the previous century. There was a culture of Anglican men often possessing interpersonal ties and where concepts such as love were not thought to be intrinsically feminine but were a part of the Christian discourse on masculinity (Delap, 2013). In other words, during the period in which my participants were growing up (or grew up in the

92 *Empathy, intersectionality, and gender schemata*

wake of), there was an understanding within Anglicanism that characteristics traditionally associated with being feminine were compatible with Christian masculinity. My participants have therefore inherited ways of thinking about gender that exist in wider society and within Anglican discourse.

Rather than being raised in an evangelicalism that continually resisted developments in gender values, my charismatic participants have been immersed in a comparatively liberal evangelicalism that was more open to such changes. I will discuss this in more depth in the next chapter. For now, though, it is worth noting that this group of participants often grew up in churches that displayed greater openness to women's ordained ministry and that these were churches that their parents had opted to take them to. In other words, from an early age, members of this group were emersed in family and church contexts that embraced at least some wider societal changes in gender values. This will have been impactful in the formation of their gender schemata.

Gender schemata and the Anglo-Catholics

The sub-theme Negatives of feminism is relevant for discussion here.

Negatives of feminism

When discussing feminism, Peter claimed:

> Sometimes the modern age equates function and being as being the same thing so that you can function and be whatever you want. Well, that's not the way it is, unfortunately for some. Our bodies are different and so they function differently, which identify us as who we are and there's no way that you can swap those around ... because biologically and genetically [men and women] are not the same.

Most of the Anglo-Catholic participants evinced a belief that men and women are distinct and should act accordingly. However, this group did not regularly elaborate on how they felt that should be worked out in contexts other than ordained ministry. Liam did explain that he typically believed women should be stay-at-home mothers if they have children but also accepted that this belief was challenged when he came to know a single mother who had to seek employment to support her children. Nevertheless, this was the exception, with participants focusing the conversation about gender roles on the priesthood rather than on gender more broadly. What evidence exists for their gender schemata points towards a sex-typed mental framework. However, because of the lack of data available to understand their assumptions about gender further, it is difficult to contextualise their thinking in light of wider cultural beliefs discussed in the Reform narratives above.

Reflection on participants' gender schemata

Discussion of my participants' gender schemata leads to the question of the relationship between their schemata and sexism. Male sex-typing is evidently related to the prejudicial attitudes towards women held by the conservative evangelical and traditional Anglo-Catholics interviewed. This is unsurprising. Gender schema theory was developed using gender stereotypes, and gender stereotypes underpin ambivalent sexism. The charismatic evangelicals possessed androgynous gender schemata and so, despite possessing something of a binary understanding of male/female traits, did not believe in the stereotypes that the Reform participants did. Hence, it is equally unsurprising that the charismatic evangelicals have not evinced sexist attitudes in line with the definition of sexism being used here.

It is notable that evidence for the Anglo-Catholic's gender schemata is less overt because several of them did not grow up in this tradition. Some scarcely had any church connection as children. Social influences on their cognitive frameworks for interpreting information pertaining to gender are more likely to be diverse in comparison with the other two groups, therefore. However, Bem (1981a) also suggests that there may be a heterosexuality subschema which particularly encourages the development of binary gender schemas. Given that just over half of this group are homosexual, this might also be a contributory factor for this group providing less evidence of gender schemata.

Participants' identities

Participants' identities became apparent from analysis of their narratives as well as from ethnographic observations. They are intersectional with each participant belonging to different (but intersecting) social groups, such as being white, male, middle class, Anglican, and a priest. The concept of intersectionality was coined by Kimberlé Crenshaw (e.g., see Crenshaw, 2017) and much of the research on intersectionality focuses on those with less privileged social statuses, leading to much valuable insight into social inequality. However, intersectional identities can be found amongst members of any social group and individuals can simultaneously hold identities of less and greater levels of privilege (e.g., Coston and Kimmel, 2012; Van Herk, Smith and Andrew, 2011). My participants belong to the CofE through their particular Anglican traditions (whether evangelical or catholic) and are priests. Hence, they inhabit multiple interlocking identities that are directly relevant to the scope of this monograph. I introduce them here but unpack them in subsequent chapters.

With respect to Reform, participants hold a religious-professional identity, a familial identity, an evangelical identity, and a gender identity. Their religious-professional identity as Anglican clergymen was apparent and multifaceted: as priests in the CofE, participants explained that they had to undergo an often lengthy discernment process that requires a confidence that

94 *Empathy, intersectionality, and gender schemata*

priesthood within the CofE is a vocation that God has called them to; an immersive experience in theological college that forms them to incorporate Anglican priesthood into their daily lives; and a vocational profession that impacts specific areas of their livelihood, such as their housing arrangements. In fact, their homes were in very close proximity to their church buildings, which were often in view from their houses and easily accessible to parishioners and colleagues. This made their personal and professional lives difficult to distinguish from each other. Indeed, priestly vocation demands that clergy understand and order the entirety of their lives around this priestly calling, given the obedience that they are expected to give to the teachings of the Church, for example, in relation to highly personal matters such as their sexuality.

However, this is clearly tied to their familial identity; the previous chapter evidenced that the role of church leader parallels that of the (leader) husband within the (heterosexual) marital context for the interviewees (see also Fry, 2019). In this respect, there is overlap between the two identities. The close proximity between vocational and familial life was highlighted when I had lunch with one participant and his family (a wife and two children) prior to the interview. During the working day, and therefore in between clergy duties, the family would take time out to eat together. In other words, priestly life and family life do not exist in entirely distinct spheres as with some professions but are interwoven.

Participants' identities as conservative evangelicals—their immediate tradition—is one that most of them had been raised in from childhood and bears a relationship to their other identities. They frequently referred to themselves as "conservative evangelica" to distinguish themselves from other Anglicans—their wider tradition—including other evangelicals. The primacy of scripture was claimed as a key tenet of this identity and the Bible was used to justify their role as leaders in church and in the family, reflecting evangelical biblicism (see Bebbington, 1989).

This group of participants are also all white, have predominantly middle-class backgrounds, and benefit from the cultural resources that this status regularly affords. All but one had attended university prior to ordination training, often Oxford or Cambridge, and 11 out of the 14 had undertaken postgraduate study, including—in two cases—doctorates. Some had attended private (including boarding) schools and all but one spoke with middle-class, south-eastern accents. To use a Bourdieusian concept, this group possess habitus[3] (and thus consumed resources) associated with dominant social groups—that is, those with greater levels of social privilege (see Bourdieu, 1977, 1986, 2001). The privileged status was exemplified by the contents of their studies. These rooms were noticeably full of books, including many academic volumes (e.g., on biblical studies, doctrine, and Church history). None of this is surprising given the historical relationship between the middle class (indeed, the ruling class) and CofE clergy (Brown and Woodhead, 2016). Indeed, ordination has historically been endowed

Empathy, intersectionality, and gender schemata 95

with an elite status (Aldridge, 1993), an understanding that was still common among the clergy when many of my participants from this group were training for the priesthood.

These identities are bound up with participants' gender identity. The introduction of women priests was an antithesis of interviewees' sense of identity as clergymen because their new colleagues are women rather than men, and—according to my participants—people should occupy different roles on the basis of sex. In other words, women's ordination contravenes participants' understanding of their (male) priestly identity because women have become placed in the same category of 'priest'. Similarly, participants believe that men and women are to take on distinct roles as husband and wife because of their traditionalist gender identity.

The charismatic evangelical participants also hold religious-professional identities for the same reasons as their Reform colleagues. They equally hold heterosexual familial, evangelical, and gender identities. However, these identities are conceived of differently. I have already noted that this group is a distinct expression of evangelicalism from its more conservative counterpart. In fact, members of this (immediate) tradition consciously distinguished themselves from their conservative evangelical colleagues in multiple ways. For example, they stated their preference for a hermeneutic of historical context in biblical interpretation, or the emphasis on spiritual gifts that many in this group feel is important to discerning a person's call to Church leadership, regardless of sex. They also typically rejected the headship model in their marriages. In this respect, their gender attitudes are more closely aligned to their Anglican identity (their wider tradition) given that contextualised readings of biblical texts have been prominent in CofE discourse on women's ordination. This is unsurprising given that the charismatic movement has historically been ecumenical and more affirming of women's ministry, as discussed in the second chapter.

Many in this group have middle-class backgrounds, although with fewer possessing postgraduate qualifications (eight in total) and fewer attending Oxford or Cambridge. Many of those who did attend these universities, did so as part of their ordination training. Participants' studies were likewise often full of academic books. Most attended training institutions that do not command the same level of prestige as Oxford and Cambridge. Thus, whilst they all possess middle-class, south-eastern accents, they also have a broader variety of educational backgrounds. Two participants are mixed race, with the rest being white. Most would also have been training for ordination around the time that clergy understood their social role as being endowed with an elite status. This group then had access to cultural resources that will have contributed to habitus associated with social dominance but to a lesser extent than the Reform participants.

Whilst the Anglo-Catholic participants also hold religious-professional identities, they did not evince the salience of their familial identities in discussions of gender and theology. None of them are married, although one is a widower,

96 Empathy, intersectionality, and gender schemata

and none of them had lived with their families for some years, with two exceptions who explained that they are in civil partnerships, although they did not discuss these in detail. As aforementioned, seven have homosexual identities. They also have an Anglo-Catholic identity rather than an evangelical one, and frequently referred to themselves as Catholics (their immediate tradition) within the CofE (their wider tradition). This meant that there was less of an emphasis on scripture and more on identifying with the Roman Catholic Church during the interviews. Similarly to the charismatics, they distinguished themselves from the conservative evangelicals by explaining that they too prefer a hermeneutic of historical context—although, as seen in the previous chapter, this is not reflected in their interpretation of apostleship. As also witnessed in the previous chapter, their traditionalist gender beliefs indicate a more rigid gender identity as with members of Reform. As a further parallel to Reform, they hold the fact that they are men as essential to the validity of their priestly roles.

This group likewise possesses middle-class status, with one notable exception. However, the individual in question, whilst coming from a working-class family, attended Oxford for his first degree, prior to ordination training. Most of this group have postgraduate qualifications (seven in total), although the majority elected not to attend Oxford for their ordination training, and none attended Cambridge. However, several of them did attend Russell Group institutions (including Oxford and Cambridge) for their university education prior to ordination training. Nevertheless, the statuses of their higher education institutions are diverse. All are white and spoke with middle-class, south-eastern accents and the majority trained or were ordained prior to Aldridge's findings on the perceived elite status of the clergy. Overall, this group consumes cultural resources associated with privileged status, but to a lesser extent than the conservative evangelicals and in ways distinct to the charismatic evangelicals. As with Reform, the introduction of women priests was antithetical to their clerical identity because their new colleagues are women rather than men, and they believe that, in the context of the Church, people should occupy different roles on the basis of sex. It thus likewise contravenes the Anglo-Catholics' understanding of their (male) priestly identity.

Participants across all three groups, therefore, possess identities that are primarily privileged, although there are three important caveats here. The first is that more than half of the Anglo-Catholics are homosexual which, as discussed in the previous chapter, has led to a sense of frustration of their marginalisation within a Church that does not officially permit same-sex sexual activity. This ought not to be overlooked given that privilege is not a "zero sum quality" but often a multi-faceted phenomenon (Coston and Kimmel, 2012, p. 97).

The second caveat is that two charismatic evangelicals are mixed race and thus do not inhabit the privileged status of their white peers in this respect. The third is that the social status of clergy has waned over the years with

Empathy, intersectionality, and gender schemata 97

churches playing less of a role in society than has previously been the case, a phenomenon that some participants reflected on. That is not to claim that clergy lack privileged status through their profession/vocation. Some of my participants also reflected on the trust and access afforded to them in different social settings beyond the Church in view of their ordained status. However, it does mean that their relative privilege as a social group ought to be juxtaposed alongside its recent relative decline.

It is also worth noting that those with higher levels of social privilege often display discriminatory behaviour as a way of maintaining their higher social status at the expense of others, a phenomenon otherwise known as symbolic—or masculine—domination within the sociological literature (Bourdieu, 2001), or as an outworking of ingroup favouritism within the social psychological literature (Tajfel and Turner, 1979, 1986). Both bodies of literature highlight different but complementary aspects of the social world that will provide useful explanatory power for interpreting participants' data, particularly in tandem. This will be unpacked in subsequent chapters. These phenomena have not been evinced in the charismatic evangelical narratives, however, which requires explanation, which I will provide subsequently.

Having explored the gender attitudes of participants (particularly with respect to beliefs and emotions), their cognitive frameworks for interpreting gender-related information, and their intersectional identities, I will offer some methodological reflections before turning to an examination of their behaviours and a further analysis of their emotions.

Methodological reflection

A clear benefit from the qualitative approach to analysing prejudice taken here is that it enables one to identify how those with prejudicial attitudes articulate them. More particularly, because participants were not selecting predetermined options for their description of gender roles, one is able to gain insight into the specifics of their gender attitudes, limiting the risk of misrepresenting participants (see Burman, 1994) and thus also limiting the possibility of oversimplifying their beliefs (see Halualani, 2008). This approach also provides insight into the specific expressions of sexism that occurs in day-to-day life. Whilst it is useful—indeed necessary—to understand the categories of sexism and their definitions, discerning the presence of sexism is not an abstract undertaking but requires one to identify how the quantitative findings translate into people's lives.

The qualitative approach has also indicated that sexism is not always a set of attitudes that are distinctly different from non-sexist ones. Rather, one can adopt attitudes that contain elements of the definitions of sexism without fully reflecting these definitions. Such a qualitative venture is long overdue considering the institution's historical significance and the role it plays in public life (see Nason-Clark, 1987a) and because prejudice is all the more difficult to tackle if its expressions cannot be identified (see Storkey, 1985).

98 *Empathy, intersectionality, and gender schemata*

Bringing cognate areas of research into dialogue with an exploration of prejudice, and doing so in a qualitative way, further advances understanding of how sexism occurs in situ. Juxtaposing prejudicial beliefs alongside other attitudes and cognitive frameworks that accompany them offers a more in-depth understanding of prejudicial ones because more of the factors that shape such attitudes become apparent. This has also contributed to an older methodological discussion regarding gender schema theory by highlighting that at least some people do possess binary gender assumptions, even when they do not hold entirely traditional or essentialist gender attitudes. This indicates that gender schema theory continues to be relevant for gender research.

Finally, on the methodological front, the fact that participants' display of empathy was consistent with their display of prejudicial attitudes—in keeping with what one would expect from previous research—provides further empirical weight for the use of this theoretical lens for understanding my participants' narratives.

Conclusion

In this chapter, I have explored three quite distinct but co-contributory components of participants' gender attitudes. Whilst they stem from different bodies of knowledge, they nevertheless converge in the present study in their relevance for understanding my participants' data. The discussion of empathy has provided further insight as to why prejudicial attitudes are present or absent within each group of interviewees. As it is an important psychological resource for challenging prejudice, where it is absent, prejudice is more likely to remain compared with where it is present. Analysis of gender schemata also provides some explanation as to why sexism pervades or is absent (at least for the evangelicals) as it highlights that the Reform participants process gender-related information in terms of clear stereotypes whereas the charismatics do not. It ought to be noted that one's religious tradition is closely related to their gender schema, with the former shaping the latter and with differences in religious traditions shaping them to different ends. This is an important point. Religious beliefs cannot be seen simply as 'add-ons' that justify pre-existing assumptions; they contribute to them in a significant way.

The discussion of intersectionality has begun to establish the relevance for participants' different identities. It is clear that one's stance on women's ordination is linked to a gender identity which relates to a religious identity. These sit alongside other identities. The extent to which they are relevant for understanding participants' gender attitudes will become apparent in due course, but it is worth bearing in mind that people's attitudes are not formed in a closed circuit. In particular, they are not formed without respect to identity. Indeed I have already established that the boundaries between my participants' gender attitudes and a variety of different social phenomena are blurred.

Notes

1 However, it is important to note that the theory does not assume that certain content is inherent to a gender schema. Rather, the nature of the content will be determined by the assumptions that any given society has about gender. In Bem's context (as in my participants'), assumptions about gender that are traditionally found within their societies still dominate—albeit in transmuted form—whilst sitting alongside less traditional assumptions and values. Hence, the ingrained stereotypes affirm traditional gender roles in the context being studied.
2 Some of the data discussed in this chapter is analysed in Fry (2019) but to different ends.
3 I.e., the accumulation of habits, dispositions, and skills which become ingrained over time (Bourdieu, 1977).

References

Aldridge, A. (1993). Negotiating status: Social scientists and Anglican clergy. *Journal of Contemporary Ethnography*, 22(1), 97–112.
Baron-Cohen, S. (2003). *The essential difference*. London: Penguin UK.
Batson, C.D., & Powell, A.A. (2003). Altruism and prosocial behavior. In T. Millon & M. Lerner (Eds.), *Handbook of Psychology, vol. 5: Personality and social psychology* (pp. 463–484). Hoboken, NJ: John Wiley & Sons.
Bebbington, D.W. (1989). *Evangelicalism in modern Britain: A history from the 1730s to the 1980s*. London: Unwin Hyman.
Bem, S.L. (1981a). Gender schema theory: A cognitive account of sex typing. *Psychological Review*, 88(4), 354–364.
Bem, S.L. (1981b). The BSRI and gender schema theory: A reply to Spence and Helmreich. *Psychological Review*, 88(4), 369–371.
Bourdieu, P. (1977). *Outline of a theory of practice*. Cambridge University Press.
Bourdieu, P. (1986). The forms of capital. In J. Richardson (Ed.), *Handbook of theory and research for the sociology of education* (pp. 241–258). New York: Greenwood.
Bourdieu, P. (2001). *Masculine domination*. Redwood City, CA: Stanford University Press.
Brewer, W.F., & Treyens, J.C. (1981). Role of schemata in memory for places. *Cognitive Psychology*, 13(2), 207–230.
Brown, R. (2011). *Prejudice: Its social psychology*. Hoboken, NJ: John Wiley & Sons.
Brown, A., & Woodhead, L. (2016). *That was the Church that was: How the Church of England lost the English people*. London: Bloomsbury.
Burman, E. (1994). Interviewing. In P. Banister, E. Burman, I. Parker, M. Taylor, & C. Tindall (Eds.), *Qualitative methods in psychology* (pp. 49–71). Buckingham: Open University Press.
Coston, B.M., & Kimmel, M. (2012). Seeing privilege where it isn't: Marginalized masculinities and the intersectionality of privilege. *Journal of Social Issues*, 68(1), 97–111.
Crenshaw, K.W. (2017). *On intersectionality: Essential writings*. New York: The New Press.
Dawkins, R. (1989). *The selfish gene*, 2nd edition. Oxford University Press.

100 *Empathy, intersectionality, and gender schemata*

Delap, L. (2013). "Be strong and play the man": Anglican masculinities in the twentieth century. In L. Delap & S. Morgan (Eds.), *Men, masculinities and religious change in twentieth century Britain* (pp. 119–154). Basingstoke: Palgrave Macmillan.

Dovidio, J.F., Allen, J.L., & Schroeder, D.A. (1990). Specificity of empathy-induced helping: Evidence for altruistic motivation. *Journal of Personality and Social Psychology, 59*(2), 249–260.

Eisenberg, N., & Miller, P.A. (1987). The relation of empathy to prosocial and related behaviors. *Psychological Bulletin, 101*(1), 91–119.

Eldredge, J. (2001). *Wild at heart: Discovering the passionate soul of a man.* Nashville, TN: Thomas Nelson.

Eldredge, J., & Eldredge, S. (2005). *Captivating: Unveiling the mystery of a woman's soul.* Nashville, TN: Thomas Nelson.

Frable, D.E., & Bem, S.L. (1985). If you are gender schematic, all members of the opposite sex look alike. *Journal of Personality and Social Psychology, 49*(2), 459–468.

Fry, A.D.J. (2019). Justifying gender inequality in the Church of England: An examination of theologically conservative male clergy attitudes towards women's ordination. *Fieldwork in Religion, 14*(1), 8–32.

Fry, A.D.J. (2021a). Postfeminist, engaged and resistant: Evangelical male clergy attitudes towards gender and women's ordination in the Church of England. *Critical Research on Religion, 9*(1), 65–83.

Garaigordobil, M. (2014). Sexism and empathy: Differences as a function of sociodemographic variables and relations between both constructs. In A. Columbus (Ed.), *Advances in psychology research, vol. 100* (pp. 59–80). New York: Nova Science Publishers, Inc.

Gilligan, C. (1993). *In a different voice.* Cambridge: Harvard University Press.

Gray, J. (1992). *Men are from Mars, women are from Venus: A practical guide for improving communication and getting what you want in your relationships.* New York: Harper Collins.

Gray, J. (2011). *Men are from Mars, women are from Venus and children are from Heaven.* New York: Random House.

Greer, G. (1970). *The female eunuch.* London: MacGibbon and Kee.

Halualani, R.T. (2008). How do multicultural university students define and make sense of intercultural contact? A qualitative study. *International Journal of Intercultural Relations, 32*(1), 1–16.

Joel, D. (2011). Male or female? Brains are intersex. *Frontiers in Integrative Neuroscience, 5.* 10.3389/fnint.2011.00057.

Lobel, T.E. (1994). Sex typing and the social perception of gender stereotypic and nonstereotypic behavior: The uniqueness of feminine males. *Journal of Personality and Social Psychology, 66*(2), 379–385.

Nason-Clark, N. (1987a). Ordaining women as priests: Religious vs. sexist explanations for clerical attitudes. *Sociological Analysis, 48*(3), 259–273.

Nathanson, A.I., Wilson, B.J., McGee, J., & Sebastian, M. (2002). Counteracting the effects of female stereotypes on television via active mediation. *Journal of Communication, 52*(4), 922–937.

Spence, J.T. (1993). Gender-related traits and gender ideology: Evidence for a multifactorial theory. *Journal of Personality and Social Psychology, 64*(4), 624–635.

Starr, C.R., & Zurbriggen, E.L. (2016). Sandra Bem's gender schema theory after 34 years: A review of its reach and impact. *Sex Roles*, *76*(9), 566–578.

Stephan, W.G., & Finlay, K. (1999). The role of empathy in improving intergroup relations. *Journal of Social Issues*, *55*(4), 729–743.

Storkey, E. (1985). *What's right with feminism?* London: SPCK.

Tajfel, H., & Turner, J.C. (1979). An integrative theory of intergroup conflict. *The Social Psychology of Intergroup Relations*, *33*(47), 33–47.

Tajfel, H., & Turner, J.C. (1986). The social identity theory of intergroup behaviour. In S. Worchel & W.G. Austin (Eds.), *Psychology of intergroup relations* (pp. 7–24). Chicago, IL: Nelson Hall.

Tannen, D. (1990). *You just don't understand*. New York: Ballantine.

Toi, M., & Batson, C.D. (1982). More evidence that empathy is a source of altruistic motivation. *Journal of Personality and Social Psychology*, *43*(2), 281–292.

Turner, J.C., & Reynolds, K.J. (2012). Self-categorization theory. In P. Van Lange, A. Kruglanski, & E. Tory Higgins (Eds.), *The handbook of theories of social psychology: Self-categorization theory* (pp. 399–417). London: Sage.

Van Herk, K.A., Smith, D., & Andrew, C. (2011). Examining our privileges and oppressions: Incorporating an intersectionality paradigm into nursing. *Nursing Inquiry*, *18*(1), 29–39.

5 Contact and contact avoidance

Introduction

Having established the beliefs that participants have about women, and the contextual factors that shape them, in the following two chapters I will continue to explore my participants' gender attitudes by assessing how they behave towards outgroups, by which I mean their female colleagues as well as their colleagues (male and female) who hold more liberal theologies of gender. The present chapter will contain an examination of my participants' narratives with respect to the theory of intergroup contact, which builds on the social psychological understanding of prejudice already discussed. The next chapter will then involve a discussion of participants' interactions through the lenses of group schisms, social capital, and spiritual capital, and will involve a further exploration of their emotions also. In this chapter, I will first introduce several additional themes relevant for discussion before I outline the theory of intergroup contact. This will be followed by a methodological reflection on the utility of adapting the theory of intergroup contact—which is based on quantitative studies—for qualitative means.

Contact and Reform

There are several themes within the Reform narratives that are relevant for discussion because they contain reports that concern the nature of participants' interaction with clergy beyond their immediate tradition, particularly wo men priests. These are: (i) Mixed experience in the discernment process; (ii) Resistance towards training institutions; (ii) Homogeneity in training; and (iv) Resistance towards the diocese.

Mixed experience in the discernment process

Participants' reports of their experiences of the discernment process for ordained ministry in their previous dioceses were rather mixed. For several of them, this meant having both positive and negative experiences during this time, whereas others had either positive or unmemorable experiences. For instance, Joshua recalled:

DOI: 10.4324/9781003081913-5

The first DDO[1] I had was not a great relationship .... The third time we met up she said, 'What's the Gospel?' and I think I used 'man' as a placeholder for 'mankind' ... that whole conversation de-railed .... I was passed on to [another] lady ... and she was fantastic .... I was [then] handed over whilst I was at [theological] college to [another] lady who was fine, but I don't think I ever met her actually.

Joshua's narrative reveals a tricky relationship that resulted from gender-related insensitivity. However, this was an infrequent occurrence amongst the Reform participants during the discernment stage. It was more common for participants to express some enjoyment of their relationships with those in the diocese who were charged with discerning participants' readiness to train for ministry. Joshua's relationship with the second person from the diocese is more typical amongst the Reform group, including in the narratives of those who meet with members in the diocese who are from different traditions to their own. This includes those who had women as vocations advisors[2] or directors of ordinands. Alistair, for example, said, "I still see [my DDO] ... at conferences ... I bumped into her at a drinks thing recently. It's lovely ... she's always very warm. We always have a little chat .... It's always encouraging."

Several other participants, however, reported something of the impersonal relationship that Joshua recalled having with the third DDO. For instance, Sam recalled that his discernment process was "brief and simple. [I spent] half an hour with the DDO [and then had] tea with the archdeacon." For these participants, relationships were brief, lacking depth, and largely unmemorable for them. Overall, this theme demonstrates that participants' interactions with others in their previous dioceses were inconsistent.

Participants did not see their relationships with the DDO as a formative part of the discernment process contributing to their sense of vocation to the priesthood. Participants could have utilised these opportunities to form relationships with the DDOs that would ultimately help them to become ministers. Instead, those interviewed clearly thought very little of the role of other Church workers in their discernment unless the relationships were affirming rather than challenging. When participants did express an appreciation for others' confirming their vocation, it was in respect to those who presented no challenge to their evangelicalism. The fact that Joshua praised the DDO who apparently took no issue with the way he articulated his theology, but not the woman who questioned his gender-normative language, illustrates this effectively. This is suggestive of an uneasiness with authority beyond their tradition, including women, given that DDOs have (soft) power—in the Foucauldian sense of the word (see Foucault, 1977)—because they influence when and if potential clergy go forward for ordination training.

Resistance towards training institutions and Homogeneity in training

There were numerous instances where the Reform participants explained that they disengaged from their training institution and community in different

104 *Contact and contact avoidance*

ways. There were also plenty of instances when they provided evidence of homogeneity in their ordination training. These two themes will be discussed together because they reflect participants' understanding of the same experience as trainee clergy. Regarding the first of these themes, Adam, who went to Ridley Hall (an evangelical college in Cambridge), explained that:

> There were times where I'd get quite frustrated at being at Ridley because my understanding and my theology wasn't always quite as welcome, which could quite often bring some sort of conflict at times. Some of that might have been self-inflicted but ... if any conversations came up about the ordination of women or the episcopacy ... it wasn't always ... easy to say anything so you just kept quiet, or if you did [espouse a traditional view] it was usually ... not that welcome.

Adam evidenced that he became evasive within his training community to some extent because his interactions with those outside of his immediate tradition could be negative. He admitted that some of this was his own fault, indicating that the nature of his interactions could have been improved. However, he also implied that fellow ordinands of a less traditionalist persuasion than himself contributed to his undesirable social experiences during his time in training. This was because of their decision to respond in an uninviting manner to those who held more conservative gender beliefs. Hence, participants' resistance towards their training colleges was partially the result of how they felt their peers received them.

It is also relevant to note that participants who went to more conservative theological colleges evinced similar levels of disengagement from their training institutions. For instance, Stanley went to Oak Hill, the most theologically conservative of the evangelical training institutions within the CofE. Nevertheless, he explained that:

> I didn't particularly want to live in a college with a bunch of 19-year-olds and I wasn't married. So the older students often were married and lived out .... I think the people who had the most influence on me were probably [the teachers] when I was doing the Conrhill [evangelical] course, which I did before I started at theological college.

Similarly, Ian said:

> I [didn't enjoy] the fact that Ridley was part of the federation of Cambridge theological colleges. I didn't do much with the other colleges, you know, it was fairly tedious ... I think you were endlessly walking on egg shells so you didn't offend people. You had radically different theological opinions and the supposed unity was a bit of a sham, and the relationships with the staff at Ridley were not always terribly easy ...

Contact and contact avoidance 105

[the Principal] didn't ask me about my prayer life, he didn't ask me about anything about what was going on.

Participants evinced an avoidance of those in their training colleges with whom they departed theologically. Those who attended Ridley Hall and Wycliffe Hall (an evangelical theological college in Oxford) also had to undertake some training with ordinands at different (usually more theologically liberal) training institutions, which they were critical about in the interviews. In fact, participants did not only resist their training institutions when they were largely made up of those from different Christian traditions or who possessed different gender attitudes and values to their own. Rather, they also resisted training institutions that were within the conservative evangelical tradition, as highlighted by Stanley's statement.

With respect to Homogeneity in training, participants frequently evinced that they either surrounded themselves with those from the same tradition as them if they attended a training institution that was theologically broader, or they provided evidence that their training college lacked theological diversity, with most of their peers holding similar positions to themselves. In fact, Simon revealed, "[Out of] all the ordinands in my year group, none of them were women .... I had deeper relationships with the men, but that's just because it happened to be that way in my year group."

Simon attended Oak Hill and reported the absence of women wanting to train to be deacons or priests, meaning he was not exposed to women who were pursuing a vocation to ordination. Indeed, the fact that he had less in-depth relationships with the female students at Oak Hill would have meant less exposure to women's perspectives on ministry, including from those who were also undergoing theological and ministerial training in a lay capacity. Similarly, Joshua explained, "my immediate contact with college was with the four other people who were on my course ... we all had similar convictions." Joshua was one of only five in his year group who undertook the BA degree in the University of Oxford's Faculty of Theology and Religion when he attended Wycliffe Hall. All five of them were conservative evangelical men, and this was his closest circle of friends at a college that he believes was around 90% male.

Additionally, Joshua explained that he often neglected to engage with the community socially, meaning that he was often physically absent from the college given much of the teaching he received was also outside of it. He expanded, admitting that staff and students challenged him for this lack of integration: "People might have come to me and said, 'You're having this on your own terms', which was true .... I'd be frustrated to see someone hovering in and out. But I have to say, personally, it was brilliant." Joshua had decided to be largely withdrawn from the college community, interacting mostly with the other four men on his course who were fellow conservative evangelicals. He also showed little consideration of the perspective of others,

106 *Contact and contact avoidance*

including the thoughts of his tutors who would have had Joshua more present in community life.

Resistance towards the diocese

Participants frequently evinced either outright resistance towards their diocese or described interactions with the wider Church that revealed ulterior motives for such contact. For instance, when asked about his interaction with the diocese, Henry explained, "My involvement is actually, at the moment, through the wider Anglican Church—GAFCON and [the] Free Church of England." Henry stated that he does not interact with the diocese voluntarily. Instead, he engages with the Global Anglican Future Conference (GAFCON), which is a schismatic international Anglican network that was established in 2008 when leaders in the Anglican Communion met in Jerusalem with the aim of steering the Communion towards historical theological orthodoxy, as they saw it (GAFCON, n.d.). Similarly, the Free Church of England broke away from the CofE in the nineteenth century in opposition to the rise of the Oxford Movement and considers itself to be an evangelical Church (The Free Church of England, 2018). Henry's involvement with the wider Church is thus through schismatic movements, rather than with his diocese, demonstrating that, not only does he refrain from engaging with his diocese, but that he is actively protesting the wider CofE through his chosen affiliations. In fact, Henry expressed that the outcry against gender traditionalist Philip North's appointment as the Bishop of Sheffield in 2017 demonstrated that, in his opinion, there is little place in the CofE for theological conservatives. One can deduce from Henry's narrative that such resistance is shaped by a sense of rejection.

Whilst other participants described a more generous level of engagement with the wider CofE, it was apparent that they desire to do so to promote their own theology within the Church. For example, when Callum was asked if he thought that the CofE needed evangelicalism, he replied, "I think it's necessary and without it the Church of England will die." He later expanded that he was writing a module for new curates in the diocese on the Old Testament/Hebrew Bible because he felt that the current course of study was theologically too liberal, and he wanted to be a voice of evangelical influence in the CofE.

Nevertheless, this does require an increased level of engagement and cooperation that was not found in Henry's narrative. Callum did explain that he had sworn allegiance to the bishop and that he would not want to leave the CofE. However, it is important to note that this level of engagement was accompanied by the expressed possibility of leaving the Established Church if there is a future schism. He also felt that the Church had become too liberal. Whilst Callum is evidently more willing to interact with the diocese than Henry, the underlying attitude is akin to that of participants also involved with GAFCON, given that Reform and GAFCON both aim to change the CofE by bringing it back to (what is perceived to be) its Reformed roots.

However, a minority of participants, whilst feeling uncomfortable with the perception of marginalisation that they experienced in the diocese as conservative evangelicals, refrain from either deliberate protest or reform. Stephen remarked:

> I am a member of Reform, but I'm ... not as fully square in their position ... on the ordination of women .... I see it as a secondary issue and therefore I'm totally ready to respect and work with people who take a different view on it .... I'm part of the New Wine network and ... they would be very much more supportive of women's ordination.

Stephen thought that Reform had become too focused on the matter of women's ministry, despite holding to conservative gender values himself. He reported helping women through the selection process towards ordination so long as they have a clear theological position on why they felt women may be ordained that is informed by the Bible. However, he does not actively partake in additional diocesan activities other than attending Reform meetings. Moreover, whilst being a member of Reform, he is a member of a group that had a more permissive stance on women's ministry. In fact, despite currently being broader with respect to its evangelicalism, New Wine has its roots in the charismatic evangelical tradition, which (as previously stated) has been more inclusive of women's ministry. Although Reform is a more closely-knit group, it is possible that being exposed to this kind of influence has impacted Stephen's approach to disagreement regarding the role of women in Church leadership. Nevertheless, Stephen was the exception rather than the rule in this case.

Most, on the other hand, tended to articulate fears of a 'slippery slope' whereby shifting theological positions on the ordination of women is thought to inevitably lead to the CofE's official acceptance of homosexuality, reflecting the concerns that Carey (2004) notes in his memoirs, discussed in the second chapter. For many of these participants, then, the question of women's ordination and consecration is tied up in the question of homosexuality, something that is presently causing significant tensions within the CofE (see Brittain and McKinnon, 2011). In fact, one participant mentioned to me in passing that he was considering rousing the other members of Reform in the diocese to write a letter of protest to the bishop after a civil partnership between two priests in the diocese had been announced in the local media.

Overall, the Reform participants evinced limited levels of contact with the wider CofE, unless there was a lack of theological disagreement or an opportunity for the advancement of the evangelical tradition within the Established Church. Unsurprisingly then, contact with women clergy or clergy-in-training was also limited.

108 *Contact and contact avoidance*

Contact and the charismatic evangelicals

In the third chapter, I noted that the charismatic evangelical participants did not evince prejudicial attitudes towards women. I will now explore the kind of contact that they have with others, including their female colleagues, to achieve a fuller picture of participants' narratives with respect to the ordination of women. The themes for discussion in the present chapter are: (i) Presence of women in ordination training; (ii) Co-operation with those in other traditions and with different theologies; and (iii) Exposure to women in church leadership.

Presence of women in ordination training

A distinctive feature of the charismatic evangelical narratives is the fact that participants trained alongside women and/or had ordained female tutors during their time at theological college. While the number of women they trained alongside varied from only a few to substantially more, participants had no trouble recalling relationships with their female peers. Richard said, "[My dissertation supervisor] is the principal at [the college] and ... she is extraordinary. She's absolutely brilliant ... she was great." Richard is grateful for the contribution that his supervisor made to his formation as a minister in ordination training.

Several participants had trained prior to 1992 but nonetheless trained with women preparing for the diaconate. For instance, Lewis said, "I think there was a deep bond between the twelve or fourteen of us [who were in the same cohort]. It was a mix of men and women, probably about four or five women, seven or eight men." The kind of relationship that Lewis had with women training for the diaconate evinces that the personal relationships this group has with women clergy have constantly been positive and involved deep friendships. Whilst he could not remember the exact number of people he trained alongside some decades earlier, Lewis was clear that those relationships were very meaningful to him, and thus formative, at the time.

Co-operation with those in other traditions and with different theologies

This group also engages with ordained colleagues from different theological traditions to their own on a regular basis. For instance, when asked whether he works with those of other traditions, Philip explained that:

> ... in post-ordination training, because it's diocesan based, the likelihood is—and it was true for us there—you assemble with people who hold different theological positions to yourself. I grew to like ... all of those people who were part of my cohort and it's an opportunity to learn empathy and place yourself in other people's shoes and listen to their story ... trying to place yourself in their shoes is a way of trying to understand how they come to their position that they hold.

Similarly, Ken said:

> ... whilst we're charismatic evangelical, we try to embrace different theological traditions and worship styles ... I robe up for Communion but we also sing [Pentecostal songs]– it's a mix ... we try and embrace the diversity in our congregation.

The charismatic evangelicals in this study engage with those of other traditions in a way that is distinct from the other evangelical cohort studied. This is perhaps to be expected given that the charismatic tradition has been ecumenical, and therefore embraced different traditions, from very early on in its origins (see Maiden, 2018).

Exposure to women in church leadership

Twelve of these participants have also had exposure to women in church leadership in various capacities. For example, Rob said, "I grew up ... with a deaconess, and she always had a blue robe on, and it never meant anything to me except that she was part of the team of people who were employed by the church." Rob had seen women in public ministry from an early age, making the phenomenon a norm for him. In fact, prior to his ministerial training, he didn't appreciate the differences in roles that liturgical clothing represented and so was unable to distinguish between the roles of ordained men and women along these lines. Similarly, Matt reported, "We had a female deaconess in the 1980s who led our youth group, so very early on I had an experience of women's ministry that was very positive." As with Rob, Matt grew up with a clear exposure to women's licensed ministry, something that he feels was a positive phenomenon.

Oscar who, like Michael, belongs to the HTB network, holds more traditional gender values that would exclude women from leading churches or dioceses but accept them as curates. However, he explained that not only does he work with women in his congregation through the selection process for ordination, but also that most of the people he sends to the diocese for discernment are women. This means that even amongst the minority of this group who have some theological objections to women's ordination, interaction with women priests (or potential priests) is common and can be supportive as well as in-depth, given that the discernment process usually takes over a year.

Contact and the Anglo-Catholics

As with Reform, the Anglo-Catholic participants have evinced prejudicial attitudes towards women. I have selected five themes for exploration in this chapter because they will provide a detailed understanding of how the participants interact with those outside of their own tradition, not least

110 *Contact and contact avoidance*

women priests. The themes for discussion are: (i) Lack of women ordinands in training; (ii) Worked with women priests; and (iii) Wider participation in the CofE.

Lack of women ordinands in training and Worked with women priests

All but one of the clergy interviewed trained for the priesthood at a residential theological college that stood in the Anglo-Catholic tradition. Eleven of the 13 recalled a distinct lack of women training for either the diaconate or the priesthood. Oliver said that during his time at the College of the Resurrection it was "All male ordinands at that point .... The College of the Resurrection ... is a male [monastic] community .... Our voice trainer ... was a ... lady .... I think she was the only female member of staff when I was there." Oliver trained prior to the first ordinations of women to the priesthood or to the diaconate. However, this absence in training was also cited by those who had trained for ordination more recently. For example, Tyrone recalled that women were not a prominent feature of training because "in the year prior [to me arriving], the college had just admitted women students and only eight years before that ... [they] allowed the wives of married students to come to chapel."

There was thus a lack of contact with those who would become their female colleagues from 1994 during the time when participants were being formed as priests. In fact, participants explained the benefits of communal living and activity, and the social support that accompanied this lifestyle at their colleges. This mirrors the male-dominated culture of the Tractarians where Anglo-Catholic theology was formed in an all-male, Anglican, academic environment and offers further evidence of the enclave-like aspect of this tradition.

This has largely remained after ordination even though participants interact with female clergy to a modest extent. Ashley explained that, despite helping women priests in the diocese in a number of ways, he does not see their ordination as valid: "I suppose my mind-set is that I'm engaging in ecumenical dialogue and activity. So, these are fellow Christians, I just don't happen to recognise their [religious] orders." In the third chapter, I noted that this group sometimes couched their opposition to women's ordination in softer terms, employing the language of doubt rather than outright rejection. Ashley's comment here is comparable, implicitly suggesting that his refusal to recognise women's ordination is almost incidental with his use of "*I just don't happen* to recognise their orders." His working with them was no different from the lay women he worked with. I interviewed Ashley in his house and on arrival there were two other women working, one of which was undertaking administration for the church and the other was tidying Ashley's house. These interactions with women likely (and collectively) reinforce the expectation that women are not priestly but better suited to other, more subservient roles in church life.

Peter stated, "I'm one of those who would be called 'impossiblist' ... only men are able to receive the grace of ordination." In other words, my participants' more recent interactions with female clergy are not only limited but accompanied by the same environment they experienced prior to ordination. Evan, in contradistinction, despite being more conservative on the matter initially, became affirming of women's ordination to the priesthood. He described his encounter with a woman discerning a vocation within the CofE:

I'd already made a friend who was a Church Army officer[3] and [she] had to do post-ordination training [with me] .... She plonked herself next to me on the sofa and we got talking, then we had dinner together and we became friends ... she was there as a Church Army officer ... and then discerned a calling, first of all to the diaconate, then to the priesthood. And I went on a journey with her .... It was her, and journeying with her, and beginning to see in her the signs of priestly nature, [that changed my mind].

Evan sensed this call in her and supported her through the discernment process. There was nevertheless a mismatch between his theological conviction regarding the role of women in the Church and what he felt he was experiencing as a result of his relationship with the Church Army officer. However, this did not prevent him from working with her to discern her sense of vocation.

Aaron, who is homosexual, stated that his mind was changed after seeing a woman preside at Communion over a long period of time when he was a chaplain and would take part in Communion services at his local church. He reported that seeing a woman preside just as well as men led him to believe that women could fulfil the priestly role. Aaron also explained that when he held a more traditional view of priesthood, it wasn't with great conviction, and he chose not to join any organisations that opposed the development of women priests. He also explained that he grew up without an understanding that men and women ought to take on defined roles because his parent's values were untraditional in this respect. It was therefore encounters with women who are perceived to have a vocation to the priesthood and its associated abilities that challenged the theological assumptions of those within this tradition who came to change their minds on the matter.

Wider participation in the CofE

Participants evinced involvement in the wider diocese. Peter explained:

[I] always endeavoured [in] my time as Regional Dean [of Forward in Faith] to ensure we always had a quarterly Mass at the cathedral because it is as much our cathedral as anybody else's ... I think it was one of the reasons

112 *Contact and contact avoidance*

why I was made an honorary canon [of the cathedral]—because I had engaged Forward in Faith ... into the life of the diocese as much as [I] could.

Peter's understanding of engagement, however, is territorial. He desired to occupy space that he felt rightfully belonged to his traditionalist peers just as much as it does to more liberal clergy. This parallels the sentiment in Ashley's narrative, discussed in the third chapter, because of the implied sense of marginalisation in this statement. In other words, Peter felt the need to make use of the cathedral to demonstrate that it is not solely the space of those who hold alternative theological positions (see also Fry, 2021b). Peter also recalled an argument with the (male) diocesan bishop, with whom he had impaired Communion by placing himself under a flying bishop. In that conversation, Peter felt the need to assert that his church building has been in Communion with the Pope much longer than it has been Anglican.

Additionally, Peter reported that this incident occurred after the bishop had expressed the desire for his church to be closed because of Peter's conservative theological position. He also stated that he felt his comment about his building being in Communion with the Pope would be a "strike against [his] name" with the diocese. This reflects something of Callum's narrative where disengagement is accompanied by a sense of rejection. These interactions are also in keeping with the resistance towards bishops evinced by the Tractarians and likewise show that interaction with those outside of their immediate tradition is limited. Once more, the enclave-like aspect of Anglo-Catholicism is apparent in my participants' narratives as is the tension with episcopal authority.

Such resistance was also noticeable when I attended a midweek Mass at the invitation of one of the participants. During the service, they turned their back to the congregation and performed some of the liturgy in Latin. This is a symbolic gesture that clearly nods to Roman Catholic tradition prior to Vatican II, where Mass in the vernacular was introduced. It was a definite look back to the Church's (perceived) historical connection to Roman Catholicism.

Intergroup contact

Having described the above themes, I will analyse them further in light of the social psychological theory of intergroup contact. In the third chapter, I outlined Allport's (1979) understanding of prejudice. It is part of his wider theory, known as the contact hypothesis, which identifies multiple behaviours that accompany prejudicial outlooks. I utilise the contact hypothesis here because participants' interactions with those beyond their tradition mirror the behaviours outlined in the theory, making it a useful body of knowledge for further interpreting the data. Indeed, the fact that the narratives frequently reflect not only the definition of prejudice found in this body of research, but also the behaviours understood to accompany prejudice, adds credence to the decision to use this theory as an interpretive lens for understanding my participants.

Prejudice can be reduced when contact between distinct social groups is made under certain conditions. More particularly, it is likely to be reduced during prolonged contact when all parties involved: (i) possess equal status; (ii) seek common goals; (iii) are willingly co-operatively dependent upon each other; and (iv) interact with the positive support of the relevant authoritative bodies (Dovidio, Gaertner and Kawakami, 2003). Co-operative dependence is especially effective at facilitating prejudice reduction because goal sharing can foster the process of re-categorisation. This is when opposing groups begin to see themselves as part of a new superordinate category, rather than as two distinct entities (Brown, 2011). Further support for these four conditions has been provided in the most recent studies, demonstrating the robustness of the theory. Meta-analysis has shown that greater levels of intergroup contact are associated with lower levels of prejudice, even when participant selection biases are accounted for (Pettigrew and Tropp, 2005). Usefully, the analysis incorporated studies that engage with a wide range of prejudices.

There is a strong likelihood of reciprocal causality between contact and prejudice because those who hold prejudice tend to avoid those against whom they are prejudiced, just as a lack of contact can reinforce prejudice (Brown, 2011). However, when contact is made it can be effective in reducing such attitudes (Brown, 2011). Nevertheless, several factors can discourage persons from engaging with outgroups. These include: (i) differences in values (Pettigrew, 1998); and (ii) wider social (including institutional) norms (Kirk, 1993).

These are important factors to remember when continuing to explore participants' interactions with women and the wider CofE. In fact, it is evident from the discussion thus far that members of Reform, and most of the Anglo-Catholics, had different attitudes and values from the wider CofE, which affirms the legitimacy of women's ordination.

In addition to this, the optimal conditions of intergroup contact do not themselves effect prejudice reduction. Rather, they facilitate four stages that more directly reduce an individual's prejudice (Pettigrew, 1998). Firstly, ingroup members learn about the outgroup, correcting any faulty caricatures that ingroup members have of them. However, this only happens when: (i) the outgroup's behaviour is evidently different from the stereotype, and when an outgroup's behaviour is strongly associated with their label; (ii) occurs frequently across a variety of different contexts; and (iii) the outgroup members concerned are seen as typical members of that group.

Secondly, there is behavioural change, which precedes other attitude changes. When contact leads to new social situations, new expectations surrounding behaviour arise, and when this includes accepting outgroup members, behavioural change can lead to other attitude changes. Thirdly, there is generating affective ties, where positive emotions—particularly

114   *Contact and contact avoidance*

empathy—can improve attitudes towards outgroups and can be cultivated during contact. Finally, there is ingroup reappraisal because contact can encourage reflection on ingroup norms, leading to the conclusion that there may be other legitimate identities or behaviours. That is, to use sociological language, plausibility structures are undermined. In other words, when contact occurs under the optimum conditions, four causal stages of prejudice reduction are set in motion.

However, a weakness in existing research is that it has often neglected to explore what contact looks like in practice (Halualani, 2008). In what follows, I will therefore explore the extent to which contact manifests in participants' narratives, offering a thicker description of it than is often afforded in quantitative research. With this in mind, I will now turn my attention to a discussion of the Reform narratives, highlighting when prejudice-reducing phenomena are either present or absent.

Intergroup contact and Reform

Mixed experience in the discernment process

Returning to the first of Reform's themes for this chapter, the reported contact with women clergy in this context was complicated. On the one hand, participants were testing a vocation to a Church that permitted them to reject the validity of women's ordination. On the other hand, for some of them, they had to satisfy women involved in the discernment process that they possessed a genuine vocation. The question of status is thus unclear. Nevertheless, given the prejudicial attitudes towards women held by members of Reform, it is fair to state that however participants understood their status compared to the women they encountered in the discernment processes, this contact appears to have done little to undermine their sexist attitudes. This is unsurprising, however, given the extent of gender inequality that, as much research has shown, pervades society.

It is also unlikely that participants had identical goals to those discerning their call. Most of those interviewed expressed a strong sense of calling and desire to enter professional ministry, whereas the role of those in the discernment process is to test whether—rather than assume that—such a vocation is there. In fact, at the time of conducting this research, once those in the diocese are satisfied that those in the selection process are ready for a national selection panel, they refer would-be clergy to the CofE's selectors as a further stage in the selection process. This means that those in the diocese are not charged with making a decision on the appropriateness of anyone for ordination per se. In addition to this, both the lack of clear equal status and the lack of common goals make the presence of co-operative dependence unlikely. Thus, even though there would have been support from the wider CofE in so far as it arranges the discernment structures for potential clergy, the other factors that undermine prejudice were absent.

Resistance towards training institutions and Homogeneity in training

The behavioural patterns discussed suggest that participants were trained in environments that were not conducive to prejudice reduction for several reasons. Firstly, participants did not possess equal status to their tutors who evidently had a level of authority over them. This is evinced in Henry's narrative. He said, "I had a bit of a clash with my tutor ... who I felt had shopped me to my bishop .... I had to go down to see the bishop .... And I felt betrayed by that ...." In this scenario, his tutor was able to have Henry sanctioned for failing to conform to the expectations that were put upon all ordinands during the process of ordination training.

Secondly, with regard to the same criterion for prejudice reduction, participants who trained at colleges other than Oak Hill reported training alongside women who did not hold a more restrictive position on women's ordination. However, given women have not been selected for ordination on equal terms with men, interaction with female ordinands is unlikely to have undermined gender prejudice.

Thirdly, there were evidently discrepancies with respect to the goals of those running the training institutions and this study's participants. The latter resisted compulsory elements of training, particularly when it involved other colleges, in addition to their refusal to partake in the social elements of college life. Again, Joshua stated, "So my immediate contact with college was with the four other people who were on my course, and ... we all had similar convictions." Hence, they also failed to share common goals with clergy-in-training of other Christian traditions/theological persuasions.

Fourthly, because of this, participants did not put themselves in positions where they would be co-operatively dependent on those with different gender beliefs from themselves. Finally, although college staff would have had participants interact with their peers from across the range of Anglican traditions, the fact that members of Reform actively rebelled against this directive would have undermined the efficacy of any interaction supported by relevant authorities. Joshua, after all, said, "People might have come to me and said, 'You're having this on your own terms', which was true .... But I have to say, personally, it was brilliant." Prejudice reduction would only have occurred if participants were willing to co-operate with authorities. As it stands, even if participants opted to interact with their theologically divergent peers, any support from college staff would most likely do little to bolster such contact because their authority carries little currency for the Reform participants.

Resistance towards the diocese

This theme indicates that participants rarely engage with the wider Church, including women ministers, women who were in the process of becoming clergy, and those supportive of women's ordination. Stephen mentioned that he helps women through the discernment process for ordination. However, in such cases, there is a lack of equal status as those he assists through the

116 *Contact and contact avoidance*

discernment process are reliant on his recommendation as their incumbent. In fact, it would be difficult for any of the participants to interact with female clergy with equal status. The discriminatory legislation that has accompanied the introduction of the ordination of women has meant that men do not need to recognise the validity of women's ordination. Indeed, legislation regarding women's consecration as bishops only dictates that clergy need to accept that the CofE has reached a decision on its appropriateness, rather than having to personally accept that it is theologically valid (see Ferns, 2014). In addition to this, the absence of interaction with female priests means that common goals would be impossible as would co-operative dependence, regardless of whether the CofE were to actively promote interaction between female priests and those who object to their ministry.

Some initial reflections on Reform

It is worth foregrounding the fact that contact avoidance increased in participants' narratives over time, exhibiting an enclave-like element. The more they have been exposed to the CofE, and the different understandings of Anglicanism that they previously had little exposure to, the more inclined they are to distance themselves from the wider Church. As a case in point, participants showed no signs of avoidance during the discernment process. However, a vast majority of them had only exercised their faith in conservative evangelical contexts up to that point. Although those they encountered in the discernment process often came from different traditions to the participants, they rarely displayed attitudes that my participants considered antithetical to their immediate Anglican tradition, making their post-ordination ministry the first significant immersion into Anglican cultures that are distinct to those that they had experienced. In this respect, the contact avoidance is a continuation of Reform's response to the ordination of women, undermines the commitment made by evangelicals at Keele, and is bolstered by negative experiences within the CofE. This in turn has implications of participants' prejudice, given that limited contact with clergy from other traditions (which includes women), means that it is unlikely to be undermined.

Moreover, human beings are predisposed to categorise objects, including persons. This categorisation relies on stereotypes that are often unfounded, however, because phenomena that constitute a particular identity are constantly evolving, meaning that such categories are ultimately mythical (Appiah, 2018). Therefore, when participants select to distance themselves from the wider CofE, they are primarily distancing themselves from the symbolic meaning that they impose on the institution. In this instance, they caricature it as a theologically liberal Church with a clear commitment to gender equality in contradiction to biblical teaching. Hence, the narratives provide evidence of the drawing of symbolic boundaries between Reform and the wider CofE as such caricaturing involves distinguishing themselves from the wider Church as they articulate beliefs in opposition to those within the CofE.

More particularly, because persons depend upon such categories for their sense of identity, not least by defining themselves through demarcating outgroups (e.g., see Tajfel, 1974), the belief of the 'otherness' of those who are not conservative evangelical is a part of the symbolic meaning that participants impose upon the CofE. Therefore, through the decision to avoid the liberalism that participants attribute to the CofE, they avoid contact with those whom they associate as more closely aligning with it, particularly their more theologically liberal colleagues, not least women priests. This precludes experiences that could undermine their prejudicial attitudes.

Intergroup contact and the charismatic evangelicals

Presence of women in ordination training

Looking at Nick's narrative, he explained:

> My friend ... was an important part [in the formation of my views on ministry and gender equality] because she had strong feminist views ... I had other friends—one in my pastoral group .... Again, she was a little older than me and she had lived through the pains of people not being ordained and she was very aware of it. She may well be a bishop one day.

Nick sees a female friend as a potential bishop. This suggests that he sees her as able to represent something of priesthood, indicating that prejudice towards women was less likely to be present given that he too was a priest (indicating an absence of outgroup dynamics). It is thus not a mere coincidence that there is an absence of traditional gender stereotyping.

Co-operation with those in other traditions and with different theologies

Nick described his working relationship with neighbouring parish clergy: "We are three Anglican churches who pretty much—apart from conservative evangelicals— ... [represent] the broad spectrum of the Church of England .... We meet regularly for clergy to encourage one another and to pray for one another." The description of his relationships with clergy in other traditions (which include women) shows that he frequently co-operates with those who possess a different theology and expressed their faith in ways that are different to his own practice as they pray with and for each other. This involves sharing things that they would appreciate prayer for. Hence, it is also a personal exchange, meaning that Nick and his colleagues go beyond the bear minimal contact required by those who work within a diverse institution. They share personal relationships.

Nick's statement here also evinces that he shares a common goal with those he meets with as they undertake the same activities on behalf of each

118   *Contact and contact avoidance*

other, showing a clear sense of mutuality. This mutuality also indicates that participants are co-operatively dependent upon each other as they are inter-reliant on their colleagues' intercessions. In one respect, the majority of clergy in such scenarios—including the women worked with—possess equal status in the immediate context of the parish because all but one has incumbent status in their respective parishes (which participants willingly recognised). Also, such interaction takes place because area meetings are a part of the ecclesial structure set up by the CofE. In other words, these interactions take place with the support of the institutional Church.

Exposure to women in church leadership

Rob said, "I grew up … with a deaconess, and she always had a blue robe on, and it never meant anything to me except that she was part of the team of people who were employed by the church." This meant that he did not distinguish between women deaconesses and male priests, instead seeing those who led in church on equal terms, regardless of their sex.

Additionally, Oscar, whilst having a theology of male headship, also explained that he assists women in the discernment process for ordination. This process is made possible because the diocese is set up in such a way where those who feel called to ordained ministry are to approach their incumbent first who then decides whether to send the potential candidate to the diocese for further discernment. This next stage is done with the support of the incumbent priest who writes references and provides ministerial experience for the candidate in the parish. In other words, the authority structures in the CofE operate in a way that encourages co-operation between the candidate and incumbent. Whilst Oscar could, in theory, choose to discourage women from going forward for vocational discernment, the fact that he does not (a factor likely shaped by his tradition's broader acceptance of women's ministry) allows for co-operation to occur.

Some initial reflections on the charismatic evangelicals

The narratives discussed above have clear links with the history of the charismatic movement within England more broadly and the CofE in particular. Participants' ease with the presence of women at theological college is unsurprising given the tradition's history of accepting women's leadership in church. It also explains their exposure to women in church leadership prior to their training for ordination. My participants' co-operation with women from other theological traditions also reflects the decision made at Keele to engage more actively with the wider CofE. Participants' tradition, therefore, contributes to their interaction with female priests. This is a point at which charismatic evangelicals' behaviour departs from that of conservative evangelicals. Despite both having common ancestry, evangelicals in the CofE have taken noticeably different paths since 1992. Whereas conservative

Contact and contact avoidance   119

evangelicals opted for a program of protest and reform, this study's charismatic evangelical participants were at least sufficiently content with this decision to avoid conflict with the CofE. Indeed, there is no charismatic evangelical group within the Established Church that formally takes an outspoken position contrary to women's ordained leadership.

With this in mind, it is unlikely that these participants hold prejudicial attitudes towards women. Previously, I explained that components of sexism were present in the narratives but that their data fell short of sexism as defined by the social psychological literature on prejudice. This is consistent with the fact that the charismatic evangelicals exhibit levels of contact with women priests that have been widely demonstrated to undermine prejudice. This group thus operates in a way that precludes the possibility of fertile soil in which prejudice could grow, even if this context results from the lack of prejudice to begin with, given the likelihood of reciprocal causality. Moreover, the narratives above indicate that these participants are more willing to engage with, rather than draw symbolic boundaries between, themselves and the wider CofE. In fact, they evinced no resistance towards their diocese during the interviews, with one exception (Michael) who simply stated that if the CofE introduced same-sex marriage ceremonies then he would leave it *if* that is what his wider network of colleagues—within the HTB network—did.

This also demonstrates that the context of beliefs is important and that one cannot simply judge an expressed view in a social vacuum. Hence, participants from all three groups cannot be understood without first appreciating the tradition that they have inherited. Importantly, one may deduce from the above discussion that gender attitudes that exhibit elements of traditional thinking are not necessarily prejudicial. Even those who have comparatively traditional gender values, such as Oscar, do not prevent—but rather facilitate opportunities for—women exploring the possibility of ordination as priests, which they understand would likely lead to incumbency positions for those women.

An additional point is thus highlighted: what a person articulates as their gender beliefs is not always sufficient on its own to determine the extent of one's prejudice. In the abstract, some of the beliefs articulated by members of this group have the potential to be identified as sexist but required further investigation. Instead, how a person behaves is also an important aspect of identifying the presence of prejudice. It is true, however, that this study can only evaluate what participants reported they had done. Nevertheless, given the level of candour and the highly personal information provided at times, one can only assume participants' honesty unless there are sufficient grounds to believe the contrary.

In fact, professed beliefs can be contradictory in nature because an individual can profess different beliefs in different contexts, making such contexts a necessary window into human thought (see Stringer, 1996). Thus, participants such as Oscar professed a value that accompanies his

120 *Contact and contact avoidance*

relationship to the HTB network whilst his behaviour was inconsistent with its espoused belief. Once more, beliefs are therefore not the only measure needed to assess prejudice. However, this does not make the elements of their gender attitudes that overlap with the social psychological definition of sexism unproblematic.

Intergroup contact and the Anglo-Catholics

Lack of women ordinands in training and Worked with women priests

Oliver has been quoted above saying that his training college consisted of "All male ordinands at that point .... The College of the Resurrection ... is a male [monastic] community .... Our voice trainer ... was a ... lady .... I think she was the only female member of staff when I was there." The relative homogeneity does mean that there would have been little opportunity for the Anglo-Catholic participants to have their gender norms challenged because of the lack of alternative perspectives available to them.

Returning to Ashley's narrative, he explained that, despite helping women priests in the diocese in a number of ways, he doesn't see their ordination as valid: "I suppose my mind-set is that I'm engaging in ecumenical dialogue and activity. So these are fellow Christians, I just don't happen to recognise their [religious] orders." Peter likewise stated, "I'm one of those who would be called 'impossiblist' ... only men are able to receive the grace of ordination." On the one hand, participants evinced co-operation with their female colleagues. On the other hand, however, they do not perceive that they do so on an equal basis with women. The fact that the CofE makes provisions for those who cannot accept the validity of women's ordination provides legitimacy to this perspective (Fry, 2021b), rather than supporting the interaction between two outgroups in a way that could encourage prejudice reduction.

Others who have more personal relationships with women priests also indicated a similar lack of co-operation. Malcolm, for example, when discussing a friendship, closed down the conversation about his interaction with women priests. He said, "All I can say is we've got to understand each other. We know exactly where we come from ... but I wouldn't say I've worked with her ... we keep in touch socially ... rather than [working] in each other's churches." The fact that Malcolm reported being on relatively good terms with this priest does not mean that they co-operate to achieve shared goals. Also, the fact that their interaction does not occur professionally means that the CofE is unable to foster the type of contact that can lead to reduced prejudice.

Evan's account, by way of contrast, shows that he changed his position on women's ordination to the priesthood after a prolonged and sustained encounter with someone who was discerning their call to ordained ministry. This process would have required goal sharing because both parties were in the process of discerning whether the woman in question had a vocation to the priesthood and Evan was evidently open to this possibility by the time this process started. This process would also have required mutual co-operation because the discernment of one's vocation to the priesthood

Contact and contact avoidance 121

involves both, the candidate's sense of call, and the affirmation of those who know them well. Furthermore, it was the structures of the CofE that enabled them to meet in the first place when the woman in question was assigned to Evan for ministerial training for the Church Army. Hence, a wider authority was instrumental in fostering their contact.

Within the context of the CofE, their statuses cannot be easily compared. Evan was a priest when he met his friend, and she was a Church Army officer. They thus represented two very distinct ministries in the CofE that are not readily comparable. It is also important to consider the fact that Evan identifies as homosexual, meaning that his own social status—particularly when the above event took place towards the end of the twentieth century—would have been more complex (see Herek, 2004). On the one hand, Evan is white, university-educated, middle class, and male. On the other hand, his homo-sexuality would have made status differences unclear, and so even though both parties were not on an identical social footing, neither could one have been clearly held in higher esteem than the other. Thus, the impact of the contact between them could not have been undermined because of unequal status, even if it would not necessarily have undermined prejudice either. Furthermore, the fact that Evan began to see "signs of priestly nature" in his friend shows that he was able to see her as representative of women pursuing a call to the priesthood.

However, the other Anglo-Catholic interviewed who changed his mind on women's ordination as priests did not provide a narrative of typical contact. As already stated, Aaron is likewise homosexual and changed his mind on the ordination of women as priests after experiencing a woman conduct Communion services in a way that led him to believe that women can fulfil the priestly role. The fact that the woman he encountered led to him changing his mind on all women priests means that Aaron saw her as representative of women who felt a call to priesthood. Moreover, he had never belonged to a group that protested the ordination of women and grew up in a family that held less tightly to traditional gender norms. Collectively, this evidence suggests that Aaron did not hold his views as strongly as most of his Anglo-Catholic colleagues. It also indicates that his gender attitudes lacked significant role-based expectations and thus it is unlikely that his views could have been convincingly labelled as prejudicial. Therefore, specific forms of contact were unnecessary for changing his opinion on women priests in the same way that it would be necessary for others. This is also consistent with Glick and Fiske's (1996) finding that heterosexuality, but not homo-sexuality, is a predictor of indirect sexism.

Wider participation in the CofE

Peter is quoted above saying:

> [I] always endeavoured [in] my time as Regional Dean [of Forward in Faith] to ensure we always had a quarterly Mass at the cathedral because it is as

122 *Contact and contact avoidance*

> much our cathedral as anybody else's ... I think it was one of the reasons why I was made an honorary canon [of the cathedral]—because I had engaged Forward in Faith ... into the life of the diocese as much as [I] could.

From this territorial approach to co-operation, one may deduce that interaction with the wider diocese is not based on goal sharing but on advancing the need of one's social group. Regarding the conflict he reported with the diocesan bishop, whilst it is difficult to discern from the data whether contact avoidance led to relationship breakdown, vice versa, or a mixture of both, in/outgroup relationships tend to be fluid rather than fixed, meaning that outgroups continually define themselves over and against each other (e.g., see Tajfel, 1974). In other words, Peter is probably engaged with a cycle of difficult relationship and contact avoidance.

A further point of interest is the fact that the Anglo-Catholic participants, including members of Forward in Faith, do engage with the diocese in a way that indicates goal sharing and support from the institutional Church. For instance, Adrian assists other clergy—including women priests—with bookkeeping skills and Peter undertakes administration for the bishop pertaining to marriage licences. However, such encounters do not foster co-operative dependence because participants do not achieve anything for themselves. Also, when undertaking such activities participants do not assume equal status between themselves as seen in Ashley's narrative.

Aaron and Evan both have a strong history of engagement with those outside of their immediate tradition. For example, Aaron recalled his time as a parish priest for a group of churches which provided the opportunity for him to work with a variety of colleagues in different traditions of the CofE. He explained, "When I was an incumbent ... I inherited a male lay reader who I got on very well with ... but theologically and liturgically we were miles apart." His parish was in the central tradition, despite him being an Anglo-Catholic, and a lay reader with whom he worked closely was of a different tradition to him.

Whilst Aaron reported that this could cause conflict, he also recalled a good personal relationship with him. Both had to work together on a regular basis to co-ordinate church services where they would share responsibilities, including preaching and the leading of worship. This means that they were co-operatively dependent on each other and shared common goals. Whilst they would not have had equal status, because Aaron was ordained and his lay reader was not, they were both male, indicating equal status in that respect. However, because of Aaron's homosexuality and his lay reader's heterosexuality, Aaron would not have been as prominent in the social hierarchy as his lay colleague, particularly in the 1980s, when this relationship was established.

Some initial reflections on the Anglo-Catholics

The above demonstrates that these Anglo-Catholic priests continue the tradition of selective adherence to bishops, despite the prominence of their

Contact and contact avoidance   123

position. Participants' interactions with the diocesan bishop are strong evidence of this. In fact, this is the same behaviour that Jones (2004) notes when Forward in Faith emerged as a sanctuary from the changing Church.

One should also note that the enclave-like existence of their theological training mirrored the similar structures that the first Anglo-Catholics experienced at Oxford. Participants' time in training was predominantly male-dominated and many of them also come from a privileged background and possess degrees from institutions such as Oxford and other prestigious institutions.

The primary continuation in behaviour between these participants and the literature was in the engaged orthodoxy that participants clearly exhibit. The Anglo-Catholic priests interviewed collectively demonstrate a relationship with the wider CofE that includes engagement as well as resistance. However, the interaction is somewhat limited in scope and regularly accompanied by a mentality of resistance. Indeed, the resistance that participants disclosed during interview was clear and occurred more regularly than the interactions they reported with the wider Church, a parallel with the Reform narratives. Collectively, this behaviour is indicative of the drawing of symbolic boundaries between gender traditionalist Anglo-Catholics and the wider CofE. This also means that whilst this group continues to exhibit the enclave-like features of their historical tradition, their narratives are better understood in light of the engaged orthodoxy model. This is unsurprising, however, given that this model does not preclude the existence of enclave-like behaviours and that I have previously noted this phenomenon amongst Reform whilst they also exhibit engaged orthodoxy (Fry, 2021a). This means that the type of contact between these clergy and their female colleagues is unlikely to undermine any prejudicial attitudes across this group as a whole.

Methodological reflection

The above themes demonstrate where and how resistance/contact avoidance and contact can take place. Whereas previous studies have charted how this happens on a large scale and thus discuss general trends and offer generalised solutions, I have charted—in specific terms—how it exhibits itself in the context of the CofE. Specific solutions for tackling prejudice in a real-life context can therefore be suggested. I will turn to such solutions in the final chapter (but see also Fry, 2021b).

The above discussion on symbolic meaning and boundaries in the Reform narratives is a further example of how the discipline of sociology can complement that of social psychology. The former adds a depth of understanding to the latter because it offers the insight that contact between persons is not perceived in an unmediated fashion by them but involves interpreting the 'other' through one's own worldview or cultural lens. Hence, insights from sociological literature and intergroup processes collectively make sense of participants' behaviour.

124 *Contact and contact avoidance*

The primary difference between this qualitative analysis and its results from the usual quantitative analyses is that I am concerned with capturing participants' subjective experiences of these events. This means that the present study is concerned with how participants understand their own experiences of contact and their attitudes towards outgroups. Quantitative studies, on the other hand, carry greater risk of misrepresenting or altogether missing how people interpret the questions being asked of them and their understanding of their experiences that lead them to answer the survey questions in the ways that they do (see Halualani, 2008). My approach thus captures much more of the social context that lies behind clergy attitudes towards gender than has often been the case with studies on intergroup contact.

This has led to a nuance in the theory of intergroup contact. The literature to date has claimed that the involvement of relevant authorities helps to foster prejudice reduction. However, in the case of Reform one sees that *a person's perception of another's authority* is key. If they do not think much of the authority of others, then they will not respond positively towards them, undermining the possibility of prejudice reduction.

Whilst the quantitative studies have demonstrated the importance of the impact of beliefs for assessing prejudice, the present study has demonstrated that an individual's beliefs divorced from their wider context do not always provide sufficient grounds to judge the extent of prejudice. This became apparent when analysing the charismatic evangelical narratives. In the present study, this has been evidenced in such a way as to show the more nuanced nature of beliefs, something that cannot be captured so readily through quantitative means where participants must select predetermined options to indicate their beliefs (see Dixon, Durrheim and Tredoux, 2005).

Moreover, many of the themes within the Reform and Anglo-Catholic narratives highlight a further benefit of adopting a qualitative approach to analysing prejudice and contact: they reveal that there are multiple factors beyond the participants' direct control that come to bear on their attitudes. These include the lack of women at theological college, the way that they feel others receive them, or their exposure to women leaders growing up, for example. An understanding of participants' wider environments helps foster greater insight into the specific phenomena that can contribute towards prejudice and contact avoidance or its lack.

Conclusion

Regarding the Reform and Anglo-Catholic participants, their reported behaviours indicate that their resistance towards the wider CofE—particularly women priests—is related to their perception of how the others in the Church with different theological convictions have received them. However, prejudice and contact avoidance are mutually reinforcing. This means that one cannot assume that their interactions with the wider CofE alone led to participants' withdrawal from their colleagues and ultimately to prejudice. Rather, prejudice is entirely capable of encouraging disengagement. Thus, while one must take seriously the claims of these participants and recognise that their colleagues may not have treated them well, one must also recognise that pre-existing prejudice most likely also encouraged distance.

Indeed, the historical assessment of women that Christianity has offered suggests that some participants were immersed in traditions that held prejudicial attitudes towards women long before the CofE opened the diaconate and priesthood to them. However, as aforementioned, group identities are not completely stable and develop in reaction to other groups, and so it is equally as likely that the negative interactions that participants reported with colleagues from different traditions to themselves have compounded contact avoidance, which will have reinforced participants' prejudice.

Whilst women are evidently the focus of that prejudice, contact avoidance is exhibited to those who operate in the wider CofE who do not hold to traditional gender attitudes and values, apparently regardless of gender or sex, because of what they represent to my gender traditionalist participants. This means that for the conservative evangelical and majority of Anglo-Catholic participants, contact avoidance has at last two main shaping influences. These are prejudice and perceptions of the wider CofE, both of which can be bolstered by negative interactions with other clergy. The former will have been shaped by gender attitudes within historical Christianity and wider society.

These findings are an evident contrast from those resulting from an analysis of the charismatic evangelical narratives. In most cases, their approaches to gender both inside and outside of the Church are more flexible and less binary. Participants in this group also articulated fuller relationships with those of different theological traditions and demonstrated a history of engaging with women in positions of religious leadership. This has helped facilitate an absence of prejudicial—and the presence of more affirming—attitudes towards women inside and outside of the CofE.

What may be concluded in light of this? In the third chapter, participants' attitudes towards women were established and it was evidenced how the conservative evangelicals and most of the Anglo-Catholics possess gender attitudes that fit a variety of the definitions/sub-definitions of sexism. As a contrast, however, the charismatic evangelical participants do not evince attitudes that meet the criteria for sexism identified in this monograph, despite the fact that a minority in this group evinced gender values that were not far removed from members of Reform.

In the present chapter, I have built upon these findings by highlighting the way that the Reform and Anglo-Catholic narratives are void of the types of contact that have been identified as undermining prejudice. It has also been noted that the charismatic evangelical narratives evince the presence of the types of contact and wider circumstances that undermine prejudice and so accompany more affirming attitudes towards women. In other words, the

126 *Contact and contact avoidance*

analysis in this chapter and the third chapter collectively show that participants' narratives are consistent with the findings in the quantitative literature. Furthermore, the analysis within this monograph builds on such studies by providing a detailed description of how these attitudes have manifested within the context of a historical and national institution in England that has been patriarchal. In this respect, it also demonstrates empirically that such sexism still exists strongly within, what Page (2010) refers to as, "pockets of opposition" (p. 158) in the CofE.

In this chapter, the data have led to consideration of context-specific insights into the environments that persons with prejudicial attitudes find themselves in and how the former contribute to the latter. Moreover, whereas other studies, such as Nason-Clark (1987a), have focused on functional sexism (i.e., a focus on the restriction of women's roles), I have demonstrated the specific, underlying attitudes that accompany traditionalist gender norms in the Established Church. In addition to this, I have identified multiple social forces behind participants' attitudes. To do so, I have charted the historical context that participants have inherited through participation in their respective traditions. However, this is supplemented by an analysis of the social psychological processes that inform the gender attitudes that participants evinced at interview.

Notes

1 The DDO is the Diocesan Director of Ordinands, the person responsible for overseeing the discernment process for potential clergy in each diocese. An ordinand is someone training for ordination.
2 A Vocations Advisor helps churchgoers within a given diocese discern their sense of Christian vocation.
3 The Church Army is an evangelistic wing of the CofE. Its candidates are ordained as 'captains' rather than as deacons or priests, meaning that they occupy a distinct structure within the Church.

References

Allport, G. (1954/1979). *The nature of prejudice.* Cambridge, MA: Perseus Books.

Appiah, K. (2018). *The lies that bind. Rethinking identity: Creed, country, colour, class, culture.* London: Profile Books ltd.

Brittain, C.C., & McKinnon, A. (2011). Homosexuality and the construction of "Anglican Orthodoxy": The symbolic politics of the Anglican Communion. *Sociology of Religion,* 72(3), 351–373.

Brown, R. (2011). *Prejudice: Its social psychology.* Hoboken, NJ: John Wiley & Sons.

Carey, G. (2004). *Know the truth: A memoir.* London: HarperCollins.

Dixon, J., Durrheim, K., & Tredoux, C. (2005). Beyond the optimal contact strategy: A reality check for the contact hypothesis. *American Psychologist,* 60(7), 697–711.

Dovidio, J.F., Gaertner, S.L., & Kawakami, K. (2003). Intergroup contact: The past, present, and the future. *Group Processes and Intergroup Relations,* 6(1), 5–21.

Ferns, S. (2014). *The five guiding principles: Guidance for candidates for ordination in the Church of England*. Ministry Division. Retrieved from https://www.churchofengland.org/sites/default/files/2017-10/the_five_guiding_principles.pdf.

Foucault, M. (1977). *Discipline and punish*. (A. Sheridan, Trans.). New York: Pantheon.

Fry, A.D.J. (2021a). Postfeminist, engaged and resistant: Evangelical male clergy attitudes towards gender and women's ordination in the Church of England. *Critical Research on Religion, 9*(1), 65–83.

Fry, A.D.J. (2021b). Clergy, capital and gender inequality: An assessment of how social and spiritual capital are denied to women priests in the Church of England. *Gender, Work & Organization*. Advanced online publication. 10.1111/gwao.12 685.

GAFCON. (n.d.). *About GAFCON*. Retrieved from https://www.gafcon.org/about.

Glick, P., & Fiske, S.T. (1996). The ambivalent sexism inventory: Differentiating hostile and benevolent sexism. *Journal of Personality and Social Psychology, 70*(3), 491–512.

Halualani, R.T. (2008). How do multicultural university students define and make sense of intercultural contact? A qualitative study. *International Journal of Intercultural Relations, 32*(1), 1–16.

Herek, G.M. (2004). Beyond "homophobia": Thinking about sexual prejudice and stigma in the twenty-first century. *Sexuality Research and Social Policy, 1*(2), 6–24.

Jones, I. (2004). *Women and priesthood in the Church of England: Ten years on*. London: Church House Publishing.

Kirk, T. (1993). *The polarisation of Protestants and Roman Catholics in rural Northern Ireland: A case study of Glenravel Ward, County Antrim 1956 to 1988* (Doctoral dissertation, Queen's University, Belfast).

Maiden, J. (2018, February 19). *The charismatic turn of the long 1960s: Contexts and characteristics* [Paper presentation]. Contemporary Religion in Historical Perspective: Publics and performances. Milton Keynes, United Kingdom.

Nason-Clark, N. (1987a). Ordaining women as priests: Religious vs. sexist explanations for clerical attitudes. *Sociological Analysis, 48*(3), 259–273.

Page, S-J. (2010). *Femininities and Masculinities in the Church of England*. (Doctoral dissertation, University of Nottingham).

Pettigrew, T.F. (1998). Intergroup contact theory. *Annual Review of Psychology, 49*(1), 65–85.

Pettigrew, T.F., & Tropp, L.R. (2005). Allport's intergroup contact hypothesis: Its history and influence. In J. Dovidio, P. Glick, & L. Rudman (Eds.), *On the nature of prejudice: Fifty years after Allport* (pp. 262–277). Hoboken, NJ: Blackwell Publishing.

Stringer, M.D. (1996). Towards a situational theory of belief. *Journal of the Anthropological Society of Oxford, 27*(3), 217–234.

Tajfel, H. (1974). Social identity and intergroup behaviour. *Social Science Information, 13*(2), 65–93.

The Free Church of England (2018). *FCE History*. Retrieved from https://fcofe.org.uk/our-history/.

6 Schism and clergy capital

Introduction

In the previous chapter, I introduced more literature related to prejudice and argued that my participants' beliefs about women were consistent with their behaviour towards them, according to what one would anticipate from the contact hypothesis. In this chapter, I will extend the discussion on intergroup contact by exploring how work on group schisms and on social capital and spiritual capital can further illuminate participants' narratives with respect to how they engage with other Anglicans. This is because participants' narratives are consistent with these bodies of knowledge. In the case of schism research, I will demonstrate how self-categorisation theory and self-discrepancy theory—which relate to prejudice via contact—enable one to understand more fully the emotions involved in participants' narratives. In fact, demonstrating that certain emotions are identifiable in the narratives adds further weight to the decision to understand the clergy interviewed through these psychological lenses and that of prejudice because the consistency with which the data reflects findings from related areas of prejudice research provides a greater level of explanatory power in interpreting the data.

Greater insight into the specific ways that contact (or the avoidance thereof) manifests in the everyday lives of clergy will also be gained through the employment of theories on social and spiritual capital. This will further increase understanding of the types of contact that my participants have with others, not least women priests, given that such capital is ubiquitously shared or denied during (inter)group processes. It will also enable further methodological reflection on the utility of employing theoretical lenses from multiple disciplines to better understand religious phenomena in the contemporary world. In this chapter, I will proceed with an outline of the various theoretical lenses being employed before bringing these into dialogue with several of the themes explored in the previous chapter and adding two more to the discussion of the Anglo-Catholics.

DOI: 10.4324/9781003081913-6

Group schisms

It is relevant to discuss group schisms because it provides an explanation as to why some groups avoid contact with others. To understand why social groups schism, one must understand that persons who consider themselves similar to each other—and thus in the same 'group' as each other—receive an identity from belonging to that group, defining themselves with respect to its typical attributes and characteristics whilst differentiating themselves from other groups, who have different attributes and characteristics. This is the essence of self-categorisation theory (see Turner and Oakes, 1986).

When group members perceive that the identity of their group has come under threat from within it, their sense of identification with that group can decrease. More specifically, perceived subversion of this identity can have a negative impact on group identification where group members struggle to continue seeing themselves as part of that group. In such circumstances they can experience dejection-related emotions such as disappointment and sadness or agitation-related emotions such as apprehension and uneasiness (Sani, 2005).

These emotions are best understood through self-discrepancy theory, the idea that persons have three selves (Higgins, 1987). First, there is the actual self, the attributes one believes they possess. Second, there is the ideal self, an idealised version of oneself that a person aspires to. Third, there is the ought self, how one thinks they should be. It is discrepancy between the actual and ideal selves that leads to dejection-related emotions whereas discrepancy between the actual and ought selves generates agitation-related emotions (Bizman and Yinon, 2002).

It is because the identities of human beings are tied up in social groups that these three selves—and related emotions—are experienced at a group level. Therefore, perceived changes to a group's identity can create discrepancy between the actual group (how someone perceives the group to be), and either the ideal group (what someone would prefer the group to be) and/or the ought group (what someone believes the group ought to be) for its members. When such discrepancies exist, group members can experience either dejection-related emotions, if the discrepancy is between the actual and ideal group, and/or agitation emotions, if the discrepancy is between the actual and ought group (Bizman and Yinon, 2002).

Emotions of dejection tend to lead to apathy and passivity, whereas emotions of agitation lead to initiative and activity (Frijda, 1986). This means that a distinction should be made between passive schismatic behaviours (e.g., withdrawal) and more active forms (e.g., protest). Schismatic intentions can be moderated by the extent to which one perceives they have a voice, or lack thereof, within the group. That is, the more one believes they will be heard, the more likely they will be to stay within the group (Sani, 2005). If participants in the present study gravitate towards schism with other Anglicans, then contact

130 *Schism and clergy capital*

with clergy outside of their immediate traditions, particularly women—and all that it can foster in the reduction of prejudice—will be limited.

Social capital and spiritual capital

Research on schisms bears relation to work on social capital because they both concern the way in which persons interact. Social capital is a pool of social resources that people have via their network of relationships, often used to exclude others and consolidate power (Bourdieu, 1983). When it is used in this way it is known as bonding capital because it is shared only amongst members of the same social group. By way of contrast, it is known as bridging capital when it is shared between groups but linking capital specifically when a social group of higher status shares with one of lower status (Putnam, 2000).

Social capital is also a helpful complementary lens to the contact hypothesis because it too is concerned with understanding the impact of human interaction and has been well utilised in research that seeks to understand how women can be discriminated against in the occupational sphere (e.g., Kumra and Vinnicombe, 2010). Moreover, conservative religious groups are made up of members that are more likely to be heavily involved in their faith community than their wider community. Trends in religious life therefore typically reinforce a lack of social cohesion with other groups. Instead, smaller and thus more exclusive communities tend to generate trust, honesty, and reciprocity internally. This includes co-operation, increased effectiveness at problem-solving, and the ability to test their own views against others. Smaller group cohesion, as expressed by conservative religious communities, is therefore often an exclusive phenomenon as it leads to social capital amongst connected members of a network, excluding those outside of it (Putnam, 2000).

Bourdieu saw religious professionals as an elite group that employed religious beliefs to justify the unequal social order that provided them with power and privilege. He referred to this as religious capital (Guest, 2007b). This has since been developed by Verter (2003), who draws on Bourdieu's notion of cultural capital to posit the distinct theory of spiritual capital. This consists of three elements: (i) the embodied state—what Bourdieu referred to as habitus, one's "knowledge, abilities, tastes, and credentials" accrued through religion (p. 159); (ii) the objectified state—commodities that are consumed in order to create habitus, such as beliefs or religious clothing; and (iii) the institutionalised state—the power that institutions possess in providing devotees with reward, usually salvation.

I have offered a more detailed discussion of the importance of social and spiritual capital for gender inequality within the hierarchy of the CofE elsewhere (Fry, 2021b). The focus of analysis in this chapter is on using capital as a method for analysing male clergy attitudes towards women, especially clergy, rather than to explore its professional implications for female clergy.

Schism and clergy capital   131

Schism, capital, and Reform

A few themes in the Reform narratives evinced the emotion set associated with schismatic behaviour as well as the type of interactions that are suggestive of refused social and spiritual capital. In light of this, the themes for discussion in this chapter are: (i) Mixed experience in the discernment process; (ii) Resistance towards training institutions; (iii) Homogeneity in training; and (iv) Resistance towards the diocese.

Mixed experience in the discernment process

I will begin with statements by Ron and Ian. The former said:

> I'd say it was very, it was kind of business like [with the DDO] really. I was aware that theologically we were in very different places. Compared to some of my contemporaries, some of the stories I hear, I don't think I had a difficult time at all from her.

The latter stated, "I started the process of getting ordained, which in those days was brief and simple, half an hour with the DDO, tea with the archdeacon." With respect to schismatic behaviours and emotions, there is no evidence that participants experienced or exhibited anything identifiable as such, even though Ron and Ian did not report this episode as if it were a positive experience. The above implies that participants had little in the way of social ties with those involved in their vocational journey at the diocesan level, indicating that there would have been little sharing of social capital. Whilst this was not necessarily unique to the Reform participants, it is nevertheless symptomatic of their general engagement with those outside of their immediate social networks. In the above case, participants did not recall much about their DDOs, even though they had nothing negative to report about them. Building on the previous chapter, this too is indicative that co-operation would have been limited between participants and diocesan clergy, increasing the likelihood that participants would continue to hold sexist attitudes. It also highlights that schism-related emotions do not need to be present for members of Reform to be distant from others.

Resistance towards training institutions and Homogeneity in training

Returning to Adam, when discussing his time in ordination training, he explained that:

> There were times where I'd get quite frustrated at being at Ridley because my understanding and my theology wasn't always quite as welcome, which could quite often bring some sort of conflicts at times. Some of that might have been self-inflicted but ... if any conversations came up about the ordination of women or the episcopacy ... it wasn't always ... easy to

132 *Schism and clergy capital*

say anything so you just kept quiet, or if you did [espouse a traditional view] it was usually ... not that welcome.

Participants did evince some schism-related emotions and behaviours. For example, Adam evidently possessed dejection and passivity in response to the theological differences he experienced with his peers at college. He also comes from a church tradition that has conservative gender norms and as a university student belonged to a church that was led by clergy who were members of Reform. He belonged to this church until he began training for ordination. His encounters with others at Ridley Hall would therefore have been the first immersive exposure to an evangelical Anglicanism that possessed different gender attitudes and values to his own. For Adam, there was an apparent conflict between the conservative evangelical Anglicanism that he had experienced and the Anglican expressions and associated gender beliefs he encountered during his time in ordination training. Given the layered nature of participants' identities, discussed in the fourth chapter, this means that Adam's experience indicates identity conflict.

Moreover, at interview, he explained that he dislikes the "silo" mentality that can be found in conservative evangelicalism and so believes that it is important to engage with others outside of his immediate tradition, hence his decision to attend Ridley Hall. In fact, Adam expressed a desire to get to know other Anglicans—including non-evangelicals—during his time in training. This suggests that he believes Anglicanism is ideally able to embrace multiple traditions. However, the fact that he was sometimes unable to do this shows that there was a discrepancy between the actual group (which did not embrace conservative evangelicalism) and the ideal group (which would ideally have done so). This discrepancy explains the dejection emotion of disappointment evident in Adam's narrative and the accompanying withdrawal from elements of college life.

Expanding on Henry's statement from the previous chapter. He reported:

> Sometimes we [ordinands] would skip lectures and ... go and talk theology in [our] study bedrooms together .... I had a bit of a clash with my tutor ... who I felt had shopped me to my bishop .... I had to go down to see the bishop .... And I felt betrayed by that .... I think it was about chapel attendance, but he outed it in my report .... We had also clashed theologically and I wondered whether he had it in for me .... [We clashed] about penal substitutionary atonement[1] .... I'd ... exposed [his faulty theology] in a lecture.

Henry demonstrated agitation in the form of apprehension when he recalled the relationship he had with his college tutor. He explained that his tutor's actions led him to conclude that he may have had a vendetta against him. Importantly, the clash was over a historical doctrine that is also important to Reform and often to evangelicals more widely (i.e., crucicentrism, see

Schism and clergy capital 133

Bebbington, 1989). This difference in doctrine would thus have been a clash between Henry's conservative evangelical and Anglican identities when he came into contact with Anglicans holding different theology.

Henry experienced a conflict between the actual group (which did not hold to a specific understanding of atonement) and the ought group (which he feels should confess penal substitutionary atonement). He explained that he believes true Anglicanism is most faithfully expressed through conservative evangelicalism, implying that Anglicanism ought to reflect his conservative evangelicalism. However, participants such as Joshua, discussed in the previous chapter, were unlikely to display such behaviour or emotions because their withdrawal from college life led their experience of training to be more socially and theologically homogenous. This means that they would not have been exposed to the same perceived threats to their evangelical Anglican identity, and so there would have been no reason for schism emotions to have presented themselves. Therefore, participants who encountered greater theological diversity at their training colleges displayed the emotions associated with schisms when their sense of identity was perceived to be under threat. Evidence for this increased as participants left the first stage of the discernment process and entered into the training phase.

These narratives also indicate that participants' social and spiritual capital were shared with their peers, so long as they were theologically similar to themselves. In the previous chapter, it was noted that Joshua spent much of his social time with the other conservative evangelicals on his degree programme and that Henry missed lectures to be with his peers who shared his theological outlook. Due to contact avoidance, however, there would be a lack of shared capital between participants and those in authority at their training college, as well as between the participants and their peers with different theological outlooks to their own.

The fact that participants avoided contact with those of different theological outlooks to themselves suggests that they would also have passed up opportunities to exchange and debate different ideas, leaving them with the impact of 'group think' where people adopt the views of one's social group unchallenged (see Putnam, 2000). This would help to sustain prejudicial attitudes.

Resistance towards the diocese

Having previously established the presence of contact avoidance between the Reform participants and those in their diocese—not least women priests—I will now show that they report schismatic behaviours towards the diocese. A key example is found in Henry's statement above. As identified in the previous chapter, Henry explained that he is a part of GAFCON and the Free Church of England, both of which have split from the CofE. They did so because they believed that it was turning from its historical roots (GAFCON, n.d.; The Free Church of England, 2018).

134 *Schism and clergy capital*

GAFCON advocates the belief that the Bible has been a central feature of Anglicanism, but also that it is no longer so, something that requires correction. On the one hand, this is not a schism because it is seeking to change Anglicanism rather than develop a new expression of Christianity. On the other hand, GAFCON is made up of individual churches and new denominations that split off from the Anglican Church in various provinces and allows those who find themselves in theological opposition to their bishop to go under an alternative evangelical bishop for pastoral and spiritual support—such as via prayer networks and resources for ministry training—unrecognised formally by the CofE (e.g., see GAFCON, 2008). It is therefore a partially schismatic movement but one that is trying to bring the Anglican Church's identity back to its perceived past, consisting of members who believe that the historical identity of the Anglican Communion has come under threat. Similarly, the Free Church of England emerged as a result of a similar perception about the CofE, as evangelical clergy opposed the assimilation of aspects of Roman Catholicism into it, a clear change in historical identity as the CofE broke away from Roman Catholicism. To re-introduce some of its theology and worship was thus seen as a break with the CofE's historical identity.

But did the Reform participants evince other traits related to schism? Henry certainly feels as though he lacked a voice within the CofE when it came to the ordination of women. When asked about his experiences of working within the CofE, he replied, "I think the mutual flourishing fox has been shot", by which he meant that the Established Church provides no place for theological conservatives with respect to matters on gender and sexuality. ('Mutual flourishing' has been a term used to promote the acceptance of theological diversity within the CofE). Henry's statement is also indicative of apprehension, an agitation emotion, given that he is uncertain about his future place in the CofE. It is also important to bear in mind that Reform specifically required that those who join it resist liberal theological developments in doctrine and morality within the CofE. This implies that the network officially believed that the CofE's historical core beliefs have been interrupted by more liberal thinking. In fact, several participants explained that they have impaired Communion with their bishop by selecting to go under the pastoral oversight of a flying bishop, whereas others who had not done so conceived that they might well do so in the future, should the CofE become theologically more liberal than they currently perceive it to be.

The fact that Henry evinced agitated emotions suggests that he perceives a further discrepancy between the actual group and the ought group. He understands the CofE to reject conservative evangelical theology yet believes that it should reflect traditional evangelical beliefs because these are—in his understanding—the historical beliefs of the Church. Callum's narrative indicates a similar experience. He identifies as being more fully part of the CofE because he is still under the oversight of his diocesan bishop and was not officially a member of Reform. He also explained that he would be happy with his bishop coming to his church and teaching. He stated that he consciously pledged allegiance to his bishop when he was ordained. Nevertheless, he explained that the CofE needs to be at least somewhat evangelical. Callum also expressed concern that the teaching he received during his assistant curacy training lacked an evangelical component which is why he agreed to design a new module for the assistant curates in the diocese. Thus, there is a discrepancy between how he thinks the CofE should be (the ought group) and what he thinks it is (the actual group).

This discrepancy is not limited to overtly theological matters. En route to a Reform meeting,[2] I was in a car with Justin and Henry, both of whom were making fun of the diocese's professional development processes. They referred to them as a waste of time, largely because they were perceived to not readily dovetail with the conservative evangelical model of ministry, which places preaching from the Bible and gospel proclamation over and above (what is perceived to be) secular managerial processes.

This theme shows with greater clarity that participants' social and spiritual capital was invested in a conservative evangelical network, largely at the exclusion of other Anglican groups. When it is shared, however, it is for the advancement of evangelicalism. It also shows that where one decides to invest their capital is dependent upon their sense of identity. The above also indicates that the decision to avoid investing capital in particular groups is not necessarily a comfortable decision for those that make it and is demonstrative of the ambivalence that members of Reform exhibit towards the Established Church as they simultaneously engage with and resist it.

Initial reflections on Reform

It is worth reiterating that contact avoidance increases in participants' narratives over time. The more they are exposed to the CofE, and the different understandings of Anglicanism that they previously had little exposure to, the more inclined they are to distance themselves from the Church. These schismatic behaviours include both passive forms of behaviour (e.g., Adam) and more active forms (e.g., Callum). As a case in point, participants showed no signs of avoidance during the discernment process. However, most of them had only exercised their faith in conservative evangelical contexts up to that point. Also, those they encountered in the discernment process displayed no values or attitudes that participants considered antithetical to their conservative evangelicalism even though they were aware that such persons often came from different traditions. Indeed, whilst participants knew theoretically that there were theological differences between themselves and other Anglicans, identity—or challenges to identity—are formed through the process of contact, meaning that contact is a prerequisite of schism (see Turner and Oakes, 1986).

Many participants explained that during their time at theological college, they were exposed to different traditions—evangelical or otherwise—and it was at this point where schismatic behaviour began to present itself.

136 *Schism and clergy capital*

However, the fact that nearly all participants attended evangelical colleges and had close friendships with conservative evangelicals means that the need to schism was not greatly felt; most of their contact would have been with like-minded people.

The same cannot be said for participants once they entered the diocese as a member of the clergy. They explained that they had to undergo training with those with more theologically liberal perspectives and often reported during the interviews that they feel like they are in a diocese that is predominantly liberal. Participants also see many of the senior clergy in this diocese as being too liberal. Thus, participants are exposed to those who are in the same broader social group (the CofE) but are believed to have departed from historical theological belief, causing a conflict of identity and thereby leading to my participants' schismatic behaviour, seeing members of the broader group as something of an outgroup without fully departing from that group.

Furthermore, despite some participants involving themselves in alternative ecclesial structures outside of the CofE, participants have not left the CofE. In the second chapter, I discussed the development of flying bishops and the two integrities. In addition to these, participants who have belonged to Reform have a network of like-minded Anglicans to support them as they carried out their ministries. This offers the participants a sense of voice and explains why they have remained in the CofE to date. Equally, international links such as GAFCON can give a sense of voice to those who have views that might otherwise be more marginal (see Guest, Olson, and Wolffe 2012). Nevertheless, this ought not to be over-estimated in light of Henry's comment above. Rather, there is enough perceived voice to keep participants within the CofE, but the bulk of the evidence is indicative of identity threat and schismatic intentions, particularly in matters pertaining to gender. It is this tension which helps to explain my participants' ambivalence towards the CofE.

Moreover, intersectionality plays a role in the navigation of one's identity where different aspects of a person's identity can mark them out from others in their social group (Appiah, 2018). This has been born out amongst the Reform participants who navigate their sense of conservative evangelicalism alongside their sense of Anglicanism, which are often in conflict. Intersectionality is therefore appropriate language with which to understand the phenomenon that contributes to the emotions explored. Whilst research on intersectionality has often focused on those of lower social status, with particular regard to gender, sexuality, and ethnicity (e.g., see Pilarski, 2011), the above demonstrates the utility in applying this theoretical lens to white, middle-class men because it helps to explain why they respond to those who have less socially favourable inter-locking identities in the way(s) that they do.

Schism, capital, and the charismatic evangelicals

The charismatic evangelicals differ significantly from the other two groups with respect to the evidence of schismatic behaviour. Indeed, the question of voice requires little discussion when analysing the charismatic evangelical themes because their engagement with the wider Church does not indicate schism or resistance. In fact, several of the participants are ministering in church plants that have emerged at the request of the diocese.

This suggests that the latter is somewhat reliant on the former, and so participants in this group perceived themselves as having a voice in the wider Church. This explains why there is an absence of agitation and dejection-related emotions in their narratives and shows that they do not experience a conflict between their evangelical and Anglican identities. Nevertheless, there are two themes to discuss briefly that will provide helpful details for understanding this group in more detail. These are: (i) Presence of women in ordination training; and (ii) Co-operation with those in other traditions and with different theologies.

Presence of women in ordination training

As discussed previously, the charismatic evangelicals trained alongside women. Returning to Nick's and Lewis' narratives once more, the former said:

> My friend ... was an important part [in the formation of my views of feminism] because she had strong feminist views ... I had other friends, one in my pastoral group .... Again, she was a little older than me and she had lived through the pains of people not being ordained and she was very aware of it. She may well be a bishop one day.

Lewis said, "I think there was a deep bond between the twelve or fourteen of us [who were in the same cohort]. It was a mix of men and women, probably about four or five women, seven or eight men."

Such relationships are suggestive of shared social and spiritual capital between this group of participants and the women that they sustained relationships with during theological college. Evidently, the charismatic evangelicals shared intellectual ideas with each other, as evinced in Nick's narrative. Lewis was describing the relationships he had within his tutor group, a group of ordinands who share in each other's spiritual lives, sometimes undertaking tasks together, such as organising chapel services or praying with each other. This is also indicative of spiritual commodities—spiritual capital in the objectified state—such as receiving prayer, which were consumed to achieve a desired outcome for the participants. These activities involve regular and sustained contact, factors that are known to undermine prejudice, and that are more likely to occur when there is a lack of it.

Co-operation with those in other traditions and with different theologies

The co-operation discussed thus far also indicates the presence of spiritual capital between participants and potential outgroups. Returning to Matt's

138 Schism and clergy capital

comment, he reported, "I have [multiple] parishes here, and a number of colleagues ... from different theological churchmanships to me ... every day one is working with those differences." In these instances, spiritual capital is shared with those who are notably of different theological traditions to the charismatic evangelical participants. It also demonstrates the co-operation that accompanies such interactions.

More specifically, participants share the objectified state with their female colleagues because they are consuming the same spiritual resources through ongoing training in the diocese or through sharing theological ideas and insights as they gather with neighbouring, including female, clergy. This will have contributed to some shared habitus—the embodied state—because sharing capital within one's network informs one's habits, dispositions, etc. (see Bourdieu, 1977). Again, this interaction suggests and helps to explain the absence of prejudice towards women priests amongst this group of clergy.

However, after the interview was over, Michael came out to me before I got into my car because he had forgotten to say something during the interview that he wanted to. As aforementioned, he felt churches in the HTB network (of which he is apart) may well split from the CofE if it became more liberal on the question of homosexuality. It could be that for some of this group, interaction with the CofE will become more limited in the future and that their more permissive attitudes towards gender do not reflect a more permissive set of attitudes towards sexuality.

Schism, capital, and the Anglo-Catholics

Building on some of the themes in the Anglo-Catholic narratives explored in the previous chapter, and adding two more to the analysis, the following are relevant for discussion here: (i) Lack of women ordinands in training; (ii) Worked with women priests; (iii) Conflict with others in the CofE; (iv) Criticism of the wider CofE; and (v) Wider participation in the CofE.

Lack of women ordinands in training and Worked with women priests

When asked whether there were women studying when he was training for ordination, Edward replied, "Not in college no, but there was in the university I think .... There were occasional lectures; women came in and did bits of pastoral studies and things in particular areas, but not on staff at the time." There were no women studying theology at his training college when he was there, including in a lay capacity. Equally, the only women teaching at the time were guest teachers who would often provide training in areas stereotypically associated with (alleged) female domains. Equally, Peter said:

> At [the College of the Resurrection], all the staff were male because then some of the [monastic] community were teaching and the other staff ...

Peter likewise encountered women during his ordination training but in a very limited capacity and not as peers.

Participants demonstrated no schism-related emotions as the result of women's ordination during their time in ministerial training. This is most likely because of the lack of in-depth contact with those who hold alternative beliefs about gender. Reflecting on Evan and Aaron's narratives, discussed in the previous chapter, they also lacked similar emotion responses when they encountered women considering (or already in) the priesthood prior to their change in gender beliefs. However, this can be explained by the presence of prejudice-reducing factors in Evan's case, and the strength of his former traditionalist views in Aaron's case.

Most of the Anglo-Catholic narratives indicate that social capital and spiritual capital have not been widely invested in social groups outside of their own since participants' ordination. As a case in point, I have previously noted Peter's exclusive use of cathedral space for Forward in Faith, which evinces a bonding approach to capital (see also Fry, 2021b). However, the narratives do show that a limited amount of social capital is invested through co-operation with women priests. For instance, Adrian helps some female clergy with bookkeeping:

> The priest who's just left [the neighbouring parish] came over because we've done very well at raising money for property and they were struggling to try [and] sweat their assets. So, I said you can come over and I'll share the story of what we've done, some of it might be helpful, and I'll show you the money books.

Nevertheless, the narratives also highlight that one's mentality shapes capital sharing between groups. For instance, Ashley was previously quoted as explaining that he does not see the ordained status of women as valid when he interacts with his female colleagues. Similarly, Adrian does not undertake activities with women that allow them to do anything uniquely priestly. It is thus important not to assume that the sharing of capital in any form is indicative of the sharing of capital in all forms. For example, participants do not collaborate with women priests to offer a Mass where the woman presides at Communion. This is because the efficacy of Communion for receiving grace would be doubted (as indeed are other sacraments administered by women), owing to the belief that only a man can be in the place of Christ at the altar. This shows that the sharing of capital amongst persons must be analysed at the level of mentality as well as of action, given that their mentality regarding women influences the extent to which they share capital with them.

140 *Schism and clergy capital*

Returning to the case of Evan, he explained:

> I'd already made a friend who was a Church Army officer and [she] had to do post-ordination training [with me] .... She plonked herself next to me on the sofa and we got talking, then we had dinner together and we became friends ... she was there as a Church Army officer ... and then discerned a calling, first of all to the diaconate, then to the priesthood. And I went on a journey with her .... It was her and journeying with her and beginning to see in her the signs of priestly nature [that changed my mind].

This narrative highlights the power that men in the CofE possess over women. When Evan's friend began the discernment process for ordination, it was shortly after women had been permitted to become priests, meaning that women were still highly dependent upon men's approval for ordination. The woman in question needed Evan to provide bridging social capital for her to benefit from his social resources, which in this case included supporting her application for the Church's discernment process. In this respect, she also needed him—as a mentor figure—to assist in her development of spiritual capital in the objectified state so that she could embody the necessary habitus that would convince others in the discernment process of her vocation.

Evan and his friend co-operate. Additionally, they also problem-solve because, as Evan explained, post-ordination training facilitated mentors, to aid mentees in solving problems that arise during one's ministry. It was clearly also a time where Evan's own gender beliefs were tested. Social and spiritual capital are therefore a part of intergroup processes where prejudice-undermining behaviours are concerned. What is unusual in this account, however, is that such behaviours tend to be exhibited in smaller and thus often more exclusive communities (see Putnam, 2000). Whilst this is a small 'community' existing of two persons, it is only exclusive in so far as the CofE arranges this kind of interaction on a one-to-one basis, rather than in respect to the usual in/outgroup divide.

Conflict with others in the CofE and Criticism of the wider CofE

Regarding the tensions and frustrations that this group of participants experienced towards the CofE, Ashley stated:

> Because of some ... issues—not just the ordination of women ... I frequently arrive at clashing with people who I think are too innovative .... The liberal catholics in [this diocese] have predominantly been hostile and unwilling to engage in any discussion whatsoever; they have gone out of their way to marginalise people like myself.

Ashley admitted that he frequently clashes with his colleagues in the diocese who he considers to be theologically too liberal, instead preferring traditional theology on matters pertaining to gender and other subjects. However, he claimed that this is because—as a theological conservative on these matters—he has been marginalised by the wider diocese (with its more liberal culture). This parallels the conservative evangelical narratives, represented by Adam, who distanced himself from his peers during theological training because he felt marginalised on account of his conservative theology of gender.

Moreover, Ashley's comment echoes a criticism held by all the other Anglo-Catholic participants (Evan and Aaron being exceptions). For many, theological liberalism is the CofE's attempt to be relevant and appeal to wider society. Ashley's comment therefore reveals agitation-set emotions, particularly frustration on the basis of the innovation he perceives to be present, and his sense of marginalisation from the wider diocese. There is thus a discrepancy between the actual group and the ought group. Ashley sees himself as an Anglican, having decided to stay within the CofE rather than join the Ordinariate, an ecclesial sphere for Anglicans wishing to join the Roman Catholic Church. He believes that the CofE is authentically catholic because there is a continuity in the contemporary Church from its historical (i.e., catholic) roots. For him, Anglican identity should therefore reflect this and retain Roman Catholic beliefs. However, he explained that Anglicanism does not reflect this because of the innovative approach that he believes his colleagues are introducing into the CofE.

Wider participation in the CofE

Nevertheless, this does not prevent these clergymen from participating in the life of the wider Church in some capacities, although this is somewhat limited, evidencing the exclusivist bonding approach to social and spiritual capital. Peter explained, "I know many women priests and I do work with them. We respect each other's views ... and there are certain things we can do together and there are certain things we can't." In other words, when it comes to priestly activities, participants are unlikely to share capital as they are unlikely to work with women performing a priestly role.

Although Adrian reported helping clergy outside of his immediate tradition with their bookkeeping, his narrative reveals dejection-related emotions. He stated that he is tired of the politics of Church life. He was particularly upset by the way he has been treated by some of his neighbouring parish priests, particularly a female incumbent, because of his gender traditionalist theology and he explained that he is counting down the days until his retirement when he can escape these politics. Hence, there is a discrepancy between the actual group, which appears to reject traditional Anglo-Catholics and the ideal group, which would allow such Anglo-Catholics to work alongside clergy from other traditions within the CofE to at least some extent.

142   *Schism and clergy capital*

This response is likely augmented by his familial relationships and context. Adrian showed me several photographs of his family in his house, detailing several difficult relationships, primarily related to mental health struggles experienced by members of his family, which are partially unresolved. Adrian also spoke of his family's working-class background, explaining how unusual it was for him to go to university. For most of the clergy interviewed, however, going to university was less remarkable, owing to the middle-class context of many of their upbringings, reflecting the wider clergy culture of the CofE. Adrian likely has an extended history of navigating different identities without fully fitting into their respective social groups. To put it another way, participants' emotion responses to women priests/the wider CofE cannot be viewed in isolation from other life experiences.

The gender traditionalists usually do little to share capital with other groups. However, when they do attempt to do so, their actions risk being undermined by the way they report being treated by others. This could lead those who would otherwise interact with other clergy, sharing capital with them, to distance themselves from the wider Church instead.

Initial reflections on the Anglo-Catholics

Participants' reported behaviours indicate that their resistance towards the wider CofE—including women priests—stems, at least in part, from their perception of how others in the Church receive them. In addition to this, the presence of schismatic behaviours demonstrates that they believe that the introduction of women's ordination was an important break with the identity of the CofE, which they feel is best represented by traditional Anglo-Catholicism. It is also apparent from the above analysis that participants rarely interact with those of different theological traditions in ways that could serve to undermine prejudice.

Nevertheless, the fact that those interviewed have remained within the CofE does suggest that they feel that they have a sufficient voice with which to be heard and demonstrates a tension of seeing the wider CofE as something of an outgroup without fully breaking away from it. That participants may have their own like-minded bishop, are part of a network (whether formally or informally) of Anglican priests with similar theology, and that the CofE maintains the two integrities are all obvious reasons for them to believe that this is the case. In fact, one of the participants has written literature on why Anglo-Catholics should remain in the CofE rather than join the Roman Catholic Ordinariate. However, participants frequently appeared frustrated with, and tired of, their sense of marginalisation. I interviewed them at a particularly poignant time because it was shortly after Philip North had received significant backlash after being announced as the next Bishop of Sheffield, because of his traditionalist gender views. It is therefore possible that this sense of voice is on borrowed time for the traditional Anglo-Catholic participants, particularly those who opted to join Forward in Faith.

Methodological reflection

It has become apparent that intersectionality as a theoretical framework sheds light on the nature of schisms. It foregrounds that members of a group can have competing identities and that schismatic behaviours and emotions occur when overlapping identities are perceived to be in conflict by the individual holding them. In the present case, this is a conflict between conservative evangelical or traditional Anglo-Catholic identities and wider Anglican identities.

Moreover, the analysis of the Reform themes bears testimony to the potentially exclusive nature of resource sharing and that religious belonging can be accompanied by a lack of a straightforward sense of belonging to other social groups, which in this case would mean other Anglicans. In this sense, theories of intergroup contact and social and spiritual capital complement each other as they highlight different aspects of withdrawal from or engagement with other groups. The former can highlight multiple types of contact. The latter highlights the types of resources that can accompany such interaction (or which are denied because of a lack of interaction). They highlight the implications of either interaction or resource sharing for intergroup dynamics.

Analysis of Reform also provides additional insight into the lack of social capital that others have noted pervades contemporary society. Putnam (2000) has argued that the practicalities of phenomena such as modern family dynamics and working patterns negatively impact social capital. Whilst this may well be the case, my analysis indicates that the role of social identity in this process ought not to be overlooked in this regard as it can lead to exclusivist social interactions.

Regarding the charismatic evangelicals, employment of social and spiritual capital as interpretive lenses highlights the presence of religiously oriented interaction and resource sharing and so highlights the nature of participants' co-operation in a way that the contact hypothesis does not. Hence, both the social psychological lens and the sociological lenses are co-dependent in the pursuit of detailed qualitative analyses of social activity. The capital lenses help one to draw out the specifics of co-operation because they are able to highlight the way in which inter-personal activities occur in a socio-religious context. That is, whereas employing the contact hypothesis highlights how contact and prejudice are reported to manifest in the everyday life of the clergy, utilising social and spiritual capital *more readily* highlights how co-operation in particular—an important facet of contact—is reported to present itself in situ religionis.

Indeed, the exploration of capital within the Anglo-Catholic narratives such as Evan's reveals the importance of the CofE as an authority in bringing together those of different traditions for fostering contact, including co-operation. This provides further evidence that social and spiritual capital are helpful complementary lenses to the contact hypothesis because they highlight the specific ways in which co-operation—a factor that reduces

144 *Schism and clergy capital*

prejudice—manifests. Hence, they highlight aspects of co-operation and thus indicate more specifically the types of co-operative contact that can undermine prejudice.

Finally on the methodological front, the literature on schisms can be (erroneously) read as indicating that individuals belong to one social group at the exclusion of another. In reality, it has focused on the processes whereby groups (can) split and—often being quantitative—has not offered a thick description of people's emotions and behaviour during the processes that can lead up to schism. This has led to a focus on group conflicts rather than insinuating that social identities are necessarily binary. By way of contrast, the employment of intersectionality, particularly as part of a qualitative analysis, enables the more complex reality to come to the fore. Of course, group dynamics are often exclusionary, but persons do also belong to multiple social groups and possess multiple social identities. This chapter contains an analysis of data that show how schismatic behaviour and related emotions manifest during the processes that can lead to full secession from a group. In doing so, the complicated reality of contact between those who belong to the same social group, whilst also belonging to groups that are in tension with it, is highlighted.

Conclusion

The discussion on my participants' emotions suggests that the Reform and traditional Anglo-Catholic participants experience a discrepancy between their various senses of Anglican identity. It is when their perceptions of Anglicanism are questioned that negative emotions manifest. If they were able to hold their evangelical or Anglo-Catholic identities together with their Anglican identity, then it may be that the latter identity will be less threatened and thus their resistance less intense. However, this partially relies on how other Anglican clergy treat them.

In the previous chapter, I argued that participants' behaviour is consistent with their prejudicial beliefs (or lack thereof) towards women. In the present chapter, I have demonstrated how effectively the work on schisms, an important part of intergroup contact, enables a further analysis of the data. In doing so, it is further apparent that participants' level of contact and resistance mirrors what one would anticipate from the contact hypothesis. In addition to this, the utilisation of complementary theoretical lenses continues to shed further light on the social world of such clergymen and evidences the connectedness between different lenses in multiple disciplines. To this I shall return later in the monograph. At present, however, I shall turn to a discussion of the international contexts in which my participants' narratives are situated.

Notes

1 Penal substitutionary atonement is the belief that God laid the wrath for people's sins on Jesus at the crucifixion.

2 I am unable to report what was said during this meeting as access to it was to recruit participants and agreed with the Chair of Reform for the diocese on the provision that I did not report anything from that meeting.

References

Appiah, K. (2018). *The lies that bind. Rethinking identity: Creed, country, colour, class, culture*. London: Profile Books ltd.

Bebbington, D.W. (1989). *Evangelicalism in modern Britain: A History from the 1730s to the 1980s*. London: Unwin Hyman.

Bizman, A., & Yinon, Y. (2002). Social self-discrepancies and group-based emotional distress. In D.M. Mackie, & E.R. Smith (Eds.), *From prejudice to intergroup emotions: Differentiated reactions to social groups*. New York: Psychology Press.

Bourdieu, P. (1977). *Outline of a theory of practice*. Cambridge University Press.

Bourdieu, P. (1983). The field of cultural production, or: The economic world reversed. *Poetics, 12*(4–5), 311–356.

Frijda, N.H. (1986). *The emotions*. Cambridge University Press.

Fry, A.D.J. (2021b). Clergy, capital and gender inequality: An assessment of how social and spiritual capital are denied to women priests in the Church of England. *Gender, Work & Organization, 21*(6), 2091–2113.

GAFCON. (2008). *The complete Jerusalem statement*. Retrieved from https://www.gafcon.org/resources/the-complete-jerusalem-statement.

GAFCON. (n.d.). *About GAFCON*. Retrieved from https://www.gafcon.org/about.

Guest, M. (2007b). In search of spiritual capital: The spiritual as a cultural resource. In K. Flanagan & P. Jupp (Eds.), *A sociology of spirituality* (pp. 181–200). Aldershot: Ashgate.

Guest, M., Olson, E., & Wolffe, J. (2012). Christianity: Loss of monopoly. In L. Woodhead & R. Catto (Eds.), *Religion and change in modern Britain* (pp. 57–78). Oxford: Routledge.

Higgins, E.T. (1987). Self-discrepancy: A theory relating self and affect. *Psychological Review, 94*(3), 319–340.

Kumra, S., & Vinnicombe, S. (2010). Impressing for success: A gendered analysis of a key social capital accumulation strategy. *Gender, Work & Organization, 17*(5), 521–546.

Pilarski, A.E. (2011). The past and future of feminist biblical hermeneutics. *Biblical Theology Bulletin, 41*(1), 16–23.

Putnam, R.D. (2000). *Bowling alone: The collapse and revival of American community*. New York: Simon and Schuster.

Sani, F. (2005). When subgroups secede: Extending and refining the social psychological model of schism in groups. *Personality and Social Psychology Bulletin, 31*(8), 1074–1086.

The Free Church of England (2018). *FCE History*. Retrieved from https://fcofe.org.uk/our-history/.

Turner, J.C., & Oakes, P.J. (1986). The significance of the social identity concept for social psychology with reference to individualism, interactionism and social influence. *British Journal of Social Psychology, 25*(3), 237–252.

Verter, B. (2003). Spiritual capital: Theorizing religion with Bourdieu against Bourdieu. *Sociological Theory, 21*(2), 150–174.

7 Gender attitudes in (inter)national perspective

Introduction

So far, I have analysed participants' gender attitudes as they manifest within the CofE and their relationship to historical beliefs and events in immediately England. In this chapter, I will explore the relationship between my participants' narratives and the international contexts in which they are situated, particularly with regard to how each tradition has been shaped by modernity. With respect to the conservative and the charismatic evangelicals, this is because these traditions have a shared history with US evangelicalism which has been formative, and because gender attitudes within US evangelicalism have been informed by its response to modernity. To understand how factors beyond the UK context come to bear on participants' gender attitudes, therefore, it is necessary to understand their relationship to US evangelicalism, including how the latter has responded to modernity. This does not mean that there is a straightforward linear influence of modernity on US evangelicalism which then impacts its English counterpart. The historical scholarship indicates that both shaped each other in tandem. It also shows that modernity has had a direct influence in England, as seen in the second chapter. Nevertheless, existing knowledge on the response of US evangelicalism to modernity provides ample material with which to explore how this interrelationship has shaped English evangelicalism within the CofE in the present. This affords new knowledge on the social factors that have shaped current gender attitudes within English evangelicalism.

None of this is to suggest that there are no clear distinctions between the evangelicalisms on either side of the Atlantic. Important differences do exist. This chapter will therefore also contain discussion that attends to the discontinuities between US and English evangelicalisms. Highlighting the differences between them will serve to underscore how factors unique to the English context (in addition to those discussed in the second chapter) also come to bear on my participants' gender attitudes. I will also explore the international context of Anglo-Catholicism because the gender attitudes of my Anglo-Catholic participants have been influenced by Roman Catholicism.

DOI: 10.4324/9781003081913-7

Gender attitudes in (inter)national perspective 147

In what follows, I shall outline the historical relationship between the evangelicalisms on both sides of the Atlantic as well as between (traditional) Anglo-Catholicism and Roman Catholicism. This will involve describing and revisiting the historical responses that these traditions have evinced towards gender developments from modernity into the present century. Having done so, I will proceed to explore participants' narratives, drawing out where the influence of the historical relationships between these traditions may be observed, before offering some methodological considerations. Before I do this, though, it is necessary to unpack further what is meant by modernity, to set the scene for an exploration of evangelical and Anglo-/Roman Catholic responses to it.

Modernity

The historical context

Whilst the concept of modernity is agreed upon, there are minor differences in the emphases afforded to it. However, it may be summarised as consisting of four key components (see Bruce, 2008). Firstly, there is differentiation, the segregation of society with the onset of the Industrial Revolution, where society became increasingly compartmentalised with new institutions performing roles previously fulfilled by the Church. Secondly, there is the process of socialisation, where populations adapted to new social and professional roles and ways of life in new urbanised areas and led to decreased contact between the classes. Thirdly, there is rationalisation, the process of explaining the world through natural rather than supernatural means, not least with the advent of modern scientific investigation with the focus on cause and effect. Finally, there is egalitarianism, where an understanding of individual responsibility gave way to the demand for equal rights.

The genesis of modernity, in some respects, can be traced back to the Reformation where rationalisation was set in motion by the coding of morality. This involved finding an internal logic for discerning ethical conduct, meaning that it was no longer solely attached to divine command. Hence, the role of religion in moral reasoning and guidance gradually decreased (Bruce, 2008). It was this same European phenomenon which led to the rise of egalitarianism in modernity where the focus in Protestant theology on human equality before God led to the development of individual responsibility, which paved the way for individual rights (Bruce, 2008).

Within the processes of modernity were contained higher levels of religious pluralism in the US context, particularly with increases in the number of Roman Catholics and Jews, the result of European migration (Ammerman, 1987). This was accompanied by the rise of biblical criticism and subjectivism as part of an intellectual revolution internationally (Ammerman, 1987). As a result, whereas before the onset of modernity the overarching belief systems in society were assumed to be an accurate account of how the world was, once the cogs of modernity began to turn, the plausibility of the existing worldview

148 *Gender attitudes in (inter)national perspective*

was undermined (Bruce, 2008). For example, the historical authenticity of the Gospels was called into question, undermining normative Christian assumptions (Marsden, 1991). This is perhaps most clearly expressed in David Strauss' (1846) *Life of Jesus,* which claimed that the Gospel accounts must be fabricated on account of the frequent reports of miracles. The French Revolution also indicated a new way of thinking about the world (Antoun, 2001), not least in matters of religion where, for example, the assumption of divine political order was abandoned in some quarters, and questioned in others (Chadwick, 1990). Indeed, this had influence beyond France (see MacCulloch, 2009).

Darwin's theory of evolution was also considered by some to undermine traditional theology (Balmer, 1994). This was augmented by the ability to trace cause and effect in scientific endeavour, which made the concept of God redundant for some (Bruce, 2008). In fact, with the plausibility of some traditional religious beliefs undermined, there were theological shifts towards liberalism within mainline Protestant denominations (Marsden, 1991), leading to changing interpretations of the authority of the Bible (Ammerman, 1987). One does not have to look far into the history of Christian doctrine from the Enlightenment period onwards before finding major challenges to key beliefs held by most Protestants. For example, the traditional articulation of the two natures doctrine (which affirms the simultaneous deity and humanity of Christ) underwent significant re-examination, sometimes to understand the person of Jesus through an exclusively naturalist lens, i.e., through the laws of nature (Macquarrie, 1990). Ideas such as Immanuel Kant's (1724–1804) rationalist Christology or Friedrich Schleiermacher's (1768–1834) humanist Christology certainly went beyond the bounds of historical orthodoxy, and even heterodoxy (see Macquarrie, 1990). Furthermore, higher criticism, which sought to analyse the Bible as a collection of historical sources without regard to its authoritative religious status (Atherstone, 2013), in this milieu permitted theologians to ask questions that challenged theological convention, and which highlighted the (biased) role of Church tradition in biblical interpretation (Barr, 1983).

Theological and sociological components of evangelical reaction in the US

These developments set the scene for evangelical reaction or "anger" (Marsden, 1991, p. 1). Christians from more conservative traditions felt that their beliefs were being relegated, and so their reaction was defensive in so far as they (selectively) resisted societal changes, forming a subculture in which to shelter amidst their sense of marginalisation (Appleby, 2011). Those evangelicals who most strongly resisted modernity have often been labelled as 'fundamentalists'. Hence, "Fundamentalism [...] is the religion of the stressed and the disoriented, of those for who the world is overwhelming" (McCarthy Brown, 1994, pp. 175–176). Whilst public discourse

Gender attitudes in (inter)national perspective   149

in both the US and UK contexts have made this term highly problematic and often inappropriate (e.g., see Fry, 2020), understanding this response to social change will prove instructive for interpreting participants' data, given the transatlantic ties between US and English evangelicalisms.

A key feature of evangelical movements labelled as 'fundamentalist' is the presence of Scottish Common Sense Realism (Towsey, 2010). It promotes a plain-meaning reading of biblical texts and democratised the Bible in the eighteenth century, making it available to a larger audience (Balmer, 2016). This ties in with another key interpretative method regularly associated with 'fundamentalists', namely literalism, formed as part of a rejection of higher criticism. However, one ought not to understand 'literal' as synonymous with being anti-allegorical, but that which is clearly verifiable (Boone, 1989). Within this hermeneutical framework, the Bible is therefore understood to be an accurate source of scientific understanding (Boone, 1989).

Separatism—the distancing of some evangelical groups from wider society, and indeed from more liberal Christian traditions[1]—was another common facet of reaction against the social changes brought about by modernity (see Marsden, 1991). Paradoxically, perhaps, this was coupled with political activism from the 1970s where 'fundamentalists' publically protested social and legislative changes, particularly those related to gender (Balmer, 2016).

Evangelical reactions against changing gender norms in the US

In the second chapter, I explained that the traditional division of labour accompanied the Industrial Revolution, as men began to work in urbanised areas, leaving women at home to tend to the domestic sphere, including the religious instruction of children (see Balmer, 1994). This led to the emphasis on the male provider that had become an established norm by the twentieth century (Gallagher, 2003). However, the rise of higher criticism occurred within a context of dramatic shifts in gender roles and the rise of feminism, where women were beginning to enjoy the possibility of public ministry, begetting a counter trend of resistance to it and an emphasis on male authority in church and at home within the more conservative evangelical circles in the early twentieth century (Gallagher, 2003). In this context, higher criticism came to be seen as a threat to the traditional (Christian) social order where women played a key role in ensuring that faith continued for future generations (see Gallagher, 2003). This response provided fertile soil for plain-meaning readings of biblical texts.

Brasher (1998) has asserted that, in the US, gender was *the* key factor giving birth to 'fundamentalism', seeing it as an anti-feminist backlash, arguing that much of the early 'fundamentalist' literature focused on gender and family ideology. She also identifies three theological components in 'fundamentalist' reaction to feminism. Firstly, there is sexual polarity, the concept that men and women are created differently, and thus for different purposes. Secondly, there is sexual dominance, the belief that men, rather

150   Gender attitudes in (inter)national perspective

than women, are ordained by God to rule or hold authority. Thirdly, there is sexual unity, the belief that men and women are in some sense equal before God. Whilst Brasher's claim that gender developments gave rise to 'fundamentalism' is somewhat overstated, it was clearly salient. The question of abortion, for example, primarily became important because of evangelical outcry against legislative procedures in the 1970s that threatened to strip tertiary educational institutions of their tax-exempt status if they continued to segregate along racial lines; the momentum gained against President Jimmy Carter's administration because of racial equality legislation was harnessed by some evangelical leaders and redirected towards the promotion of traditional patterns of gender (Balmer, 2016).

Nevertheless, by the 1980s, patriarchal and hierarchical language pertaining to gender roles had softened (Balmer, 1994; Gallagher, 2003). In fact, the emergence of symbolic headship and pragmatic egalitarianism was apparent. This is the idea that theologies of male leadership and authority over women are more rhetorical than actual, and that Christians who claim to practice the headship model within the marital context are, in fact, more likely to mirror the *comparatively* egalitarian gender patterns of wider society (see Gallagher and Smith, 1999; Gallagher, 2003). This can be seen as the outworking of engaged orthodoxy, introduced in the second chapter. It results from the evangelical movement of the 1940s which sought to break away from the culture of separatism and engage more seriously with wider society, leading to the simultaneous embrace and rejection of intellectual and social culture beyond the evangelical tradition, whilst retaining elements of so-called fundamentalism (Smith et al., 1998). Grudem (1994), despite promoting the traditional headship model, nonetheless offers a clear example of this softening. In his *Systematic Theology*, he writes:

> [...] in recent years a major controversy has arisen within the evangelical world: may women as well as men be pastors? May they share in the offices of the church? [....] We must affirm at the outset that the creation narrative in *Genesis 1:27 views men and women as equally created in the image of God* [....] We must also admit that evangelical churches have often failed to recognize the full equality of men and women, and thereby have failed to count women equal in value to men [....] My own conclusion on this issue is that the Bible does not permit women to function in the role of pastor or elder within a church. (p. 937, emphasis original).

Note here the incorporation of the feminist demand for equality as well as the subjective expression of Grudem's own response on the matter of female Church leadership as his "own", rather than as a matter of fact derived from a plain-meaning reading of scripture. This is despite the latter approach often accompanying US evangelical discourse where plain-meaning reading is advocated (see Boone, 1989).

Gender attitudes in (inter)national perspective 151

It was within this broader twentieth-century context that the processes of modernity began to undermine the previous sex segregation present at the start of the Industrial Revolution, reduced the number of children women had, and reduced the number of women becoming mothers altogether (Bruce, 2008). In response, evangelicals began to insist that there was a gender difference in creation where men should lead and women follow, and that Christian scripture mandated this pattern as a timeless prescription (Gallagher, 2003). However, this was not always done softly. Hence, Ammerman (1987) notes how, in one 'fundamentalist' congregation, issues of family were frequently addressed from the pulpit where appeals were made to the Bible as asserting that the role of women was as the domestic caregiver. In other words, having accepted the emergence of women as the primary caregivers and religious instructors of children as a result of the emerging working conditions for men, evangelicals began to resist the very process that led to this development when it then gave women an increased presence in society beyond the domestic sphere.

Evangelicalism and modernity in the transatlantic context

Historically, the evangelicalisms on both sides of the Atlantic have had common roots and, since the 1940s, it has been especially evident that they enjoyed similar trajectories (Bebbington, 1994). Hence, there are a few areas worthy of note when considering how evangelicalism in the English context has been shaped by its relationship with its US counterpart in addition to noting where they have been distinct. The first area worthy of consideration is a continuity and relates to Church leaders. Both British and US evangelicalisms have had shared preachers for centuries, with more recent examples including the US evangelist Billy Graham and Anglican priest John Stott, both in the twentieth century (Bebbington, 1994; see also MacCulloch, 2009). The clear interaction between these evangelicalisms was also evinced by US students coming to Britain to study under evangelical biblical scholars such as F. F. Bruce[2] (Guest, 2007a). This means that theological claims, assumptions, and methods have been shared by evangelicals in both countries. Unsurprisingly, then, another continuity has been the rejection of higher criticism in some evangelical corners where this method was distrusted. These evangelicals were inclined towards a more literalist reading of scripture (Bebbington, 1994) and related controversies, such as the authoritative status of biblical texts, were as in the US (Bebbington, 1989).

However, this is to be juxtaposed alongside an important distinction. Evangelicals in England resisted modernity as in the US context, but the term 'fundamentalist', whilst not being altogether absent, was nonetheless used infrequently (Bebbington, 1989). The terms 'conservative' and 'liberal' emerged to describe evangelicals, with the former holding to a more literalist reading of scripture than the latter (Bebbington, 1994), indicating a cultural shift that departed from a more traditionalist articulation of theological belief within

152 *Gender attitudes in (inter)national perspective*

English evangelicalism. Darwinism also proved to be less of a contested matter in England (Bebbington, 1989). Moreover, both conservative evangelicals and comparatively liberal evangelicals displayed the ability to be innovative, even though the former tended towards greater societal resistance than the latter (Bebbington, 1989).

In other words, elements of US 'fundamentalism' could be seen within English evangelicalism, particularly its more conservative expression, but less intensely. In this respect, English evangelicalism has been more akin to the evangelicalism that Smith et al. (1998) describe. These softer manifestations can be understood in light of two phenomena: (i) factors unique to the English context that come to bear on expressions of evangelicalism as found within the CofE; and (ii) the more recent relationship that English evangelicals have had with the type of evangelicalism Smith et al. (1998) have explored. I shall begin by unpacking the English distinctives.

One area worthy of note in this regard is the institutional context. Due to the institutional nature of evangelicalism in England, tensions between liberal and conservative evangelicals did not prove as divisive as in the US (Bebbington, 1989). Historically, important evangelical figures, such as John Newton—whose conversion to Christianity whilst a slave trader led him to write the well-known hymn 'Amazing Grace'—entered the ranks of the CofE and intentionally fostered vocations within it (Noll, 1994). Evangelical leaders seeking to foster vocations within the CofE were not isolated to this point in history, however. Evangelical camps proved formative in the faith of privately educated boys during the twentieth century, many of whom would then pursue ordination to the Anglican priesthood (Brown and Woodhead, 2016), demonstrating something of an extended history of evangelical integration with the Established Church.

Four other factors equally highlight the importance of the institutional context for understanding evangelical Anglicanism today (see Bebbington, 1989). First, bodies such as the Evangelical Alliance and the Islington Conference drew liberal and conservative evangelicals together, showing a level of intra-evangelical engagement, despite some theological differences on matters salient at the time. Second, the Oxford Group—a precursor to the charismatic movement—met outside of church times rather than clashing with Sunday services, evincing that evangelical movements have developed alongside, rather than in competition with, the institutional Church. Third, in 1966, Westminster Chapel preacher Martin Lloyd-Jones had called on all evangelicals to leave their denominations to join a unified evangelical free church, a call which was immediately rebutted by the high-profile Anglican priest (and evangelical) John Stott. Fourth, off the back of this development, at the 1967 National Evangelical Anglican Congress in Keele, evangelical Anglicans agreed to affirm its commitment to the CofE and to play a more active role within the institution. However, with the decline of traditional forms of Christianity in the latter half of the twentieth century, scapegoats were sought in the form of theological liberalism, exemplified by John Robinson's book

Gender attitudes in (inter)national perspective   153

Honest to God, which sought to reframe the language Christians used for thinking about God (Brown, 2010), indicating that resistance towards theological innovation sat alongside a commitment to engage.

Further signs of evangelicalism's institutional compatibility in England can be discerned from the CofE's historical relationship with Methodism (see Olsen, 1990). During the eighteenth-century revival, many Methodists were content with the CofE, appreciating its ecclesiology and liturgy; the leader of Methodism, John Wesley, also avoided holding meetings inside church hours, with only a short list of exceptions to this, such as if the local Anglican Church was staunchly Calvinistic,[3] or for those who lived more than two miles away from it (Olsen, 1990). In addition to this, a proposed union between Anglicans and Methodists in the 1960s was rejected by conservative evangelicals only because they felt that the conditions were unfavourable to their Methodist brethren (Olsen, 1990). That this was the reason for rejection of the union underscores that CofE evangelicals have not only been willing to work within the Established Church but that, in principle at least, they were happy working collaboratively with those beyond their immediate tradition. This willingness to engage was not limited to the Church, however. As the conservative evangelical wing of the Church grew during the twentieth century, their opposition to wider society's innovations declined, also revealing greater harmony between conservative evangelicals and their social surroundings by the mid-twentieth century or so (Olsen, 1990).

Another area worthy of note, therefore, is the history of evangelical social engagement. English evangelicalism often engaged with the social concerns of the nineteenth century. However, when conservative evangelicals believed that this would detract from evangelism, it ceased to be a priority (Turnbull, 2007). Although, this began to change during the interwar years due to more internal concerns, such as the holiness movement where personal sanctification was stressed to the detriment of social justice (Bebbington, 1995). This was reversed, to some extent, at Keele in 1967, where evangelicals also affirmed that the outworking of the Gospel included loving service (Bebbington, 1995).

There is also the recent history of evangelical engagement with the Bible. The evangelical scholarly engagement documented by Perrin (2016) has highlighted important developments in the twentieth century regarding how evangelicals read scripture. Although these do not exclusively occur in the English context, they primarily pertain to it and therefore serve to deepen understanding of the influences on my evangelical participants' biblical interpretation. One important event that Perrin describes is the introduction of discussions on academic hermeneutics to the 1977 National Evangelical Anglican Congress by biblical scholar and Anglican priest Anthony Thiselton. The reaction amongst some conservative evangelicals was one of hesitancy, being concerned that it would lead to an increase in theological liberalism; although, other evangelicals embraced Thiselton's agenda with greater levels of enthusiasm. John Stott popularised aspects of Thiselton's work in this area, encouraging Bible readers to recognise their own cultural assumptions and

154 *Gender attitudes in (inter)national perspective*

engage with the task of learning what biblical texts 'meant' when they were originally written in addition to seeking its application for believers in the current day (Perrin, 2016).

A common feature that Perrin observed amongst her evangelical participants is the treatment of the Bible as a continuous narrative starting from the texts of the Hebrew Bible and continuing down to the present day. As I will show in due course, these contemporary facets of biblical interpretation are also found within my participants' narratives. Additionally, Perrin has noted how attempts to increase the theological literacy of lay evangelicals by church leaders have existed on both sides of the Atlantic, bearing witness to the difficulty of sharply dividing some phenomena as being uniquely British as opposed to American. She also found that leaders within English evangelicalism frequently employ double-reading hermeneutics, an attentiveness to the original meaning of a text alongside contemporary application. This sits alongside grammatico-historical practices amongst Perrin's participants, which can be considered a subset of historical criticism but is also rooted in resistance towards the historical-critical method (see also Porter, 2011). This method asks questions of cultural context but predates the historical-critical method and so is in this sense pre-critical (Perrin, 2016; see also Barton, 2007).

Grudem (2002) has written on the Greek word κεφαλή. Whilst the meaning of this word is disputed in New Testament scholarship (e.g., see F. F. Bruce, 1984), he argues that κεφαλή must mean "head" (p. 26), denoting male authority. Some of his argument rests on undermining other interpretations of the Greek word. As a part of his attempt to dismiss the possible interpretation of κεφαλή as 'source', which he notes is a translation favoured by some egalitarians, Grudem cites a personal letter he received from a lexicographical scholar. He explains that this scholar also rejects the possibility that κεφαλή may be understood as 'source'. The primary weakness with this line in Grudem's argument here is that the letter in question makes no attempt to elaborate on why one should not understand κεφαλή in this way, but only asserts an opinion. Nonetheless, he concludes from this that, "this must be counted a significant statement because it comes from someone who, because of his position and scholarly reputation, could rightly be called the preeminent Greek lexicographer in the world" (p. 189). In other words, his own reasoning is based on the fact that someone who he considers possessing an excellent ability in the subject matter at hand agrees with him, rather than solely on the coherence and rigour of an intellectual argument, despite possessing formal theological training himself and intending his text to be an academic piece. This is a clear example of conservative evangelical intellectual engagement being only partial, thus reflecting something of the culture described by Perrin but within the US context.

English evangelicals have historically reflected elements of the culture found within US evangelicalism, including 'fundamentalism', but these have occurred alongside important distinctions. To extrapolate, the combination of these unique factors appears to have shaped the softer expression of English evangelicalism when compared to some forms of US evangelicalism.

Gender attitudes in (inter)national perspective 155

This is because institutional, intellectual, and societal engagement would foster a less wholesale rejection of values, beliefs, and practices found beyond evangelicalism, particularly given the insights from, and evidence of, engaged orthodoxy noted in previous chapters.

Indeed, the above demonstrates that 'fundamentalism' in England did not have the leadership presence that it did in the US and that there was not the same tendency towards it as there was across the Atlantic (Bebbington, 1994). Nonetheless, 'fundamentalism' was not altogether absent in the English context as conservative evangelicals in the CofE in the 1920s and 1930s could share some of the tenets associated with it (Atherstone, 2013). It was not until the 1950s when English evangelicals appeared to be embarrassed by their links to US evangelicalism (Atherstone, 2013; see also Numbers, 2006). Thus, so-called fundamentalism did exist in England and the CofE was not entirely moderate (Bebbington and Jones, 2013). However, it was a marginal movement, ultimately rejected by evangelicals within the CofE (Atherstone, 2013; Numbers, 2006).

Nevertheless, not all evangelicalism in the US is 'fundamentalist' and the discontinuities that English evangelicalism has with so-called fundamentalism is not only the result of factors unique to the English context. As aforementioned, the relationship between the two not only predates 'fundamentalism' but has a shared trajectory from the 1940s in particular, the period where some strands of US evangelicalism were seeking self-reform so as to become a more socially engaged tradition. Given the shared leadership between British and US evangelicalisms that continue through this time, and the affinities that my participants' narratives have with this US tradition (evidenced below), it is clear that US evangelicalism has shaped its English counterpart.

Having outlined in summary form the way in which US and English evangelicalisms have developed historically in relation to modernity, it is important to explore how they have responded to changing gender roles, to understand how the broader context of modernity has been impactful on participants' gender attitudes.

Reform in transatlantic perspective

There are five themes (including two sub-themes) of relevance for understanding how the international context of English evangelicalism shapes the Reform narratives. These are: (i) Created order of male headship and female submission; (ii) Ambivalent attitudes towards feminism; (iii) Deutero-intellectualism; (iv) Resistance towards training institutions; and (v) Resistance towards the diocese.

Created order of male headship and female submission

Returning to this theme, when speaking of the Genesis 2 creation narrative (found within the Hebrew Bible), Justin alluded to and expounded on 1 Timothy 2 (a New Testament epistle). He said:

156 *Gender attitudes in (inter)national perspective*

.... You've got the household of the family and the household of God, and I love the way that 1 Timothy particularly connects those two things: the household of faith [and] the household of God ... those two households ... are to mirror and reflect and live out the creational ordinance and that would include, therefore, male headship and women submitting. So, I think you want to see that in the home, and I think you want to see that in the Church.

This was accompanied by his statement that "My basic conviction is that the Bible teaches that men and women are equal in worth and different in role." Amongst this group, such sentiments were often followed up with comments akin to Greg's qualification that male headship is "self-sacrificing, servant leadership that takes responsibility at cost to the leader rather than a self-serving, status-driven, arrogant type of headship." These comments reflect the complementarian views asserted by US authors Piper and Grudem (1991) (see also Grudem, 2002). It also echoes some of the ideas found in the work of Eldredge (2001) and Eldredge and Eldredge (2005), also US authors. The fact that Greg believes that the role of a man, at least within the context of marriage and the local church, involves an element of sacrifice is not far removed from the concept of men needing to be spiritual warriors. Both concepts lean on the idea of a macho masculinity that embraces trials in heroic fashion.

However, this sense of a Christian masculinity has a historical precedent in England. The popularised muscular Christianity that imbued middle-class Anglicanism in the twentieth century (see Delap, 2013; McLeod, 2012) has no doubt found outlet in the present conservative evangelical gender attitudes under discussion. However, the fact that such ideas originated in secular sporting culture (McLeod, 2012) presents evidence that the ideas articulated by the Reform participants are not strictly taken from Judaeo-Christian scripture as they claim. Rather, it further demonstrates that the Reform participants have inherited a tradition that assimilates the historical gender norms of wider society, which are then projected onto texts (see also Fry, 2021a). Given that participants claimed to read authors such as Grudem and Piper and explained that they have been influential in the formation of their own attitudes, it is likely that the historical context of Anglicanism has provided fertile soil in which the seeds of complementarianism may grow. To put this another way, some historical trajectories provide ways of thinking that make the assimilation of similar ideas more likely because they are consistent with existing assumptions. As discussed in the fourth chapter, human beings are predisposed to assimilate information that is congruent with previous experiences and related assumptions and beliefs.

Additional evidence of US influence is apparent on consideration of the fact that Brasher's (1998) three-fold observation is also reflected in the Reform narratives. Sexual polarity is seen in the account of men and women being created to fulfil different roles. Sexual dominance is evinced in the

Gender attitudes in (inter)national perspective 157

claim that men, rather than women, are to lead in the Church and family. Sexual unity is demonstrated in the assertion that both sexes have been made by God as equals.

A distinction between my participants and data from the US context, though, is the comparative lack of emphasis on women as caregivers. Those interviewed are typically located in expensive areas with respect to property prices and occasionally referenced this as a need for some families in their congregations to have two working parents, even if they felt that this was not ideal. This suggests a certain level of pragmatism in their theological position and further indicates that some of the participants' theology responds to their wider social context rather than being born solely from scripture.

Historical developments can help explain the lack of a traditional caregiver model in the narratives. English evangelicalism adapted to the increase of women in the workforce during the previous century, meaning that the concept of professional women became less of a contrarian idea within this tradition (Summerfield, 1998). Indeed, English evangelical gender values, whilst remaining somewhat conservative throughout the twentieth century, nonetheless adapted to include the idea of the working woman (Brown, 2001), an evident break with traditional gender values that saw the domestic sphere as the locus of women's primary vocation.

In contrast to studies on US conservative Protestantism (e.g., Ammerman, 1987), participants reported rarely promoting such theology from the pulpit. Instead, they explained that they only teach it when a related passage would come up incidentally in their sermon series. Participants further reported that they believe it is usually proper to teach through one book of the Bible at a time to their congregations so that scripture (supposedly) sets the preaching agenda rather than the preacher. When asked whether he teaches his gender beliefs to his congregation, Justin said:

> Yes. Not always and not never. Sometimes. So, if we're preaching through 1 Timothy, we're going to hit [gender roles]. We preached through Genesis 1–4 in the autumn; amongst many things we taught about, we taught on that. We don't choose sermon series so that we can teach on that ... as we read the scriptures, we come across it.

It could be, therefore, that participants' biblicism[4] is a contributing factor to this. However, participants also often expressed awareness that this teaching could be divisive for members of their congregations and so it could be that this too is a reason for refraining from politicising their gender beliefs from the pulpit. Moreover, Ammerman (1987) has argued that public protest against changing gender values in the US took place in a context of increased momentum for reasserting traditional gender patterns. My participants, on the other hand, belong to an institution that has been clear on its decision to ordain women to the priesthood and consecrate them as bishops and that had become increasingly supportive of women's ordination throughout the twentieth century.

158   *Gender attitudes in (inter)national perspective*

Notwithstanding, this has not only been embedded in the culture of the CofE but also in the wider Anglican Communion, given that an increasing number of Anglican Churches were ordaining women prior to 1994 (Fletcher, 2013). Indeed, the institutional context demonstrates that evangelicals became consciously committed to work within the CofE's structures by 1967, and the fact that Reform aimed to transform the CofE from within (Jones, 2004) underscores this. Further, the fact that the CofE is also committed to including those who objected to women's ordination in the life of the Church and has made provisions for them (e.g., Avis, 2004; Maltby, 1998), presumably makes the relative (albeit limited) peace that conservative evangelicals have with the Established Church possible. Hence, these should be understood as further factors contributing to this lack of public militancy. To put it another way, the US evangelical influence on participants' gender attitudes is moderated by a series of English (and Communion)-based factors.

Ambivalent attitudes towards feminism: Negatives of feminism and Positives of feminism

Participants' articulation of their theology of male headship was also accompanied by their ambivalent attitude towards feminism. When asked about feminism, Justin said:

> My understanding ... is it will often go well beyond [equality] in saying that equal in worth means equal in role and that is where I disagree and that's where I sense the feminist movement is unable to make that distinction of equal and different .... But I'm sure there have been ... insights it's brought.

This critique of feminism has clear affinities with evangelical reaction against growing gender inequality in later modernity which sought to promote traditional gender roles (i.e., differentiation). However, Justin follows this up by explaining that:

> ... we're trying to be distinct, happily and healthily distinct, rather than weirdly and curmudgeonly distinct—'Isn't the world evil? Isn't the world terrible?' No. We want to set up an alternative: 'Look at this Christ-radical society where all are welcomed and where we acknowledge we're different.'

Note the softer tone in his criticism of feminism when compared with some historical US responses to it; this is disagreement rather than backlash. This can be explained by the institutional context discussed directly above. Equally, it can be attributed to the softening response to feminism found within US evangelicalism from the 1980s, either directly or through greater levels of engagement with wider society afforded by engaged orthodoxy in

Gender attitudes in (inter)national perspective   159

the English context (see Fry, 2021a). Again, these need not be mutually exclusive. The combination of these factors is the most likely scenario given that their immediate context is the CofE and that they engage with US evangelical authors to inform their theology of gender. These factors also help to explain in greater depth the incorporation of some feminist ideals into their narratives as evinced in their Positive attitudes towards feminism (see also Fry, 2021a).

Deutero-intellectualism

The Reform participants are not anti-intellectual, having academic qualifications in theology, often from prestigious institutions, and being engaged in academic theological reading post-ordination. Nevertheless, there are clear instances of disregard for, or inconsistency in, a rigorous intellectual approach to their theology on matters of gender. For instance, when asked about his hermeneutics of texts such as Ephesians (a New Testament epistle that discusses gender roles), Simon said, "I think responsible hermeneutics makes sense of the situation of the time." Here, Simon demonstrably expressed an appreciation of the role of historical criticism in interpreting the Bible. He advocated the necessity of going beyond a mere plain reading of scriptural texts when forming one's theology. Nevertheless, he also said, "The best sense that I can make of the biblical texts … are that it's most appropriate for a man [rather than a woman] to be leading the church in the role of vicar." In other words, Simon believes that only men should be ordained to lead churches. However, this interpretation of the passages Simon cites in support of his claim relies on a plain-meaning reading. For example, 1 Timothy 2:11–14, which Simon stated as a relevant passage, reads:

> Let a woman learn in silence with full submission. I permit no woman to teach or to have authority over a man; she is to keep silent. For Adam was formed first, then Eve; and Adam was not deceived, but the woman was deceived and became a transgressor.
> (New Revised Standard Version, *Anglicized Edition*)

In practice, however, there is no attempt to nuance how one might read this in light of the context in Ephesus (where the recipients of this letter were based—see Drury, 2001), despite the fact that conservative evangelical scholars (with similar beliefs regarding gender) nonetheless contextualise the passage. For instance, some comment that it is not directly applicable to contemporary Church structures (e.g., Mounce, 2000). Nevertheless, this was not consistently found amongst participants when they explained their interpretation of the relevant biblical texts. In this respect, participants evinced awareness of the intellectual developments within evangelicalism outlined by Perrin (2016) but reflect a pre-critical hermeneutic. Such developments appear to have shaped the way they articulated their Bible reading

160   Gender attitudes in (inter)national perspective

practices even though the practices themselves do not appear to reflect an incorporation of such methods.

In fact, there are other types of examples of participants' inconsistency in thinking through their gender attitudes. Participants claimed that their rationale for adopting complementarian theology is that God has created men and women to fulfil different roles. However, one can see in the 1 Timothy text cited above that the author had an additional justification for prohibiting women from teaching men: it is because a woman was deceived at the Fall. Indeed, whilst the text does not claim that women are gullible, the English word "for" in this passage has the force of 'because' and the original Greek word it represents (γὰρ) also connotes a causal relation (see Balz and Schneider, 1990). Despite this, such reasoning does not enter into the narratives. Justin reported that:

> Picking up on 1 Timothy 2 .... I think the point [Paul is] making there is not that Eve was gullible—so [I] don't [not] have women in charge because they're gullible—the point he's making [is that] there is an inversion of the created order.

It is therefore apparent that the Reform participants continue in the tradition of evangelicals such as Grudem (2002) who do engage intellectually, to some extent, yet fail to consistently offer an intellectually informed hermeneutic. This is consistent with historical evangelical suspicion of higher criticism and the associated changes in gender roles. A plain-meaning reading of relevant biblical texts is what one ought to expect to see emerging within a tradition that has been shaped by that context.

Moreover, the impact of Scottish Common Sense Realism is apparent. Greg's interpretation of Genesis 2, discussed in the third chapter, is heavily reliant on 1 Timothy 2. His interpretation is not readily relatable to the text's historical context, and thus those interviewed reveal the interpretive process found within US evangelicalism. Furthermore, two of Boone's (1989) markers of 'fundamentalism' are present, namely, the idea that the Bible is reliable for all knowledge (including scientific understanding), and a literal (although not necessarily anti-allegorical) reading of biblical texts. With respect to the first marker, that Genesis is understood to offer a description of how men and women naturally 'are' is indicative of a belief that it can offer scientific insight into the sexes. With respect to the second marker, the literal interpretation is tantamount to the Scottish Common Sense Realism hermeneutic. This further testifies to the clear shaping of conservative evangelicalism within the CofE by its US counterpart.

Resistance towards training institutions and Resistance towards the diocese

In the previous chapter, I outlined how gender-related developments within the CofE, especially within the context of a perceived embrace of theological liberalism, pose a threat to the sense of identity experienced by Reform

Gender attitudes in (inter)national perspective 161

clergy. I also argued that this leads to some schismatic behaviour. For example, Henry explained that during his time at theological college:

> Sometimes we [ordinands] would skip lectures and ... go and talk theology in [our] study bedrooms together .... I had a bit of a clash with my tutor ... who I felt had shopped me to my bishop .... I had to go down to see the bishop ... And I felt betrayed by that .... I think it was about chapel attendance but he outed it in my report .... We had also clashed theologically and I wondered whether he had it in for me .... [We clashed] about penal substitutionary atonement ... and I'd ... exposed [his faulty theology] in a lecture.

Equally, post-ordination, when ministering in his current diocese, Henry explained that his involvement with the wider Church is through schismatic movements: "My involvement is actually, at the moment, through the wider Anglican church—GAFCON and [the] Free Church of England." This parallels what has been observed within US 'fundamentalism'. It was the rise of theological liberalism in the US, where evangelicals felt that they were being marginalised from society, which led to their resistance towards modernity. In particular, changes to gender values provoked an evangelical counter-response as society became more egalitarian. This is exactly what one sees with the emergence of Reform in opposition to women's ordination (see Jones, 2004) and participants' decisions to disengage from their diocese, impair Communion with their bishop, and/or join other schismatic groups.

However, whereas US evangelicals were responding to developments in gender values throughout the twentieth century (Balmer, 2016), conservative evangelicals in England's Established Church only began to more firmly resist gender developments in the late twentieth century (see Jones, 2004). This is an interesting difference between English Anglican evangelicalism and US evangelicalism given that gender roles in wider society were changing rapidly in both countries from the 1960s onwards (see Brown, 2001). However, the CofE's privileged position within English society buffered its evangelical constituents from being directly impacted by such changes within religious contexts. When the 1975 Sex Discrimination Act was introduced, religious institutions were exempted from its implications, meaning that the CofE has not been legally required to appoint women on equal terms with men (see Legislation, n.d.). In fact, it was only when the CofE decided to introduce the priesting of women, despite being under no legal obligation to do so, that conservative evangelicals began to evince schismatic behaviour on this issue.

It is true that the CofE had discussed the possibility of including women into its ordained hierarchy on several occasions before the 1992 General Synod (e.g., see Francis and Robbins, 1999), and calls for the Church to consider it may be traced to the 1950s (e.g., Thrall, 1958). Nevertheless, as aforementioned, evangelicals within the CofE had made a conscious decision during

162 *Gender attitudes in (inter)national perspective*

Keele to commit themselves to the Established Church. It was, therefore, only once the CofE had made a clear decision to change its gender values and attitudes in practical ways—and when it thus became evident that conservative evangelicals had distinct gender norms from their denomination—that such schismatic behaviours began to occur.

Therefore, a further similarity between the evangelicalisms of the two countries is that they both exhibit resistance towards liberal strands of Christianity. Moreover, the narratives indicate that resistance is more dominant than engagement with the wider Church in my participants' narratives; when they do choose to interact, it is evidently on their own terms. In fact, during the interview process, I discovered that one member of Reform—who was not interviewed—planted a church out of another one in the diocese without the bishop's consent, making it an illegal church with respect to canon law.[5] However, the diocesan bishop attempted to open dialogue with him to bring the illegal plant officially into the diocese. The minister refused to do so without certain demands (undisclosed to me) being met, a stance approved of by the participants who discussed these events with me. Whilst the minister in question was an atypical example, participants' approval offers further evidence of their resistance towards the diocese even though it is vicarious in this specific instance. This reflects something of the double separatism seen in the US context. Again, all of this highlights the polyphony of international and domestic social factors shaping my participants' gender attitudes, with the latter moderating the former.

The charismatic evangelicals in transatlantic perspective

There are two themes that are of relevance for understanding how the international context of English evangelicalism shapes the charismatic evangelical narratives. These are: (i) Hermeneutic of historical context; and (ii) Hermeneutic of canonical context.

Hermeneutic of historical context and Hermeneutic of canonical context

Participants in this group evinced differences in the way that they read the Bible when compared to the conservative evangelicals. They reported reading the Bible in light of its historical context. For instance, Shaun said:

> I think you have to look at the cultural context of those passages [about gender] and why Paul had the restrictions that he did, which go further about women having their heads covered and men not, and women not speaking in church let alone teaching, and then explore the culture where women had even less place in society and had no rights at all.

Likewise, this group also read biblical passages in light of the overarching themes found within the rest of the Bible. For example, Nick said:

In my opinion, God's overriding message on gender in the New Testament in particular is one of liberation for women and ... a lot of the time, when Peter is writing and when Paul is writing, and in the life and ministry of Jesus, what we see is women being treated in a way that the culture around them would never have treated them; [it] would never have given them the respect, the honour or the time that those people—because of who they were and who Jesus was—gave to women.

The first of these themes is evidence of a more thorough although somewhat simplified engagement with biblical criticism. Shaun explained that the passages used to prohibit women from occupying positions of Church leadership need to be understood in light of the even more restrictive culture that existed beyond the Early Church. He believes that this allows one to see that the New Testament writers were in the habit of providing greater levels of equality for women than had been the case previously in their culture. The second theme builds on the ideas found within the first. For this group of participants, this increased equality is part of a redemptive trajectory that the Christian Church ought to follow through to its logical conclusion, meaning the full ordained ministry of women within its institutional structures.

The approach outlined in the former theme stems from biblical criticism, whereas the approach in the latter has its roots in the redemptive trajectory hermeneutics discussed in the second chapter. They both show an intellectual engagement with biblical studies, albeit it in a way that maintains their tradition's roots; my participants still claim to hold to the Bible as their ultimate source of theological authority. In juxtaposition, this information highlights the affinities that this group has with the evangelicalism emerging from the US in the 1940s. In fact, the authors that this group reported reading were primarily based in the US, such as Webb (2001) and his book *Slaves, Women and Homosexuals*. However, the influence of the transatlantic context cannot be viewed in isolation. My charismatic evangelical participants did not resist their training institutions as did their Reform colleagues. During their time at theological college, participants would have been taught these hermeneutical methods and provided with access to academic literature that discusses them. In fact, there is a clear affinity with the hermeneutic of approaching scripture as a unified narrative as discussed by Perrin above, which—as aforementioned—developed primarily within the English evangelical context. There is, therefore, a combination of US evangelicalism and the English (including institutional) context shaping charismatic evangelical gender attitudes.

Anglo-Catholicism, modernity, and Roman Catholicism

In the second chapter, I discussed several factors that contributed to the emergence of the Anglo-Catholic tradition and its identification with the historical Christian Church, particularly with Roman Catholicism. The crisis

164 *Gender attitudes in (inter)national perspective*

of faith, the proposed reduction of Irish bishops by the British Government, and increased involvement of women within the life of the CofE, all appeared prior to the new articulation of catholicity and (male) apostolic succession. I also discussed evidence that Roman Catholic teaching has historically formulated theology that runs contrary to gender equality, for instance, by asserting: that there has existed a continuous trend of male priesthood since the New Testament period; that women are unlikely candidates for fulfilling the role of the male Christ at the altar; that feminism is to blame for enmity between the sexes during the mid-twentieth century; that women are trying to gain power via feminism; and that feminism compounds sex and gender. This was accompanied by the statement that it was acceptable for women to seek fulfillment beyond the domestic sphere, so long as the home remained the place of their primary vocation. The CDF also allowed for some distinction between gender and sex, whilst also accusing feminism of compounding the two (see Beattie, 2004).

Anglo-Catholicism in international perspective

There are four themes, including two sub-themes of relevance for discussion here, namely: (i) Ecumenical objection to the ordination of women; (ii) Sacramental objection to the ordination of women; (iii) Apostolic objection to the ordination of women; and (iv) Ambivalent attitudes towards feminism.

Ecumenical objection to the ordination of women

When discussing the CofE's decision to ordain women as priests, Edward remarked:

> My problem is—as a catholic—that the Church of England claims to be part of the universal Church. [Ordaining women is] an action that's not done by the universal Church, either Roman Catholics or the Orthodox, so to me the first level is a question of appreciating the catholic age of what the Church does and the Church hasn't done that universally.

Comments such as these show that Roman Catholic teaching on women's ordination is a marker for their own theology on the matter; they believe that the appropriateness of this development is dependent on other historical denominations also agreeing to it. Whilst some participants included the Orthodox Church as a reference, this was not consistent across the narratives, and those who did mention it regularly neglected to offer evidence for how that Church has influenced their own thinking in this area. When asked about the influences on their gender beliefs, my participants regularly cited various forms of Roman Catholic teaching. This indicates that Roman Catholicism over and above other denominations is an important factor in shaping their gender attitudes to the exclusion of other branches of Christianity beyond

Gender attitudes in (inter)national perspective 165

Anglicanism. This is readily explained by Tractarian origins, which 'looked back to' Roman Catholic theology when it first emerged in the nineteenth century. In this respect, as with the evangelical narratives, one can note the fusion of an international religious tradition and the domestic context contributing to the formation of participants' gender attitudes.

Sacramental objection to the ordination of women and Apostolic objection to the ordination of women

Regarding the first of these themes, Peter said, "It's the sacramental ministry that is the problem for me ... I would not receive Communion from a woman celebrating [at the altar]." Similarly, Oliver explained that "my own position about the ordination of women is that I am still uncertain about it sacramentally."

Returning to the second of these themes, Malcolm stated:

I take the view that, first of all, if you look at scripture, Christ did not defy convention, did not make women apostles. The apostles themselves, when they had to fill a vacancy, nobody as far as one knows either suggested Mary or Mary Magdalene as possibles to fill it. It was clearly a male leadership in the Church and then for 2000 years, if you look at tradition, the Church did not ordain women.

The traditional Anglo-Catholic understanding of (male) priesthood reflects the statement produced by the CDF that insisted on the legitimacy of male priesthood only, as it is the priest who stands in the place of the male Christ before the altar to administer the sacraments. Hence, the influence of Roman Catholicism in shaping my participants' gender attitudes is clearer still.

Ambivalent attitudes towards feminism: Negatives of feminism and Positives of feminism

During his interview, when asked about his response to feminism, Ashley said, "My view is that it's just an extension of the secular feminist agenda, and therefore I take the view now that most of the feminist theological writings are post-Christian, if not anti-Christian." Peter said in response to the same question: "Our bodies are different and so they function differently, which identify us as who we are and there's no way that you can swap those around." These statements reflect the CDF which blamed the feminist movement for enmity between the sexes. They also mirror its claim that changing societal conceptions of sex are threatening the biological reality of male and female bodies.

When speaking more positively of feminism, Anthony said:

I think that feminism gives us a way where we can say that [marginalised] voices can be heard and can be empowered and should be given a place

166 *Gender attitudes in (inter)national perspective*

where they've not been, and I think that has been wrong when they haven't been given that voice.

As explained in the third chapter, there is an affirmation of women seeking a vocation or profession beyond the domestic sphere. Again, this mirrors the CDF statement that women can seek fulfilment beyond the home. The evident influence of Roman Catholicism on participants' gender attitudes is also indicative of the shaping influence that this religious tradition has had on the hostile sexism that my participants evinced in their discussion of feminism, unpacked in the third chapter. Moreover, as with the evangelical cohorts, their gender attitudes are shaped by the international context of their particular expression of Anglicanism.

Methodological reflection

The clear influence of religious traditions beyond the English context found within my participants' data begs a further question: how does one understand the relationship between participants' respective Anglican traditions, their international counterparts, and wider social developments? For instance, many of the influences from US evangelicalism also have affinities with wider gender beliefs found within English society, so where does the influence of US evangelicalism stop and the influence of wider English society begin? Indeed, given the presence of engaged orthodoxy found within the evangelical narratives, what fusion of evangelical and wider societal ideas can be attributed to US evangelicalism and what can be attributed to wider English society? As this approach to wider societal interaction, whilst having its genesis in the US, leads to greater levels of engagement with one's surrounding culture, including some incorporation of it, where the influence of one ends and the other begins seems unclear. After all, the softer expressions of traditional gender attitudes can be found within postfeminism in the English context (as discussed in the third chapter) as well as within the works of popular US evangelical authors.

I previously explained that developments within historical Anglican culture have paved the way for the assimilation of gender attitudes found within US evangelicalism. The same is surely true with respect to this question, where the wider cultural milieu of Anglican clergy shapes their gender attitudes, making ideas found within the US that share affinities with them more plausible. This can also be said for the Anglo-Catholics—who likewise share an appreciation for feminism as well as a clear critique of it, indicating a postfeminist outlook—with respect to its relationship with Roman Catholicism.[6]

That is not to claim, however, that the direction of influence is exclusively one way. For those participants who grew up in religious traditions that have been shaped by those that exist beyond the UK, and who were thus exposed to them from an early age, it may well be the case that the gender attitudes found within them make those within wider English society more plausible.

Gender attitudes in (inter)national perspective   167

Equally, as one's religious tradition is formational in their identity, those who find themselves immersed in it are likely to modify their own attitudes in light of group norms (see Haslam, Reicher and Platow 2011). Also, there has been ongoing historical interaction between traditions with their international counterparts, including before participants were born. This makes it likely that historical US influence, for example, made it easier for the evangelicals to adopt ideas found in authors such as Wayne Grudem. It is thus important to avoid making overly simplistic causal inferences.

Rather, what is clear is that, regardless of the exact direction(s) of travel of causation, my participants' gender attitudes cannot be adequately understood apart from an appreciation of the impact that US evangelicalism or Roman Catholicism has had upon them, in tandem with factors unique to the English context, whether they be institutional influences or wider cultural norms. It is necessary to separate these different shaping factors out to fully appreciate the constituent parts of my participants' gender attitudes. Nevertheless, because these attitudes are evidently formed in a complex social web, it would be misleading to claim that: certain aspects of their gender attitudes are exclusively those of wider society; others belong exclusively to certain other religious traditions; and others still only to their immediate tradition. That is, the multiple factors that shape participants' beliefs and behaviours in this area, some of which may have already been shaped by each other, converge and manifest in the narratives being explored in this monograph.

Conclusion

In this chapter, I have explored how factors beyond the English context have come to shape the gender attitudes of my participants. This has involved isolating aspects of their narratives to show how the international context evidences factors that have some explanatory power for understanding the influences on the gender attitudes of theologically conservative male clergy within the CofE. However, the insights afforded by doing so are to be juxtaposed alongside the appreciation that the way in which one's social world contributes to the formation of their attitudes—that is their beliefs, emotions, and behaviours—is complex. There is a polyphony of factors that contribute to the attitudes being explored in this study. With that in mind, it is now appropriate to gather the various attitude-shaping historical, sociological, and psychological factors that have been identified thus far to more fully explore their inter-relationship through further theorising the origins of participants' gender attitudes.

Notes

1 Distancing from other Christian traditions is sometimes known as double separatism.

168 *Gender attitudes in (inter)national perspective*

2 Sometimes scholars such as Bruce are referred to as neo-evangelical because of their thorough engagement with higher criticism.
3 That is, believing that salvation and condemnation were predetermined by God and thus that one can do nothing to save their own soul.
4 A view of the Bible as the ultimate authority for all theological truth (Bebbington, 1989).
5 Canon law is CofE-related legislation.
6 However, this was not ubiquitous across this group's data given that, as explained in the third chapter, around 50% more of my Anglo-Catholic participants articulated an appreciation of feminism than criticised it.

References

Ammerman, N.T. (1987). *Bible believers: Fundamentalists in the modern world.* New Brunswick, NJ: Rutgers University Press.

Antoun, R.T. (2001). *Understanding fundamentalism: Christian, Islamic, and Jewish movements.* Walnut Creek, CA: Rowman and Littlefield.

Appleby, R. Scott. (2011). Rethinking fundamentalism in a secular age. In C. Calhoun, M. Juergensmeyer & J. Van Antwerpen (Eds.), *Rethinking secularism* (pp. 225–247). Oxford University Press.

Atherstone, A. (2013). Evangelicalism and fundamentalism in the inter-war Church of England. In D.W. Bebbington & D.C. Jones (Eds.), *Evangelicalism and fundamentalism in the United Kingdom during the twentieth century* (pp. 55–75). Oxford University Press.

Avis, P. (2004). The Episcopal Ministry Act of Synod: A "bearable anomaly"? In P. Avis (Ed.), *Seeking the truth of change in the Church: Reception, communication and the ordination of women* (pp. 152–170). London: T&T Clark.

Balmer, R. (1994). American fundamentalism: The ideal of femininity. In J. Hawley (Ed.), *Fundamentalism and gender* (pp. 47–62). Oxford University Press.

Balmer, R. (2016). *Evangelicalism in America.* Waco, TX: Baylor University Press.

Balz, H., & Schneider, G. (1990). *Exegetical dictionary of the New Testament, vol. 1.* Grand Rapids, MI: William B. Eerdmans Publishing Company.

Barr, J. (1983). *Holy scripture: Canon, authority, criticism.* Oxford: Clarendon Press.

Barton, J. (2007). *The nature of biblical criticism.* Louisville: Westminster John Knox Press.

Beattie, T. (2004). *The new Catholic feminism: Theology, gender theory and dialogue.* London: Routledge.

Bebbington, D.W. (1989). *Evangelicalism in modern Britain: A history from the 1730s to the 1980s.* London: Unwin Hyman.

Bebbington, D.W. (1994). Evangelicalism in its setting: The British and American movements since 1940. In M.A. Noll, D.W. Bebbington, & G.A. Rawlyk (Eds.), *Evangelicalism: Comparative studies of popular Protestantism in North America, the British Isles, and beyond 1700–1900* (pp. 365–388). Oxford University Press.

Bebbington, D.W. (1995). The decline and resurgence of evangelical social concern 1918–1980. In J. Wolffe (Ed.), *Evangelical faith and public zeal: Evangelicals and society in Britain 1780–1980* (pp. 175–197). London: SPCK.

Bebbington, D.W., & Jones, D.C. (2013). Conclusion. In D.W. Bebbington & D.C. Jones (Eds.), *Evangelicalism and fundamentalism in the United Kingdom during the twentieth century* (pp. 366–376). Oxford University Press.

Gender attitudes in (inter)national perspective 169

Boone, K.C. (1989). *The Bible tells them so: The discourse of Protestant fundamentalism*. New York: SUNY Press.

Brasher, B.E. (1998). *Godly women: Fundamentalism and female power*. New Brunswick, NJ: Rutgers University Press.

Brown, C.G. (2001). *The death of Christian Britain: Understanding secularisation, 1800–2000*. London: Routledge.

Brown, C.G. (2010). What was the religious crisis of the 1960s? *Journal of Religious History, 34*(4), 468–479.

Brown, A., & Woodhead, L. (2016). *That was the Church that was: How the Church of England lost the English people*. London: Bloomsbury.

Bruce, F.F. (1984). *The Epistles to the Colossians, to Philemon, and to the Ephesians*. Grand Rapids, MI: William. B. Eerdmans Publishing Company.

Bruce, S. (2008). *Fundamentalism*. Cambridge: Polity.

Chadwick, O. (1990). *The spirit of the Oxford Movement: Tractarian essays*. Cambridge University Press.

Delap, L. (2013). "Be strong and play the man": Anglican masculinities in the twentieth century. In L. Delap & S. Morgan (Eds.), *Men, masculinities and religious change in twentieth century Britain* (pp. 119–154). Basingstoke: Palgrave Macmillan.

Drury, C. (2001). The pastoral epistles. In J. Muddiman & J. Barton (Eds.), *The Oxford Bible commentary: The Pauline epistles* (pp. 244–263). Oxford University Press.

Eldredge, J. (2001). *Wild at heart: Discovering the passionate soul of a man*. Nashville, TN: Thomas Nelson.

Eldredge, J., & Eldredge, S. (2005). *Captivating: Unveiling the mystery of a woman's soul*. Nashville, TN: Thomas Nelson.

Fletcher, W. (2013). There for the burials; there for the births: Women in leadership in the Anglican Communion. In K. Pui-lan, J. Berling, & J. Plane Te Paa (Eds.), *Anglican women on Church and mission* (pp. 55–75). Norwich: Canterbury Press.

Francis, L.J., & Robbins, M. (1999). *The long diaconate, 1987–1994: Women deacons and the delayed journey to priesthood*. Leominster: Gracewing Publishing.

Fry, A.D.J. (2020, July 6). Religious 'fundamentalism': The origins of a dubious category. *Religion and Global Society*. The London School of Economics and Political Science. Retrieved from https://blogs.lse.ac.uk/religionglobalsociety/2020/07/religious-fundamentalism-the-origins-of-a-dubious-category/.

Fry, A.D.J.. (2021a). Postfeminist, engaged and resistant: Evangelical male clergy attitudes towards gender and women's ordination in the Church of England. *Critical Research on Religion, 9*(1), 65–83.

Gallagher, S.K. (2003). *Evangelical identity and gendered family life*. New Brunswick, NJ: Rutgers University Press.

Gallagher, S.K., & Smith, C. (1999). Symbolic traditionalism and pragmatic egalitarianism: Contemporary evangelicals, families, and gender. *Gender and Society, 13*(2), 211–233.

Grudem, W.A. (1994). *Systematic theology: An introduction to biblical doctrine*. Nottingham: InterVarsity Press.

Grudem, W.A. (2002). The meaning of κεφαλὴ ("head"): An evaluation of new evidence, real and alleged. In W. Grudem (Ed.), *Biblical foundations for manhood and womanhood* (pp. 145–202). Wheaton, IL: Crossway.

170 Gender attitudes in (inter)national perspective

Guest, M. (2007a). *Evangelical identity and contemporary culture: A congregational study in innovation*. Eugene, OR: Wipf and Stock Publishers.

Haslam, S.A., Reicher, S.D., & Platow, M.J. (2011). *The new psychology of leadership: Identity, influence and power*. East Sussex: Psychology Press.

Jones, I. (2004). *Women and priesthood in the Church of England: Ten years on*. London: Church House Publishing.

Legislation. (n.d.). *Sex Discrimination Act 1975*. Retrieved from https://www.legislation.gov.uk/ukpga/1975/65.

MacCulloch, D. (2009). *A history of Christianity: The first three thousand years*. London: Penguin.

Macquarrie, J. (1990). *Jesus Christ in modern thought*. London: SCM Press.

Maltby, J. (1998). One Lord, one faith, one baptism, but two integrities? In M. Furlong (Ed.), *Act of Synod- act of folly? Episcopal Ministry Act of Synod 1993* (pp. 42–58). London: SCM Press.

Marsden, G. (1991). *Understanding fundamentalism and evangelicalism*. Grand Rapids, MI: William B. Eerdmans Publishing Company.

McCarthy Brown, K. (1994). Fundamentalism and the control of women. In J.S. Hawley (Ed.), *Fundamentalism and gender* (pp. 175–201). Oxford University Press.

McLeod, H. (2012). The "Sportsman" and the "Muscular Christian": Rival ideals in nineteenth century England. In P. Pasture, J. Art, & T. Buerman (Eds.), *Beyond the feminisation thesis: Gender and Christianity in modern Europe* (pp. 85–96). Leuven: Leuven University Press.

Mounce, W.D. (2000). *Word biblical commentary: Pastoral epistles*. Waco, TX: Thomas Nelson.

Noll, M.A. (1994). *The scandal of the evangelical mind*. Grand Rapids, MA: William B. Eerdmans Publishing Company.

Numbers, R. (2006). *The creationists: From scientific creationism to intelligent design*. Cambridge, MA: Harvard University Press.

Olsen, G.W. (1990). *Religion and revolution in early-industrial England: The Halevy thesis and its critics*. Lanham, MD: University Press of America.

Perrin, R. (2016). *The Bible reading of young evangelicals: An exploration of the ordinary hermeneutics and faith of Generation Y*. Eugene, OR: Pickwick Publications.

Piper, J., & Grudem, W. (Eds.). (1991). *Recovering biblical manhood and womanhood: A response to evangelical feminism*. Wheaton, IL: Crossway.

Porter, M. (2011). *Sydney Anglicans and the threat to world Anglicanism: The Sydney experiment*. London: Routledge.

Smith, C. with Emerson, M., Gallagher, S., Kennedy, P., & Sikkink, D. (1998). *American evangelicalism: Embattled and thriving*. Chicago, IL: University of Chicago Press.

Strauss, D.F. ([1846] 2010). *The Life of Jesus, critically examined*. New York: Cosimo Inc.

Summerfield, P. (1998). *Reconstructing women's wartime lives: Discourse and subjectivity in oral histories of the Second World War*. Manchester: Manchester University Press.

Thrall, M.E. (1958). *The ordination of women to the priesthood: A study of the biblical evidence*. London: SCM Press.

Towsey, M. (2010). "Philosophically playing the Devil": Recovering readers' responses to David Hume and the Scottish Enlightenment. *Historical Research*, 83(220), 301–320.

Turnbull, R. (2007). *Anglican and evangelical?* New York: Continuum International Publishing Group.

Webb, W.J. (2001). *Slaves, women and homosexuals: Exploring the hermeneutics of cultural analysis.* Nottingham: InterVarsity Press.

8 Summary, reflections, and implications

Introduction

In this penultimate chapter, I will summarise what has been argued thus far before I provide a fuller explanation of the social factors that shape the attitudes held by the clergy interviewed. I will expand the theoretical lenses employed by positing how they, and the strands of analysis, fit together as I offer an argument that accounts for the entirety of the evidence explored. I will then offer some recommendations for the CofE for its response to the findings presented in this monograph.

Summary of findings

I have established that the most conservative attitudes towards women that clergy possess regularly meet some—if not all—of the social psychological criteria for sexism. I have also demonstrated that clerical sexism occurs alongside insubstantial contact with women in less traditional roles (not least as priests) and that those male priests who are more affirming of egalitarian gender roles articulate ongoing relationships with such women. Moreover, I have highlighted that the emotions commonly understood to accompany prejudicial attitudes are present in the narratives of those clergy who express sexist outlooks. Indeed, it has become apparent throughout the above analysis that clergy attitudes are in keeping with the findings of scholarship on prejudice and intergroup processes.

I have also shown the value that a qualitative analysis of prejudice and intergroup processes can bring to an exploration of the social world. More specifically, I have demonstrated that in-depth interviews reveal the nuances and paradoxes that people experience in their lives, something that the previous quantitative studies have not provided. For instance, participants' ambivalence towards certain topics, as well as their reticence to answer some of the questions asked of them, became apparent as did the reasons for these phenomena. These instances cannot be captured with quantitative methods and have shed light on clergy attitudes towards women. Providing participants with greater agency in how they answer questions has also provided

DOI: 10.4324/9781003081913-8

Summary, reflections, and implications 173

further insight into clergy prejudice towards, or affirmation of, women in different contexts. Additionally, capturing participants' answers in their own words has enabled connections to be drawn between their attitudes towards, including levels of contact with, women and multiple theoretical frameworks that have not previously been utilised either for exploring gender attitudes at all or for exploring them in combination with the other theoretical frameworks explored.

I have shown that: social capital and spiritual capital are important aspects of contact for those priests who regularly engage with female clergy; that such capital is shared during the type of contact that predicts affirming attitudes towards women; and that they are absent when the type of contact that undermines prejudice is also absent. Indeed, they are absent when prejudicial attitudes are present. The above analysis has also demonstrated the presence of symbolic boundaries between gender traditionalists and their denomination and that these have been coupled with the ambiguous nature of theologically conservative male clergy interactions with the wider Church, contributing to the presence of engaged orthodoxy. I have also shown that the more negatively gender traditionalist clergy view outgroups, the more likely they are to resist other Anglican groups, and vice versa for those who have more affirming attitudes towards women clergy.

Furthermore, the impact that the CofE's historical traditions have on its current clergy has been noted. I have argued that the traditions clergy inherit shape their current attitudes towards women in different contexts. In particular, those who possess prejudicial gender attitudes are those who belong to traditions that have an extended history of resisting—and even feeling threatened by—shifts in gender norms, including greater gender equality. By way of contrast, those who have inherited a tradition that has generally been more affirming of gender equality tend to be affirming of women adopting any number of roles. It is also important to note, however, that participants are not merely passive agents in this process, as discussed in the methodology section, but can opt into their respective traditions. In doing so, they can employ certain elements of these traditions, rearticulating them for the present.

Theorising the findings

This leaves the question of why these attitudes exist in the first place. I have previously argued that system-justifying motives underlie prejudicial beliefs amongst the Reform participants (Fry, 2019). However, system-justifying behaviour and motives overlap with, and occur alongside, what I theorise below (see Jost, Banaji and Nosek, 2004). Moreover, system justification theory cannot account for much of what I have observed with the charismatic evangelical and Anglo-Catholic participants whereas the model discussed next does. I have argued in this monograph that the data analysed demonstrates that research on intergroup contact and self-categorisation provide a robust

174 *Summary, reflections, and implications*

framework with which to analyse this study's participants. What follows is primarily a reflection of the data gained from those participants who evinced sexism. I will then consider why more affirming attitudes towards women—particularly priests—exist amongst other participants.

Social identity theory, self-categorisation theory, and threatened self-esteem

In the sixth chapter, I drew on research on self-categorisation theory and outlined the role of group schisms in participants' narratives. What I did not explain was the role that self-esteem plays in social groups. Social identity theory states that all persons are predisposed to ingroup bias, exhibiting favouritism to those with whom they identify and thus consider part of the same social group as themselves (Tajfel and Turner, 1979, 1986). This stems from the need to see positive distinctives about their ingroup to maintain higher levels of self-esteem; however, this also involves making generalisations about members of outgroups, seeing them as homogenous units and viewing them unfavourably. This is because one's sense of group identity is interactive rather than stable, and so is formed in response to outgroups, meaning that social groups are dependent on outgroups to shape their sense of identity (Turner and Oakes, 1986). This leads to discriminatory behaviour towards outgroups, especially from groups with higher social status (Tajfel and Turner, 1979, 1986) because higher-status groups possess greater social resources, something which they want to maintain in order to justify their higher levels of self-esteem (Jost and Banaji, 1994). These stereotypes are the route by which prejudice emerges (see Allport, 1979; Glick and Fiske, 1996; Tajfel and Turner, 1979). Hence, the pursuit and maintenance of self-esteem is the primary underlying force behind prejudicial attitudes. However, these processes occur at the unconscious level.

Self-categorisation theory builds on social identity theory. The reactions to the ordination of women in the early 1990s show that the perceived departure from a group's historical norms triggers threats to a person's sense of self and belonging, making this the source of the negative emotion sets that I discussed previously (see Sani and Reicher, 2000). In other words, people avoid and react prejudicially towards outgroups, including those who are perceived to be breaking with the ingroup, to maintain their self-esteem, sometimes because there is a sense of threat to the status of their group, whether that be to the privileged place that their group enjoys in society or to the perceived historical identity of their group (or both). The narratives of the clergy partaking in this study that exhibit gender prejudice evince a perceived threat to both.

This is more readily understood in light of threatened self-esteem. People react by behaving negatively towards a person or group when they perceive that their self-esteem is threatened (Baumeister, Smart and Boden, 1996; Bushman and Baumeister, 1998). This is unsurprising given that self-esteem is contingent upon various sources that provide a person with their sense of

Summary, reflections, and implications   175

identity (Crocker et al., 2003; Crocker and Knight, 2005). Therefore, participants' sexist attitudes are motivated by the threat that an outgroup poses to their sense of self-esteem, which is wrapped up in their identity as Anglican priests who hold either a conservative evangelical or a traditional Anglo-Catholic interpretation of their denomination.

These interpretations are shaped by different theological presuppositions. In the case of the conservative evangelicals, it is the authority of scripture, whereas in the case of the Anglo-Catholics it is unity with Rome. For those who displayed sexist attitudes, their particular understanding of Anglicanism—including priesthood—is one where only men are ordained to run the ecclesial hierarchy, an idea that can be reinforced by appeals to scripture and/or tradition. It is the fact that women's ordination poses a threat to this historical understanding of the Church that makes women priests objects of clerical sexism. The advent of women priests therefore threatens their identity as priests, as men, and as either evangelicals or Anglo-Catholics in the CofE. This leads to prejudicial attitudes.

However, there are three additional points that require discussion to clarify my argument. Firstly, there is the nature of self-esteem. It is a potentially tricky concept to define and appears to be often misunderstood by non-specialist audiences, perhaps because of the ease of access one has to 'pop psychology'. It is therefore imperative to define more precisely how I am using the term. It is a 'sociometer' that measures one's sense of worth in relationship to others (Leary and Baumeister, 2000). In this regard, self-esteem is that which monitors one's social context to discern the extent of a person's relational value, making the pursuit of self-esteem the pursuit of high appraisals (Leary, 2005). I therefore argue that the clergy who evince sexism do so because of their perception that the introduction of women into what has historically been a male-only sphere diminishes their privileged status as men, as priests, and as conservative evangelicals or traditional Anglo-Catholics.

Secondly, self-esteem is either contingent or non-contingent. The former refers to self-esteem that is dependent on external sources, whereas the latter—also referred to as trait self-esteem—denotes one's sense of self-worth over time (Mruk, 1995). Threatened self-esteem, and therefore this research, is concerned with contingent self-esteem. Thus, the clergy who evince sexism do so because their contingent self-esteem is being threatened by the advent of women's ordination to the priesthood and consecration as bishops.

Thirdly, I have demonstrated that whilst women are the objects of sexism, it is both women and ministers in other (Anglican) theological traditions more broadly that are avoided by the clergy with conservative gender attitudes. I have already demonstrated that the CofE takes on symbolic meaning for the participants who evince sexist attitudes, and that this leads them to avoid individuals who they associate with the CofE, particularly women. Therefore, the avoidance of the wider Church ought to be understood as participants distancing themselves from what the wider Church symbolises for them, namely the theological liberalism that has led to the admission of women to

176 *Summary, reflections, and implications*

the priesthood and the episcopate, the very phenomena that threatens their self-esteem.

Social capital and spiritual capital

In this context, social and spiritual capital are best understood as a product of the interaction between individuals who share a particular contingency—or contingencies—of self-worth. The clergy with prejudicial attitudes interact most with those who are fellow male priests in their respective traditions. Naturally, this is where social capital and spiritual capital are most evident. The influence of social and spiritual capital on participants' self-esteem, however, is circular, not linear: social capital and spiritual capital reinforce the sense of social identity shared with ingroup members through the process of bonding members together in an exclusive manner (see Putnam, 2000). The bonding process reinforces shared identity because group commitment (the result of self-categorisation) reinforces contingent self-esteem (Ellemers, Kortekaas and Ouwerkerk, 1999), which—as I have noted—is dependent upon belonging within a social group. By denying resources to those beyond the group, the ingroup is better positioned to maintain higher levels of self-esteem over and against outgroups. Whilst the link between social capital and self-esteem has been previously noted (e.g., Gonzales and Hancock, 2011), these studies are rare and only relatively recent.

There exists a lack of knowledge on the relationship between spiritual capital and self-esteem and on the relationship between religion, self-esteem, and social capital. This research, however, demonstrates how these bonds manifest in the lives of devotees and the impact that it has on them. Spiritual capital is evidently not only useful for understanding the privilege enjoyed by certain social groups, which previous research has demonstrated (e.g., Page, 2017); it also enables one to identify the very phenomena that reinforce a group's self-esteem when it is used in an exclusivist manner such as member-specific networks or Communion. In this respect, social capital and spiritual capital can also provide insight into the specific behaviours that can mitigate threats to contingent self-esteem because it is the process of ingroup bonding and the reinforcement of group identity that enables individuals in any given ingroup to maintain and increase self-esteem (see Tajfel and Turner, 1979, 1986). Given that this leads to less contact with outgroups, the sexist attitudes of the clergy are also shaped by the specific ways in which they consume social capital and spiritual capital.

The historical context

I argue that priests with a sexist outlook are influenced by the threat to their contingent self-esteem brought about by the ordination of women. This argument is further advanced by considering the traditions they have opted into. I have outlined at length the negative, and at times hostile, reactions that evangelicalism has had towards changing gender norms, an attitude that is consistent with self-esteem threat. I have also demonstrated how this aspect of the tradition's history is expressed by conservative evangelical clergy in the present. There is thus an evident continuity of resistance towards increasing gender equality that has been identified in the narratives of the Reform participants.

Similarly, I have explained that Anglo-Catholicism emerged as a reactionary movement against the perceived threat to the status of the (then all male) clergy in English society, indicating that this tradition historically resists perceived threats to their status. Moreover, one must take note of the fact that resistance among theologically conservative clergy towards society, and towards the CofE, has historically been at its most prominent during times of increased equality for women. This is more than a mere coincidence.

The privileged status that white, middle-class men continue to enjoy in society is well documented. I have demonstrated that most of those interviewed match this description. In fact, this is true for all those participants who evinced sexism, despite a minority of participants, such as Adrian, having working-class roots. In addition to this, clergy understand themselves as having an elite status, akin to that which academics enjoy (Aldridge, 1993), which has historically been associated with the middle class. Many of the participants were either ordained or in the process of ordination training when the research for Aldridge's article was underway. The remainder of the participants revealed that they worked in close proximity to, and under the leadership of, those who inherited this understanding of clergy status. For instance, those who were a part of Forward in Faith or Reform have opted into a network that has been run by the generation of clergy that Aldridge describes. The clergy who displayed sexism are therefore operating in a context where their privileged status was assumed.

This privileged status would have encompassed the concept of 'maleness' in particular because historically the clergy have always been male, and even the younger participants surrounded themselves with those who take the view that only men are suitable for at least some forms of Church leadership. I have demonstrated that this was true prior to ordination training, during training, and after their ordination. In other words, even for those clergymen who were ordained into a Church that also ordains women, the privilege of men in that institution was normative. Given that maleness is a part of the privileged identity of these clergymen, the idea of women priests or bishops would indeed be a threat to their contingent self-esteem because it would require them to share social resources (used to achieve status) with an outgroup.

The fact that the clergymen interviewed have opted into their respective traditions indicates that tight coupling contributes to their self-esteem as well as to the responses that participants have towards women as a result of self-esteem threat. As discussed in the methodology, Swingewood (2000) argues that one opts into a social framework that binds groups together because it

178 *Summary, reflections, and implications*

serves their motives. It is unsurprising that men of privilege with a sense of priestly vocation would choose to immerse themselves in groups such as Reform or Forward in Faith because by joining (or remaining in) such groups or their associated traditions these men can continue to operate in a social sphere that affords them a privileged status. Membership of such social networks provides these clergymen with higher levels of contingent self-esteem through a sense of shared worth and belonging with those who they perceive to be similar to themselves (i.e., white, tertiary-educated, male Protestants).

Embracing their respective multiple traditions (i.e., Anglican *and* conservative evangelical/traditional Anglo-Catholic) also means that these priests embrace the heritage related to each one (see Vasey-Saunders, 2015). Participants' contingent self-esteem is therefore shaped by where they situate themselves on the crossroads of history and the present. Moreover, whilst self-categorisation theory acknowledges that self-esteem is impacted by one's perception of the historical norms of their social group, I argue that this idea needs to be further developed: the historical traditions *themselves,* when they are embraced by the clergy, impact upon their contingent self-esteem because by opting into a conservative tradition their status as male priests becomes a part of their self-worth. Hence, the fact of women's ordination becomes a self-esteem threat.

Engaged orthodoxy

The conservative evangelical—and the majority of Anglo-Catholic—clergy interviewed evidently hold an ambiguous attitude towards their denomination. Considering the analysis so far, the tension between rejection and acceptance of the Established Church that these clergy navigate is best understood as resulting from the fact that their identity lies in their Anglican priesthood, but that this identity is also under threat via some members of the wider (Anglican) group. However, as aforementioned, social identities are dependent on outgroups to compete with and react against, to reinforce the identity of the ingroup (see also Bielo, 2011). This means that those clergymen who evince engaged orthodoxy are dependent on the very institution that threatens their identity to preserve their Anglican-evangelical or traditional Anglo-Catholic identity. Participants' engaged orthodoxy is thus an outworking of an intergroup paradox. Evangelical identity has been shown to thrive off this tension in the US context (Smith et al., 1998), and its applicability has been demonstrated in the English context (Guest, 2007a). Nevertheless, the current analysis shows that this model applies to other types of conservative Protestants, namely traditional Anglo-Catholics. It also provides an explanation of how engaged orthodoxy relates to self-esteem: clergy who hold sexist attitudes also do so because their sense of identity (and thus their self-esteem) is dependent upon an ambivalent attitude towards their denomination. It is the negative response to the wider CofE that provides the fertile soil in which sexism grows, given the lack of contact and social resource sharing that accompanies this side of ambivalence.

Summary, reflections, and implications 179

This, of course, becomes somewhat circular over time, however, as prejudice itself encourages contact avoidance.

Affirming clergy

I refer to those who did not evince a sexist outlook as 'affirming clergy' because they were happy to accept women as priests and bishops, and in a broader variety of other roles in society without reservation. I have previously established that these clergymen have their identities as male priests in either the charismatic evangelical tradition or in Anglo-Catholicism. They too operate within networks that are predominantly white, middle class, and tertiary educated. This is consistent with the embrace of a tradition that reflects a level of privilege. However, there is apparently no threat to their contingent self-esteem from women's ordination as priests or consecration as bishops given that they do not evince any of the criteria for intergroup tensions or associated prejudices. There are two distinct, yet related, phenomena within the data that explain this.

Firstly, these participants evidently work with their female colleagues beyond their specific traditions. Indeed, there was a lack of women priests within their traditions in neighbouring parishes. Much of the work on prejudice and intergroup contact has demonstrated that working with outgroups, particularly on projects that require mutual dependence, undermines prejudice and leads members of different social groups to view each other as belonging to one, superordinate group (e.g., see Brown, 2011). Nevertheless, it can be difficult to ascertain whether those who do so are less prejudiced to begin with or whether contact undermines their prejudice. This is because the quantitative studies indicate that both can be simultaneously true (Brown, 2011). Thus, it is likely that both work in tandem.

Secondly (and more specifically), affirming clergymen from both the evangelical and the Anglo-Catholic traditions demonstrate a bridging approach to their social capital and spiritual capital. That is, rather than reinforcing an exclusive group identity through bonding, these participants form relationships with those outside of their immediate social group to share capital with them. An examination of social capital and spiritual capital between social groups—or between groups that one may expect to have distinct social identities (i.e., bridging capital)—has highlighted the specific ways in which prejudice-reducing contact becomes manifest by highlighting the specific instances of contact that are present.

In addition to this, the affirming clergy interviewed did not evince engaged orthodoxy to the same extent as the other groups. The most likely explanation for this is that the CofE and their female colleagues are simply not considered to be outgroups, or at least are not outgroups unworthy of creating bridging capital with. This suggests that such participants would be able to pursue and/or maintain self-esteem through the social resources that they access via others in the CofE, including female clergy.

180 *Summary, reflections, and implications*

There is an additional matter that must also be considered. The charismatic evangelical participants were not typically part of a formal network that met on a regular basis. This means that there are fewer opportunities for them to share social or spiritual capital with colleagues in the same tradition as themselves. It also means that there are fewer opportunities for this aspect of their identity to be reinforced to the same extent as with Reform or Forward in Faith. Thus, the divide between them and potential outgroups within the wider Church will be less pronounced. Notwithstanding, that they have inherited a tradition that has also tended to be affirming of women in positions of church leadership ought not to be overlooked.

The two Anglo-Catholic participants who did not evince sexism explained that they had changed their theology based on their interactions with women priests, whether that contact was direct or indirect. Evan's theological assumptions about women were evidently challenged amidst ongoing contact of the kind that undermines prejudice, which included sharing capital. He also saw his Church Army friend in priestly terms, meaning that he recognised her potential to provide spiritual capital through divine grace bestowed on believers through the priest's presiding at the Eucharist. According to Anglo-Catholic belief, this provides grace for salvation.

Aaron's case was less obvious because the contact with a woman priest that led him to change his attitude in this area was indirect. However, the spiritual capital lens can provide further insight. He explained that the way that his colleague presided at Communion impressed him because there was no difference between the way that she consecrated the bread and wine and what he considered best practice. He, therefore, was able to receive spiritual capital from her. Thus, for Aaron, seeing a woman priest providing this capital competently has contributed to his more affirming attitude of women's ordination to the priesthood and consecration as bishops. Whilst traditional Anglo-Catholics doubt the efficacy of the sacraments when performed by a woman, Aaron did not believe he had a reason to do so once he saw a woman appear to preside at the altar in the same manner as men.

Both cases are also a matter of self-esteem because these participants would have been able to share in the spiritual resources that women priests offer through administering Communion, helping them to attain a specific religious status as a recipient of divine grace. Aaron's role as a military chaplain at this stage in his ministry is also relevant. As he was regularly away, he was unable to immerse himself in a network such as Forward in Faith, and as the only priest in much of his working context, he would not have been afforded the same opportunities to reinforce his assumptions about the role of women in the Church like many of his traditional Anglo-Catholic colleagues.

An integrated methodology

Therefore, in keeping with the epistemological underpinning of this monograph, there are evidently numerous factors that shape male clergy attitudes

Summary, reflections, and implications 181

towards women, particularly clergy. This epistemology specifically claims that it does not offer sole insight into the social world. In doing so it provides an important opportunity to understand human thinking and interaction from multiple yet complementary angles. Critical realism—particularly the stratification of reality—and tight coupling have thus provided an effective platform for the exploration of a multiplicity of factors that shape human attitudes towards gender. Collectively, these theoretical lenses offer an explanation of social causality that recognises human agency as well as the role of contextual factors for shaping events and attitudes. Moreover, by highlighting multiple segments of the social world and explaining how they fit together, the argument within this monograph possesses higher levels of explanatory power for understanding the data than would otherwise be the case.

An integrated theory of participants' gender attitudes towards female clergy

Previous scholarship has argued that self-esteem, intergroup contact, and prejudice are intimately related psychological phenomena. I have argued that historical social attitudes shape self-esteem and the related attitudes towards—including contact with—outgroups. I have further argued that social capital, spiritual capital, and engaged orthodoxy do likewise. In light of this, I will articulate a theory of the causes of theologically conservative Anglican male clergy attitudes towards female clergy that integrates the above into a conceptual whole. Although I have explored participants' gender attitudes towards women beyond the CofE, much of the evidence for their attitudes involve specifically female clergy within the Established Church. Therefore, much of the sexism discussed has been context-dependent, with the gender-related prejudice identified being manifest towards women clergy.

As has been established, the contingent self-esteem of those interviewed is reliant upon their intersectional identities as male Anglican priests, either as evangelicals or as Anglo-Catholics. These identities are shaped by each tradition's history, and the clergy decide to opt into (or remain in) their respective traditions in the pursuit of self-esteem. This leads them to interact with those who are also male evangelical/Anglo-Catholic Anglican priests. During this contact, social capital and spiritual capital are shared amongst their ingroups and, for those most resistant to other groups, symbolic boundaries are drawn between themselves and other groups that they encounter within the CofE, particularly women as they do not inhabit a male identity. This enables members of such groups to further pursue or maintain their self-esteem by distinguishing themselves from others. However, the emergence of symbolic boundaries also involves navigating a tension between contact and avoidance with outgroups to affirm one's social identity by contrasting their ingroup to others, whereas those who do not draw symbolic boundaries with the wider Church to the same extent engage in the process of bridging social and/or spiritual capital. Both sets of actions serve the advancement of the group's contingent self-esteem.

182 *Summary, reflections, and implications*

Furthermore, whether a group reacts negatively or positively towards an outgroup depends upon the extent to which their self-esteem is threatened by the outgroup in any given social sphere. In the present case, whether a group is threatened by the outgroup in question (female clergy) is primarily shaped by the extent to which their tradition (i.e., ingroup) has historically engaged with women in positions of authority in the Church sphere. Those from traditions that have affirmed and engaged with women in such positions have not inherited intersecting identities that rely on male-only spheres of religious authority. Rather, they have benefited from social resources through such interactions. In contradistinction, those who do not engage with such women have inherited intersecting identities that rely on male-only spheres of authority in the Church, hence the threat to their self-esteem with the arrival of women's ordination to the priesthood. Therefore, if a social group feels able to share social or spiritual resources, then the threat of the other group is limited because the ingroup's contingent self-esteem is still advanced. However, if these resources are not shared then one's social group is understood to be in fiercer competition with others.

Moreover, how a group manages their social and/or spiritual capital shapes prejudice, or the lack thereof, because bridging capital leads to the types of contact that undermine prejudice, whereas bonding capital facilitates contact avoidance. Moreover, because prejudice encourages contact avoidance, the way social and/or spiritual capital is managed leads to a cycle of either positive interaction or avoidance of outgroups. Thus, it is the process of behaviours related to capital that is pivotal for intergroup relations and participants' attitudes towards other groups of clergy, particularly women. This aspect of attitude formation is therefore multifaceted with behaviour shaping attitudes in addition to being a component of them.

This is juxtaposed alongside the role of emotions during contact which can lead to contact avoidance in the form of schismatic behaviours, the result of identity conflict and an accompanying perceived lack of voice. This likewise helps facilitate prejudice and can be caused by outgroup responses to those with gender traditionalist outlooks. Equally, sufficient levels of a perceived voice within intergroup processes can encourage interaction and thus serve to undermine prejudice. The above must sit alongside the role of gender schemata which, being formed early in life, provide individuals with ingrained assumptions about gender (through family, religious, and other networks) that are difficult to alter, particularly (although not exclusively) for heterosexual persons because these schemata effectively filter gender-related information so that people tend to incorporate information that is congruent with pre-existing assumptions about gender. The type of schemata will either encourage rigid stereotypes that contribute to prejudice, or they will enable one to see gender more flexibly, resist at least some stereotyping and thereby undermine the possibility of prejudicial gender attitudes. They can therefore contribute to the cyclical nature of prejudice and contact avoidance if they are sex-typed and thus consist of stereotypes.

Summary, reflections, and implications 183

There is, however, a nuance to my theory. Intergroup relations are circular rather than linear. There is no clear point at which relations within a group or between groups start or stop. My articulation of an integrated theory is thus concerned with separating the distinct components of my participants' gender attitudes so that they may be examined, understood, and explained.

A further reflection on engaged orthodoxy

Those acquainted with Smith et al.'s (1998) model will be aware that they dismiss the idea that social discontent lies behind the ambivalent engagement that conservative Protestants exhibit towards their wider social context. Their argument certainly holds given their data in the US comes primarily from working-class communities. However, the present analysis indicates that, in the English context, their dismissal does not apply. Whilst this monograph has not evidenced status discontent theory in the way that Smith et al. explore it, it has nevertheless found that the sense of threat to one's social status is at the core of clergy gender prejudice. This highlights the need to apply caution before translating a theoretical lens derived from another culture into a different context. It also highlights the distinct challenges that arise when examining the narratives of religious professionals because the question of status is central, particularly in the English context where Anglican clerics have enjoyed privileged status for centuries.

However, in his later work, Smith (2017) recognises the utility of a critical realist epistemology in enabling one to distinguish between a causal factor and the multiplicity of ways in which it can influence the social world, depending on the context in which it is at work. This means that whilst the manifestation of a causal mechanism shaping conservative Protestant reactions to changes within modernity may vary from one culture to another, the causal factor itself is constant. The pursuit of self-esteem would be the latter. In fact, Smith et al. (1998) recognise that self-esteem has been identified as an important factor in intergroup relations. Nevertheless, the way that this works itself out does vary between groups of higher and lower social status, which explains the differences between my findings and Smith et al.'s.

Implications

The fact that sexism has been found in the narratives of a significant number of the clergy partaking in this research poses an important question for the Established Church. In the introduction, I explained that gender equality is a normative value in contemporary England, and that affiliation with the CofE is not only at a historic low but now less than half of the country consider themselves to be a member of the CofE, practising or otherwise (British Social Attitudes, 2018). The publication of the 2021 census results further underscores this pattern of Anglican decline (Office for National Statistics, 2022). Whilst some evidence indicates that de-secularisation may be an

184 *Summary, reflections, and implications*

emerging phenomenon within England, the position of the CofE is nevertheless a precarious one, not least because much church growth exists outside of mainline denominations (see Goodhew and Cooper, 2018). Moreover, de-secularisation is not the equivalent of re-sacralisation (Brown, 2018), and so the place of the Established Church in England will likely remain precarious.

Additionally, as the evangelical tradition within the CofE is the largest one, the gender attitudes explored in this monograph could arguably become even more commonplace amongst the clergy. It is therefore prudent and timely for the CofE to re-evaluate its training for ordinands and clergy, the reflective practices of clergy, and its ecclesial practices in a way that fosters more positive attitudes towards women. I will therefore outline some ways that the Church could approach this concern.

Implications for training[1]

This study has identified that the sharing of social and spiritual capital is an important factor for understanding clergy attitudes towards women. It has also demonstrated that contact which involves co-operation and goal sharing likewise aids understanding of this and is present in the narratives of clergy who hold affirming attitudes towards women clergy. In light of this, the discernment process for ordained ministers must consider the proven ability for potential ordinands to collaborate and share resources with those who are socially distinct from themselves as a required criterion for selection for training. Whilst (the recently amended) selection criteria for ordained ministry has required evidence of collaboration as a prerequisite of selection for ordination, it has not specified that examples must be provided from interactions with people quite distinct from themselves (see Church of England, n.d.). Also, whilst those training for ministry must adhere to the Five Guiding Principles, this does not amount to agreeing to work closely with those who have different theological positions. Rather, clergy are only required to assent to the fact that the CofE has reached a firm decision on the appropriateness of women's ordination and consecration regardless of one's personal beliefs on the matter.

Nevertheless, prejudice reduction is unlikely to occur if it is coerced rather than purely voluntary (Brown, 2011). Notwithstanding, if would-be clergy must evince a willingness to engage with those who are likely to identify with different social groups to themselves, then this will not present itself as a significant issue because those approved for ordination training will be more willing to do so.

The CofE's theological colleges are currently required to ensure that ordinands are willing to serve within the breadth and diversity of the CofE. Whilst placements form a part of an ordinand's theological training, several participants explained that during their placements they had very little engagement with clergy from other traditions that required sustained contact

Summary, reflections, and implications   185

and/or co-operation. It is therefore important that training institutions do ensure exposure to breadth and diversity alongside active co-operation with those from other traditions, as part of all ordinands' placements. This could involve the design of activities that require the sharing of social and spiritual capital, co-operation, and goal sharing over extended periods.

It is also worth affirming some of the current ways that the CofE is including women in the life of the Church. The increase of women in theological education institutions in recent years has the ability to cultivate a more affirming culture of women's ministry. Tutors and lecturers in the Church's training institutions will be sharing spiritual resources with ordinands through the process of teaching and enabling them to form priestly identities. The increased presence of women bishops may also help facilitate higher levels of gender equality given that their ways of working could, in theory, challenge assumptions about the possibility of their priestly status as a woman priest did for Aaron.

Implications for ecclesial practices

The CofE functions in a way that allows gender traditionalists to boycott the authority of women as priests and bishops. This is a form of schism in functional terms because they are permitted to place themselves under the authority of a gender traditionalist bishop, meaning that they do not come under the jurisdiction of their diocesan bishop to the same extent that other clergy do. This has been arranged for the sake of supposed unity; the Established Church has claimed that if different traditions co-exist with their differences, it can consider itself to be a unified denomination (see Carey, 2004). Equally, the CofE has made it clear that it expects gender traditionalists to accept that the Church is clear in its commitment to ordaining women to the priesthood and consecrating them as bishops (see Ferns, 2014).

In light of this, it would be consistent with current ecclesial practice for the CofE to adopt something similar to what Linda Woodhead refers to as the 'franchise model'[2] for gender traditionalist clergy. This is the idea that such traditions within the CofE should seek to sustain themselves under revised diocesan boundaries, rather than rely on the wider Church.[3] Woodhead explained that this will also allow such churches greater autonomy because they can decide how to direct their resources and have their own bishops with theological convictions that they are more comfortable with. It therefore also provides a firmer divide between gender traditionalist pockets of the Established Church and the wider CofE.

The merit in this idea lies in the fact that identities rely on exclusivity for their existence. It is, therefore, possible that clergy who express sexism will not readily change their outlook towards the CofE, simply because they need to oppose it to maintain their present sense of identity. In this model, they will remain a part of the CofE and Anglican Communion whilst also gaining in autonomy. However, in this scenario, future women priests in positions of

186 *Summary, reflections, and implications*

ecclesial authority (such as bishops) will no longer have to relinquish authority to flying bishops because the dioceses will no longer incorporate congregations with gender traditionalist clergy by default. This would allow women to operate in a context where female authority was normative and unquestioned. Importantly, the autonomy experienced by gender traditionalist clergy in this context undermines the risks of dejection occurring as the result of marginalisation, leading to further withdrawal, which can bolster prejudice.

A preliminary, sociologically-informed reflection on the implications and Christian theology

This is not the place to offer a substantial reflection on Christian theology. However, the CofE is a religious institution and so theology is presumably an important aspect of its ecclesial practices. If my suggestions are to appeal to the Church, it is important to offer at least an initial starting point for a theological conversation that considers my solution to the issue of sexism. Sociologist of religion and Episcopalian priest Randal Balmer (2016) has offered a similar reflection on another topic, but which has some relevance for the present purpose. He argues that conservative Protestants must avoid working with mainline churches if their congregations are to thrive in the US context because, Balmer believes, a partisan and separatist approach to religion protects different churches from being too similar, thus allowing them to compete in the marketplace of religion and attract more followers. Balmer realises that for his ideas to be implemented, a theological lens must be offered to the US Church to justify his sociological position because, like the CofE, it appeals to theology to justify their actions. Balmer uses Jesus' prayer for Christian unity in John 17 as his starting point. He then explains that this is to be realised at the Second Coming[4] rather than during earthly life. Balmer thus argues that it is theologically acceptable for conservative Protestants to avoid interacting with other theological traditions in the present.

There are two issues with this, however. The first is that actively discouraging any contact between gender traditionalist and female clergy would only help facilitate prejudice. Therefore, in this model, all clergy wishing to be ordained within the CofE ought to adhere to the suggestions made for the selection process above and those I have outlined elsewhere (Fry, 2021b). Secondly, Balmer's suggestion is lacking one key component. Many biblical scholars agree that there is an eschatological significance to much of the New Testament, but they also argue that an inaugurated eschatology exists, meaning that the implications of the Second Coming start to manifest on Earth at the present time, despite being fully realised in the future (e.g., see Dunn, 1998). I thus posit that my final suggestion for tackling clerical sexism readily reflects this theological tension because it offers a looser form of affiliation with the CofE whilst falling short of an official break within it and the wider Anglican Communion.

Summary, reflections, and implications 187

Additional considerations

It is also worthwhile articulating a warning that relates to how gender traditionalists are viewed within the Established Church. All persons are predisposed to distinguish themselves from some and align themselves with others, forming ingroups and outgroups, which can (but does not necessarily) facilitate prejudice. This stems from the evolutionary need to live in manageable-sized communities (Harari, 2011). The Reform and Anglo-Catholic narratives indicated the presence of instances when other clergy had drawn clear distinctions between themselves and the participants. Such behaviour risks reinforcing outgroup prejudice amongst gender traditionalists towards women through bolstering their sense of belonging to a distinct group *and* amongst those with egalitarian gender attitudes towards gender traditionalists for the same reason. It is counterproductive to create fertile soil in which prejudice towards gender traditionalists can grow whilst attempting to address gender prejudice because it swaps one type of prejudice for another.

Indeed, as I have highlighted above, participants possess multiple (intersecting) social identities. It is not true in any straightforward way that all gender traditionalist participants hold exclusively privileged identities. I have already discussed the impact of Adrian's sense of marginalisation as a gay man with a working-class background in the third chapter. It is therefore important for the CofE to consider how it will seek to reduce prejudice and adopt the above suggestions in such a way that does not risk creating yet more prejudice amongst the clergy or a sense of marginalisation for those who also possess social identities that fall foul of other social norms.

Moreover, as the Established Church, the CofE's role is to be accessible to all, yet its historical gender values and related attitudes have alienated a generation of women, which has led to subsequent generations lacking the significant connection with the CofE that their ancestors had (see Brown & Woodhead, 2016). This disconnection was apparent in the 2012 vote on consecrating women as bishops. The then Prime Minister, David Cameron, told the CofE to "get on with it" (Wintour and Davies, 2012), i.e., allow women to become bishops. Rowan Williams, the Archbishop of Canterbury at the time, also expressed his concern that the rejection of consecrating women to the episcopate would not be understandable to wider society (Wintour and Davies, 2012). In this respect, the present research highlights the disjunction between the English Church and the people it is supposed to serve. The above suggestions, and those I have discussed elsewhere (Fry, 2021b), possess the potential to help correct this.

Conclusion

In this chapter, I have unpacked the causes of participants' gender attitudes. In doing so, I have argued that self-esteem is a significant factor shaping how

188 Summary, reflections, and implications

male clergy from theologically conservative traditions within the CofE respond to the advent of women's ordination as priests and their consecration as bishops. I have also posited that self-esteem works in combination with social capital, spiritual capital, and symbolic boundaries in fostering the types of contact (or its lack) that can either undermine or support sexism. Moreover, I have argued that where one searches for self-esteem is dependent upon their intersectional identities and the historical inheritance of those identities. This pursuit of self-esteem can lead to actions that are described by the model of engaged orthodoxy and it is the familial and religious context of a person's early life that make gender attitudes within a given social sphere more or less plausible because of the gender schemata that these can foster.

Notes

1 Further implications for training can also be found in Fry (2021b).
2 This is from my notes on an unpublished public lecture given by Woodhead on 19 October 2016 on her co-authored book *That Was the Church That Was: How the Church of England Lost the English People* at Newcastle Cathedral.
3 Personal communication, 27 October 2018.
4 The Christian belief in the return of Christ to judge the world and restore it to a sinless state.

References

Aldridge, A. (1993). Negotiating status: Social scientists and Anglican clergy. *Journal of Contemporary Ethnography, 22*(1), 97–112.

Allport, G. (1954/1979). *The nature of prejudice.* Cambridge, MA: Perseus Books.

Balmer, R. (2016). *Evangelicalism in America.* Waco, TX: Baylor University Press.

Baumeister, R.F., Smart, L., & Boden, J.M. (1996). Relation of threatened egotism to violence and aggression: The dark side of high self-esteem. *Psychological Review, 103*(1), 5–33.

Bielo, J.S. (2011). *Emerging evangelicals: Faith, modernity, and the desire for authenticity.* New York: NYU Press.

British Social Attitudes. (2018). *Chapter summary: Religion.* Retrieved from http://www.bsa.natcen.ac.uk/latest-report/british-social-attitudes-28/religion.aspx.

Brown, R. (2011). *Prejudice: Its social psychology.* Hoboken, NJ: John Wiley & Sons.

Brown, D. (2018, October 28). *Real or imagined? Measuring long-term patterns of political secularisation and desecularisation* [Paper presentation]. Society for the Scientific Study of Religion, Las Vegas, NV, United States.

Brown, A., & Woodhead, L. (2016). *That was the Church that was: How the Church of England lost the English people.* London: Bloomsbury.

Bushman, B.J., & Baumeister, R.F. (1998). Threatened egotism, narcissism, self-esteem, and direct and displaced aggression: Does self-love or self-hate lead to violence? *Journal of Personality and Social Psychology, 75*(1), 219–229.

Carey, G. (2004). *Know the truth: A memoir.* London: HarperCollins.

Church of England. (n.d.). *Understanding discernment*. Retrieved from https://www. churchofengland.org/life-events/vocations/preparing-ordained-ministry/understanding-discernment.

Crocker, J., Luhtanen, R.K., Cooper, M.L., & Bouvrette, A. (2003). Contingencies of self-worth in college students: theory and measurement. *Journal of Personality and Social Psychology, 85*(5), 894–908.

Crocker, J., & Knight, K.M. (2005). Contingencies of self-worth. *Current Directions in Psychological Science, 14*(4), 200–203.

Dunn, J. (1998). *The theology of Paul the apostle*. Grand Rapids, MI: William B. Eerdmans Publishing Company.

Ellemers, N., Kortekaas, P., & Ouwerkerk, J.W. (1999). Self-categorisation, commitment to the group and group self-esteem as related but distinct aspects of social identity. *European Journal of Social Psychology, 29*(2–3), 371–389.

Ferns, S. (2014). *The five guiding principles: Guidance for candidates for ordination in the Church of England*. Ministry Division. Retrieved from https://www. churchofengland.org/sites/default/files/2017-10/the_five_guiding_principles.pdf.

Fry, A.D.J. (2019a). Justifying gender inequality in the Church of England: An examination of theologically conservative male clergy attitudes towards women's ordination. *Fieldwork in Religion, 14*(1), 8–32.

Fry, A.D.J. (2021b). Clergy, capital and gender inequality: An assessment of how social and spiritual capital are denied to women priests in the Church of England. *Gender, Work & Organization, 21*(6), 2091–2113.

Glick, P., & Fiske, S.T. (1996). The ambivalent sexism inventory: Differentiating hostile and benevolent sexism. *Journal of Personality and Social Psychology, 70*(3), 491–512.

Gonzales, A.L., & Hancock, J.T. (2011). Mirror, mirror on my Facebook wall: Effects of exposure to Facebook on self-esteem. *Cyberpsychology, Behavior, and Social Networking, 14*(1–2), 79–83.

Goodhew, D., & Cooper, A-P. (Eds.). (2018). *The desecularisation of the city: London's churches, 1980 to the present*. Oxford: Routledge.

Guest, M. (2007a). *Evangelical identity and contemporary culture: A congregational study in innovation*. Eugene, OR: Wipf and Stock Publishers.

Harari, Y.N. (2011). *Sapiens: A brief history of humankind*. London: Penguin Random House.

Jost, J.T., & Banaji, M.R. (1994). The role of stereotyping in system-justification and the production of false consciousness. *British Journal of Social Psychology, 33*(1), 1–27.

Jost, J.T., Banaji, M.R., & Nosek, B.A. (2004). A decade of system justification theory: Accumulated evidence of conscious and unconscious bolstering of the status quo. *Political Psychology, 25*(6), 881–919.

Leary, M.R. (2005). Sociometer theory and the pursuit of relational value: Getting to the root of self-esteem. *European Review of Social Psychology, 16*(1), 75–111.

Leary, M.R., & Baumeister, R.F. (2000). The nature and function of self-esteem: Sociometer theory. In *Advances in Experimental Social Psychology, 32*, 1–62.

Mruk. C. (1995). *Self-esteem: Research, theory, and practice*. New York: Springer.

Office for National Statistics. (2022). *Religion, England and Wales: 2021 Census*. Retrieved from https://www.ons.gov.uk/peoplepopulationandcommunity/culturali dentity/religion/bulletins/religionenglandandwales/census2021.

190 *Summary, reflections, and implications*

Page, S-J. (2017). Anglican clergy husbands securing middle-class gendered privilege through religion. *Sociological Research Online, 22*(1), 1–13.

Putnam, R.D. (2000). *Bowling alone: The collapse and revival of American community*. New York: Simon and Schuster.

Sani, F., & Reicher, S. (2000). Contested identities and schisms in groups: Opposing the ordination of women as priests in the Church of England. *British Journal of Social Psychology, 39*(1), 95–112.

Smith, C. (2017). *Religion. What it is, how it works, and why it matters*. Princeton, NJ: Princeton University Press.

Smith, C. with Emerson, M., Gallagher, S., Kennedy, P., & Sikkink, D. (1998). *American evangelicalism: Embattled and thriving*. Chicago, IL: University of Chicago Press.

Swingewood, A. (2000). *A short history of sociological thought*, 3rd ed. Aldershot: Palgrave.

Tajfel, H., & Turner, J.C. (1979). An integrative theory of intergroup conflict. *The Social Psychology of Intergroup Relations, 33*(47), 33–47.

Tajfel, H., & Turner, J.C. (1986). The social identity theory of intergroup behaviour. In S. Worchel & W.G. Austin (Eds.), *Psychology of intergroup relations* (pp. 7–24). Chicago, IL: Nelson Hall.

Turner, J.C., & Oakes, P.J. (1986). The significance of the social identity concept for social psychology with reference to individualism, interactionism and social influence. *British Journal of Social Psychology, 25*(3), 237–252.

Vasey-Saunders, M. (2015). *The scandal of evangelicals and homosexuality: English Evangelical Texts, 1960–2010*. London: Routledge.

Wintour, P., & Davies, L. (2012, November 21). *David Cameron: Church of England should "get on with it" on female bishops*. The Guardian. Retrieved from https://www.theguardian.com/world/2012/nov/21/david-cameron-church-female-bishops.

9 Conclusion

Introduction

In the previous chapter, I theorised the social factors that shape participants' gender attitudes and discussed their implications. In this final chapter, I will articulate a more general theory of the social factors that shape gender attitudes based on my findings, before signposting to possible directions of future research and offering some final concluding thoughts. As explained in the introduction, the data gathered for analysis in this monograph contains the assumption that the nature of the traditional biological categories of 'man' and 'woman' as binary sexes are self-evident, even when assumptions about gender are more flexible. There was no consideration of those who do not biologically fit into such a binary and rarely of those who are not cisgender. The data informing scholarship on sexism that I have employed likewise views sex in binary terms. When I discuss gender attitudes, therefore, I am specifically concerned with the attitudes that people have towards men and women who fit such a binary, with respect to the roles that they feel each sex ought to occupy within society. My theory therefore applies to those who view sex in a somewhat binary way, including those whose assumptions about gender are nevertheless more flexible.

Intersecting social strata

In the previous chapter, I outlined a series of factors that converge to shape male clergy gender attitudes. All but two of these factors are ubiquitous across society. All persons pursue self-esteem and partake in intergroup processes in line with their (multiple) identities and which shape these identities and the attitudes held towards others. This means that the drawing of symbolic boundaries will be commonplace also. Nearly all persons will belong to a social network from which they derive social resources, meaning that the vast majority within a society will undergo bonding and/or bridging processes. All persons have schemata with which they interpret the world around them. My theory of how one's gender attitudes are formed is therefore applicable beyond the context of theologically conservative male clergy within the CofE.

DOI: 10.4324/9781003081913-9

192   *Conclusion*

Nevertheless, two factors that are not as commonly found are inherited religious traditions and spiritual capital. It is true that contemporary English society has been shaped by Christianity, particularly Anglicanism, and it is true that there is evidence that the non-religious can possess spiritual beliefs (Theos, 2013) and undertake spiritual practices (Heelas and Woodhead, 2004). There is also evidence that some possess eclectic belief systems where they weave strands of different worldviews together into an individualised system of belief (Lyon, 2000).[1] However, among the wider population, these do not consistently amount to inherited historical religious traditions with clearly defined communities that one actively and intentionally participates in (e.g., see Altglas, 2014), even though some alternative spiritualities may well have these elements (e.g., see Harvey and Vincett, 2012). In other words, taking society as a whole, one cannot be said to have their gender attitudes formed by historical beliefs that are embedded in the religious social networks within which they operate whilst drawing symbolic boundaries between these groups and others. A more general theory will therefore need to think more broadly than the concepts of 'religious tradition' and 'spiritual capital' allow.

Notwithstanding, people do belong to social groups that will similarly have inherited particular ways of thinking about gender, even if the group identities have not been formed in response towards changing gender norms. At a rudimentary level, inherited religious traditions are not distinct in function from other types of group belonging with specific regard to their ability to confer a social identity that shapes values, beliefs, behaviours, and emotion responses and which offers social resources to those within that group.

Extrapolating my theory for the wider population then, gender attitudes are formed in the process of intergroup relations. An individual's contingent self-esteem is reliant on membership of groups that reflect their (intersecting) identities. Such identities are shaped by the historical development of the social group, which one opts into (or remains within) in the pursuit of self-esteem. This leads them to interact with those who share this identity. During this contact, social resources (including social capital) are shared amongst an ingroup and, for those most resistant to other groups, symbolic boundaries are drawn between themselves and other groups that they encounter. This enables members of such groups to further pursue or maintain their self-esteem by defining themselves over and against other social groups as they consume social resources exclusively. However, the emergence of symbolic boundaries also involves navigating a tension between contact and avoidance with outgroups to affirm one's social identity by defining their ingroup by way of contrast to others. Those who do not draw symbolic boundaries with other groups more readily engage in resource sharing, such as bridging social capital, which also serves the advancement of the group's contingent self-esteem.

Whether a group reacts negatively or positively towards an outgroup depends upon the extent to which their self-esteem is threatened by the outgroup in any given social sphere,[2] which itself is shaped by the historical norms of the group. Those that have historically shared social resources with outgroups will not feel threatened by them but can advance self-esteem through interacting with them. Those groups that have not historically interacted with outgroups to share resources will experience threatened self-esteem if they perceive that they will need to share social resources with them, given that such resources will have been used exclusively to bolster their self-esteem. How a group manages their social resources shapes prejudice, or the lack thereof, because resource sharing leads to the types of contact that undermine prejudice, whereas the exclusivist consumption of social resources facilitates contact avoidance. Moreover, because prejudice encourages contact avoidance, the way social capital and other social resources are managed leads to a cycle of either positive interaction or the avoidance of outgroups. Whether one possesses sexist attitudes or not depends upon the extent to which the ingroup identity is formed along gendered lines. If the ingroup does demarcate itself from others based on the gendering of the sexes, then sexism is more likely to be present. If it does not, then sexism is less likely to occur.

The above sits alongside the role of the schemata that contain gender-related information which provide individuals with ingrained assumptions about gender. If the schemata encourage rigid stereotypes, then sexism is more likely to be present and such persons are more likely to identify with groups where such attitudes exist, thereby reinforcing sexism. Those who possess schemata that enable one to see gender more flexibly will resist at least some stereotyping and are less likely to have prejudicial gender attitudes or be a part of a group that does.[3]

On occasions where a group is at risk of being internally divided along gendered lines, the above is juxtaposed alongside the role of dejection and/or agitation emotions during contact, which can lead to contact avoidance in the form of schismatic behaviours. This results from identity conflict and an accompanying perceived lack of voice. It likewise helps facilitate prejudice and can be caused by responses to ingroup members by other perceived ingroup members. Equally, sufficient levels of a perceived voice within such group processes can encourage interaction and thus serve to undermine prejudice.

Although intergroup processes apply to men and women, there is reason to expect the more exclusivist/avoidance-oriented response (and related sexism) outlined above to be identified more frequently amongst men than women. The processes behind my participants' sexism (for those who exhibited it) are more typical of groups that are higher in social status. It is true that I have explained previously that 'othering' my participants could indeed lead to prejudice. This could relate to their sex or to their religious tradition. Indeed, some studies have indicated that women can exhibit hostile sexism towards men (e.g., Fernández, Castro and Lorenzo, 2004) as well as 'benevolently' sexist attitudes towards them (e.g., Glick and Fiske, 1999). However, there is less evidence that women hold prejudicial attitudes

194   *Conclusion*

towards men than vice versa. This might be owing to the fact that sexism towards women is more evident within society, leading to more social research on it.

Nevertheless, as women do not possess the same level of social status as men in many contexts, one should expect that they are less likely to 'other' them in the pursuit of self-esteem as this is more likely to be done by groups with higher social status (although by no means exclusively by them). Also, some women internalise sexist attitudes towards them. In such cases, this can be accompanied by more favourable appraisals of groups with higher status (Jost and Banaji, 1994), meaning that negative appraisals of men by such women are less likely. Further research will need to be undertaken to confirm whether the more exclusivist/avoidance-oriented aspects of the process (and related sexism) described by my theory actually occur less often amongst women than men.

Moreover, in this process, the role of sexuality ought not to be overlooked given that—as aforementioned—heterosexuality more than homosexuality is associated with indirect sexism, owing to the dependence on the opposite sex experienced by heterosexual persons (see also Glick and Fiske, 1999). In the above process, one should therefore expect certain types of sexist attitudes (where present) to be more frequently manifest amongst some groups and not others. Of course, there will be other factors to consider here in relation to intersecting identities and related (often context-dependent) social status regarding the specific ways in which gender attitudes are formed and manifest.[4]

My research has shown the importance of understanding gender attitudes in terms of intersecting social strata. By this, I mean that the social world consists of multiple segments (as affirmed by the stratification of reality) which converge to inform people's social identities in a variety of ways. The way in which they shape an individual's or group's identity comes to bear upon their gender attitudes. Both sexism and more affirming gender attitudes can thus be understood to be significantly shaped by this convergence. That is, gender attitudes result from intersecting social strata. In keeping with the epistemological underpinning of the present research, such a term recognises the complexity of the social world and so leaves open the possibility for other—as of yet unidentified—factors contributing to gender attitudes. For this reason, the term is broad, allowing for the possibility of multiple social influences as well as conveying the presence of social (identity, particularly group) processes. These components are indicated by the idea of intersection, implying the presence of multiple factors, whilst also echoing the language of intersectionality.

Directions for future research

There are multiple avenues for future research in addition to that stated above. In this monograph, I have explored the issue of gender inequality within the hierarchy of the CofE. In doing so, I have identified numerous influences that contribute to this inequality. In the present study, clergy attitudes in one diocese have been observed. The advantage is evident on considering the analytical depth it has provided. This has also helped to highlight the advantage of employing qualitative methods instead of requiring participants to align their answers with pre-determined survey categories. The fact that the diocese in question contains traditions that represent the CofE as a whole and has a mixture of urban, suburban, and more rural areas has been beneficial as it helps provide a representative picture of the wider CofE.

Notwithstanding, there are additional areas that can be studied, and methods utilised. For instance, it would be beneficial to compare the results of this study to those of one conducted in a more homogenous diocese—for instance, that has a higher proportion of evangelicals—not least because there could conceivably be less ingroup exclusivity if either, outgroups are less distinct from the ingroup, or the ingroup represents the majority in that area. This could highlight some subtle differences in intergroup processes, shedding light on how such dynamics play out when distinctives are less pronounced in a context where in and outgroups have overlapping identities (as CofE clergy from different traditions do).

Additionally, participant and further structured observations would complement the methods I have employed because they would provide additional evidence of how clergy gender attitudes play out in situ. For instance, attending services at churches from the breadth of the traditions explored would provide data on how clergy approached related topics from the pulpit, as would analysis of their sermons where these have been recorded. One difficulty of this approach, however, would be attending a sufficient breadth of churches at a time where gender-related topics were being preached on. Another challenge would be that not all churches record sermons. Only my evangelical participants regularly did this, meaning that gathering sufficient data that allows for a comparison with traditional Anglo-Catholics would be difficult.

In the seventh chapter, I demonstrated how religious traditions shape the Bible reading practices employed and the implications of this for gender attitudes. Elsewhere I have discussed the way that wider society can shape Bible reading for my conservative evangelical participants (Fry, 2021a). In light of my findings, it would be appropriate for future research to explore how clergy can be aided to reflect more fully on their hermeneutical strategies and the ways in which these can contribute to gender inequality. Given that some of the participants do not follow the strategy they uphold as appropriate but employ plain meaning reading at the expense of more fully contextualised readings, there is certainly scope to work with adherents of the traditions explored to facilitate reflection on the inconsistencies between the hermeneutical strategies that they consider to be appropriate and their actual practices.

It will also be pertinent to examine other traditions within the CofE. The present study has examined an unusual group of charismatic evangelicals

196 *Conclusion*

who have incorporated other theological traditions into their own theological and spiritual praxis. However, only a minority came from more explicitly charismatic groups, such as the HTB network, that are less likely to reflect this heterogeneity because it is a more organised branch of the CofE that trains assistant curates to then lead or start other churches within this tradition. It is possible that narratives such as Oscar's and Michael's are then more representative of other charismatic evangelicals. Examining other Anglican traditions will also present a fuller picture of how the CofE facilitates gender (in)equality. This monograph has only explored more theologically conservative quarters of the Church and so can only offer an understanding of these wings. Some of these wings appear more resistant to decline and so are becoming a larger proportion of the CofE (e.g., see Brierley, 2018). Nevertheless, exploring less conservative traditions for comparison would provide a more panoramic picture of the Established Church. Moreover, Christian traditions (particularly evangelical/Pentecostal ones) beyond the CofE are on the rise (see Goodhew and Cooper, 2018). An examination of Pentecostal churches would therefore be an appropriate venture, not least because they too can articulate traditional gender attitudes (e.g., see Aune, 2006). It is certainly worthwhile seeking to understand how growing Christian churches view the roles of women in church and wider society and how this is enacted.

Furthermore, it is the laity who typically interact more fully in life outside of the Church. Whether they are working in a non-religious context, engage with other parents at school or in children's groups, or whether they are involved in their local communities through organisations such as sports clubs, they are often more immersed in non-religious life than are clergy. It is therefore important to understand how their gender attitudes manifest in life beyond the Church given that gender (in)equality is not solely an ecclesial or religious concern. Indeed, because the social interactions of laity will be different from those of the clergy, their social identity, social capital, contact, etc. could conceivably shape their gender attitudes in quite different ways compared with Church leaders.

It ought also to be stated that there is a distinct lack of women's voices in this monograph. I have justified this by explaining that an understanding of male gender attitudes is necessary given the power that they wield in the Church, an approach which has led to data rich in candour, affording new knowledge to emerge about gender attitudes within one of England's most historical institutions. Nevertheless, both female clergy and female laity will undoubtedly provide crucial insight into the manifestation and impact of gender inequality within the CofE today. Their experiences will also provide valuable insight around the discussions of policies that are designed to erase sexism from the Church. This must also include the voice of theologically conservative women. Whilst sexism can be internalised, causing women to perpetuate their inequality (e.g., see Jost and Banaji, 1994), any feminist endeavour is obviously counter-productive if it denies women the platform to voice their gender attitudes and values. Whilst there is literature that shows how sexism can be internalised, it is quantitative in design and so gives a large-scale picture of prejudice internalisation, producing a statistical average that will not be applicable universally even if generally true. It is theoretically possible for women to hold traditional gender norms without having internalised sexism, or at least without having done so fully. After all, some of my participants exhibited aspects of sexism without possessing all the criteria associated with sexist attitudes.

Furthermore, this monograph has been concerned with gender attitudes in relation to the social roles occupied by men and women amongst those who take a somewhat binary view of the sexes. This has meant that clergy attitudes towards those whose gender identity does not match the sex they were assigned at birth (or indeed who are intersex) have not been explored here. There is therefore scope for future research to utilise the methods and theories explored in this monograph in an examination of clergy attitudes towards those who are not cisgender. Moreover, beyond an exploration of Christian contexts, I have posited a theory of gender attitude formation. There are multiple contexts within and beyond religious settings where this can be further explored to understand how such attitudes and processes manifest elsewhere. There is also scope to develop this theory in its application to attitudes concerning those who do not fit the binary model of sex beyond Christian spheres.

Conclusion

In this monograph, I have demonstrated that the gender attitudes of male Anglican clergy are diverse, even within some of the more conservative traditions, although some of these traditions are more homogenous than others. The extent of the heterogeneity of the three traditions studied is related to the way that each of the traditions is structured; those with regular meetings and clear network boundaries consist of clergy with views that are more similar to each other than those that are more loosely organised.

The CofE must understand that its own heritage contributes to current clergy attitudes towards women; clerical sexism is not only the result of the actions of individuals or specific traditions within the Established Church. This ought not to be surprising to the CofE given the widespread Christian belief in an inaugurated eschatology where the world is yet to be fully redeemed from its imperfections. If this is to be acknowledged, then it would be consistent with the Church's present teaching to work to eradicate the specific expressions of sexism I have identified within its ordained hierarchy, particularly given its assertion that it is theologically appropriate for women to possess any office within it.

Nevertheless, it is important to understand that the attitudes and actions of the clergy are the result of intergroup processes. These are universal social processes (see Bielo, 2011) and so in this respect, the root of clerical sexism

198 Conclusion

stems from phenomena that are not entirely atypical of the wider population. Thus, it is important to understand that—whilst they have agency—like all other human beings, they have not inherited a blank social canvas and so are influenced towards particular ways of understanding the world. I do not argue this to excuse the presence or consequences of sexism. Rather, the failure to acknowledge similarities in social processes between these and other groups could lead to the 'othering' of such clergy. It would be inconsistent to criticise participants for othering outgroups whilst doing likewise. Indeed, if sexism is to be challenged then one must understand that the research on prejudice demonstrates the transformative power of contact, particularly—in light of my findings—bridging social/spiritual capital over and above bonding capital. It has been clear from Adam's and Adrian's narratives, for example, that social exclusion compounds their gender attitudes, and I have argued elsewhere that sharing capital could soften more conservative attitudes towards women (see Fry, 2021b).

That it is possible to possess a relatively conservative gender attitude and yet not meet all the social psychological criteria for sexism has also been highlighted. Similarly, some participants have evinced the presence of one type of sexism in their narratives but not the other. Others still have evinced some of the criteria but not all for any one of the types of sexism that have been explored in this monograph (although that is not, of course, to suggest that such gender attitudes are unproblematic). Attitudes associated with sexism can thus impact one's thinking in subtle ways, even amongst those who cannot be said to straightforwardly possess a sexist outlook. It is therefore necessary to understand that, for sexism to be sufficiently challenged, an awareness of how wider discourses can impact one's own gender attitudes needs to be cultivated.

In addition to this, it is apparent that the origins of clerical sexism lie not so much in Judaeo-Christian scripture which has passages prohibiting women from undertaking certain activities, but in the social milieu that leads devotees to favour particular hermeneutical strategies over others (cf. Peek and Brown, 1980; see also Fry, 2019). This study has also led to evidence that the method employed in empirical studies is important for capturing the extent of nuance and depth that are present in the social world. One's choice of methodological design can capture details not initially obvious or expected. This has been particularly true for employing theories used in quantitative research for qualitative means. It is therefore important to consider how well-tested and utilised quantitative studies may be adapted for capturing as of yet neglected features of people's lives qualitatively, which can lead to the nuancing of theories based in quantitative research.

The importance of applying different theoretical lenses to interpret data has also become apparent. It is because participants' narratives reflect attitudes associated with a variety of social theories that I decided to pursue multiple lines of enquiry. In doing so, I have found a series of interlocking relationships between various social phenomena that have previously gone unnoticed. This

Conclusion 199

also reinforces the necessity of selecting methods of data collection that are conducive to a qualitative—or thick description—of people's social world as this approach has led to the exploration of such relationships.

Finally, it ought to be stated that gender equality is an ongoing concern. The CofE is a national institution and one of England's oldest. There have been many examples (both widely publicised and little known) where it has used its status to advocate for marginalised or comparatively vulnerable groups. It opposed Margaret Thatcher's government when its actions led to increased poverty (e.g., see Ganiel and Jones, 2012) and it has sought to safeguard human life during the COVID-19 pandemic by closing its church buildings (e.g., see Church of England, 2020). However, its strategy for admitting clergy to its ordained offices is entirely inconsistent with the wider legal structures in place for other organisations. Therefore, given the CofE's established position in the life of the nation, it is appropriate to more directly address the patriarchy that evidently exists within its structures. If it were to do so, the Church would be providing a potent symbol that gender equality is indeed increasing in English society.

Notes

1 These groups need not be mutually exclusive.
2 This means that one group could exhibit prejudice to some groups and not others. It need not mean that some groups exhibit prejudice to all outgroups or that they view all outgroups favourably.
3 I explained in the fourth chapter that evidence of gender schemata as articulated by Bem is mixed. Nevertheless, the data discussed in this monograph do affirm it, at the very least indicating its appropriateness for understanding my participants. In any case, individuals beyond those recruited for this study will possess schemata that contain gender-related information, and which help them to interpret such given that, as is established within cognitive psychology, all persons develop schemata for interpreting the world around them. I therefore continue to acknowledge the role that schemata will play in people's gender attitudes but refer to them in more general terms, recognising that it is theoretically possible that one's conceptions of gender could be ordered through other kinds of schemata to those which Bem discusses.
4 For example, there is little research on the relationship between sexism and sexual identities beyond the heterosexual-homosexual binary. Although, the research that does exist indicates that bisexual persons, for instance, can be more likely to exhibit ambivalent (including indirect) sexism than homosexual persons but are less likely to do so than heterosexual persons (see Cowie, Greaves and Sibley, 2019).

References

Altglas, V. (2014). *From yoga to kabbalah: Religious exoticism and the logics of bricolage*. Oxford University Press.

Aune, K. (2006). Marriage in a British evangelical congregation: Practising post-feminist partnership? *The Sociological Review, 54*(4), 638–657.

Bielo, J.S. (2011). *Emerging evangelicals: Faith, modernity, and the desire for authenticity*. New York: NYU Press.

200 Conclusion

Brierley, P.W. (2018). *UK Church statistics no. 3: 2018 edition*. London: Christian Research.

Church of England. (2020, May 14). *Churches could 're-open in July'*. Retrieved from https://www.churchnewspaper.com/82384/archives.

Cowie, L.J., Greaves, L.M., & Sibley, C.G. (2019). Sexuality and sexism: Differences in ambivalent sexism across gender and sexual identity. *Personality and Individual Differences, 148*, 85–89.

Fernández, M.L., Castro, Y.R., & Lorenzo, M.G. (2004). Evolution of hostile sexism and benevolent sexism in a Spanish sample. *Social Indicators Research, 66*(3), 197–211.

Fry, A.D.J. (2019a). Justifying gender inequality in the Church of England: An examination of theologically conservative male clergy attitudes towards women's ordination. *Fieldwork in Religion, 14*(1), 8–32.

Fry, A.D.J. (2021a). Postfeminist, engaged and resistant: Evangelical male clergy attitudes towards gender and women's ordination in the Church of England. *Critical Research on Religion, 9*(1), 65–83.

Fry, A.D.J. (2021b). Clergy, capital and gender inequality: An assessment of how social and spiritual capital are denied to women priests in the Church of England. *Gender, Work & Organization, 21*(6), 2091–2113.

Ganiel, G., & Jones, P. (2012). Religion, politics and law. In L. Woodhead & R. Catto (Eds.), *Religion and change in modern Britain* (pp. 299–321). London: Routledge.

Glick, P., & Fiske, S.T. (1999). The ambivalence toward men inventory: Differentiating hostile and benevolent beliefs about men. *Psychology of Women Quarterly, 23*(3), 519–536.

Goodhew, D., & Cooper, A-P. (Eds.). (2018). *The desecularisation of the city: London's churches, 1980 to the present*. Oxford: Routledge.

Harvey, G., & Vincett, G. (2012). Alternative spiritualities: Marginal *and* mainstream. In L. Woodhead & R. Catto (Eds.), *Religion and change in modern Britain* (pp. 165–172). London: Routledge.

Heelas, P., & Woodhead, L. (2004). *The spiritual revolution: Why religion is giving way to spirituality*. London: John Wiley & Sons.

Jost, J.T., & Banaji, M.R. (1994). The role of stereotyping in system-justification and the production of false consciousness. *British Journal of Social Psychology, 33*(1), 1–27.

Lyon, D. (2000). *Jesus in Disneyland: Religion in postmodern times*. Cambridge: Polity Press.

Peek, C.W., & Brown, S. (1980). Sex prejudice among white Protestants: Like or unlike ethnic prejudice? *Social Forces, 59*(1), 169–185.

Theos. (2013). The spirit of things unseen: Belief in post-religious Britain. *Theos*. Retrieved from https://www.theosthinktank.co.uk/cmsfiles/archive/files/Reports/Spirit%20of%20Things%20-%20Digital%20(update).pdf.

Bibliography

Aldridge, A. (1987). In the absence of the minister: Structures of subordination in the role of deaconess in the Church of England. *Sociology, 21*(3), 377–392.

Aldridge, A. (1989). Men, women, and clergymen: Opinion and authority in a sacred organization. *The Sociological Review, 37*(1), 43–64.

Aldridge, A. (1992). Discourse on women in the clerical profession: The diaconate and language-games in the Church of England. *Sociology, 26*(1), 45–57.

Aldridge, A. (1993). Negotiating status: Social scientists and Anglican clergy. *Journal of Contemporary Ethnography, 22*(1), 97–112.

Allport, G. (1954/1979). *The nature of prejudice.* Cambridge, MA: Perseus Books.

Alsop, R., Fitzsimons, A., & Lennon, K. (2002). *Theorizing gender: An introduction.* Cambridge: Polity.

Altglas, V. (2014). *From yoga to kabbalah: Religious exoticism and the logics of bricolage.* Oxford University Press.

Ammerman, N.T. (1987). *Bible believers: Fundamentalists in the modern world.* New Brunswick, NJ: Rutgers University Press.

Antoun, R.T. (2001). *Understanding fundamentalism: Christian, Islamic, and Jewish movements.* Walnut Creek, CA: Rowman and Littlefield.

Appiah, K. (2018). *The lies that bind. Rethinking identity: Creed, country, colour, class, culture.* London: Profile Books Ltd.

Appleby, R.S. (2011). Rethinking fundamentalism in a secular age. In C. Calhoun, M. Juergensmeyer, & J. Van Antwerpen (Eds.), *Rethinking secularism* (pp. 225–247). Oxford University Press.

Atherstone, A. (2013). Evangelicalism and fundamentalism in the inter-war Church of England. In D.W. Bebbington & D.C. Jones (Eds.), *Evangelicalism and fundamentalism in the United Kingdom during the twentieth century* (pp. 55–75). Oxford University Press.

Aune, K. (2006). Marriage in a British evangelical congregation: Practising post-feminist partnership? *The Sociological Review, 54*(4), 638–657.

Aune, K. (2008a). Evangelical Christianity and women's changing lives. *European Journal of Women's Studies, 15*(3), 277–294.

Aune, K. (2008b). Making men men: Masculinity and contemporary evangelical identity. In M. Smith (Ed.), *British evangelical identities past and present, vol. 1.: Aspects of the history and sociology of evangelicalism in Britain and Ireland* (pp. 153–166). Milton Keynes: Paternoster Press.

202 Bibliography

Aune, K., & Guest, M. (2019). Christian university students' attitudes towards gender: Constructing everyday theologies in a post-feminist climate. *Religions, 10*(2), 133–154.

Avis, P. (2004). The Episcopal Ministry Act of Synod: A "bearable anomaly"? In P. Avis (Ed.), *Seeking the truth of change in the Church: Reception, communication and the ordination of women* (pp. 152–170). London: T&T Clark.

Bagilhole, B. (2003). Prospects for change? Structural, cultural and action dimensions of the careers of pioneer women priests in the Church of England. *Gender, Work and Organization, 10*(3), 361–377.

Bagilhole, B. (2006). Not a glass ceiling more a lead roof: Experiences of pioneer women priests in the Church of England. *Equal Opportunities International, 25*(2), 109–125.

Baker, J. (Ed.). (2004). *Consecrated women? A contribution to the women bishops debate.* Norwich: Canterbury Press.

Balmer, R. (1994). American fundamentalism: The ideal of femininity. In J. Hawley (Ed.), *Fundamentalism and gender* (pp. 47–62). Oxford University Press.

Balmer, R. (2016). *Evangelicalism in America.* Waco, TX: Baylor University Press.

Balz, H., & Schneider, G. (1990). *Exegetical dictionary of the New Testament, vol. 1.* Grand Rapids, MI: William B. Eerdmans Publishing Company.

Barr, J. (1983). *Holy scripture: Canon, authority, criticism.* Oxford: Clarendon Press.

Barticioti, F. (2016, December 1). Archive for the movement of the ordination of women [Blog post]. *LSE History.* http://blogs.lse.ac.uk/lsehistory/2016/12/01/archive-of-the-movement-for-the-ordination-of-women/.

Baron-Cohen, S. (2003). *The essential difference.* London: Penguin UK.

Barton, J. (2007). *The nature of biblical criticism.* Louisville: Westminster John Knox Press.

Batson, C.D., & Powell, A.A. (2003). Altruism and prosocial behavior. In T. Millon & M. Lerner (Eds.), *Handbook of Psychology, vol. 5: Personality and social psychology* (pp. 463–484). Hoboken, NJ: John Wiley & Sons.

Baumeister, R.F., Smart, L., & Boden, J.M. (1996). Relation of threatened egotism to violence and aggression: The dark side of high self-esteem. *Psychological Review, 103*(1), 5–33.

Beattie, T. (2004). *The new Catholic feminism: Theology, gender theory and dialogue.* London: Routledge.

Bebbington, D.W. (1989). *Evangelicalism in modern Britain: A history from the 1730s to the 1980s.* London: Unwin Hyman.

Bebbington, D.W. (1994). Evangelicalism in its setting: The British and American movements since 1940. In M.A. Noll, D.W. Bebbington, & G.A. Rawlyk (Eds.), *Evangelicalism: Comparative studies of popular Protestantism in North America, the British Isles, and beyond 1700–1900* (pp. 365–388). Oxford University Press.

Bebbington, D.W. (1995). The decline and resurgence of evangelical social concern 1918–1980. In J. Wolffe (Ed.), *Evangelical faith and public zeal: Evangelicals and society in Britain 1780–1980* (pp. 175–197). London: SPCK.

Bebbington, D.W., & Jones, D.C. (2103). Conclusion. In D.W. Bebbington & D.C. Jones (Eds.), *Evangelicalism and fundamentalism in the United Kingdom during the twentieth century* (pp. 366–376). Oxford University Press.

Bem, S.L. (1981a). Gender schema theory: A cognitive account of sex typing. *Psychological Review, 88*(4), 354–364.

Bibliography 203

Bem, S.L. (1981b). The BSRI and gender schema theory: A reply to Spence and Helmreich. *Psychological Review, 88*(4), 369–371.

Benn, W. (2016). Evangelical episcopacy. In L. Gatiss (Ed.), *Positively Anglican: Building on the foundations and transforming the church* (pp. 43–54). Watford: Church Society.

Berger, P.L. (1967). *The sacred canopy.* New York: Anchor.

Bhaskar, R., & Collier, A. (1998). Introduction: Explanatory critiques. In M. Archer, R. Bhaskar, A. Collier, T. Lawson, & A. Norrie (Eds.), *Critical realism: Essential readings* (pp. 385–394). London: Routledge.

Bielo, J.S. (2011). *Emerging evangelicals: Faith, modernity, and the desire for authenticity.* New York: NYU Press.

Bizman, A., & Yinon, Y. (2002). Social self-discrepancies and group-based emotional distress. In D.M. Mackie & E.R. Smith (Eds.), *From prejudice to intergroup emotions: Differentiated reactions to social groups.* New York: Psychology Press.

Blomberg, C. (2011). The New Testament in North America. In A. Köstenberger & R. Yarbrough (Eds.), *New Testament studies in the 21st century: Essays in honor of DA Carson on the occasion of his 65th birthday* (pp. 277–299). Wheaton, IL: Crossway.

Boone, K.C. (1989). *The Bible tells them so: The discourse of Protestant fundamentalism.* New York: SUNY Press.

Bourdieu, P. (1977). *Outline of a theory of practice.* Cambridge University Press.

Bourdieu, P. (1983). The field of cultural production, or: The economic world reversed. *Poetics, 12*(4–5), 311–356.

Bourdieu, P. (1986). The forms of capital. In J. Richardson (Ed.), *Handbook of theory and research for the sociology of education* (pp. 241–258). New York: Greenwood.

Bourdieu, P. (2001). *Masculine domination.* Redwood City, CA: Stanford University Press.

Brasher, B.E. (1998). *Godly women: Fundamentalism and female power.* New Brunswick, NJ: Rutgers University Press.

Braun, V., & Clarke, V. (2006). Using thematic analysis in psychology. *Qualitative Research in Psychology, 3*(2), 77–101.

Braun, V., & Clarke, V. (n.d.). *Questions about thematic analysis.* The University of Auckland. Retrieved from https://www.psych.auckland.ac.nz/en/about/our-research/research-groups/thematic-analysis/frequently-asked-questions-8.html.

Brewer, W.F., & Treyens, J.C. (1981). Role of schemata in memory for places. *Cognitive Psychology, 13*(2), 207–230.

Brierley, P.W. (2018). *UK Church statistics no. 3: 2018 edition.* London: Christian Research.

British Social Attitudes. (2018). *Chapter summary: Religion.* http://www.bsa.natcen.ac.uk/latest-report/british-social-attitudes-28/religion.aspx.

Brittain, C.C., & McKinnon, A. (2011). Homosexuality and the construction of "Anglican Orthodoxy": The symbolic politics of the Anglican Communion. *Sociology of Religion, 72*(3), 351–373.

Brown, A. (2014, July 14). Church of England General Synod approves female bishops. *The Guardian.* https://www.theguardian.com/world/2014/jul/14/church-england-general-synod-approves-female-bishops.

Brown, C.G. (2001). *The death of Christian Britain: Understanding secularisation, 1800–2000.* London: Routledge.

204 Bibliography

Brown, C.G. (2006). *Religion and society in twentieth-century Britain*. Harlow: Pearson Longman.

Brown, C.G. (2010). What was the religious crisis of the 1960s? *Journal of Religious History, 34*(4), 468–479.

Brown, D. (2018, October 28). *Real or imagined? Measuring long-term patterns of political secularisation and desecularisation* [Paper presentation]. Society for the Scientific Study of Religion, Las Vegas, NV, United States.

Brown, R. (2011). *Prejudice: Its social psychology*. Hoboken, NJ: John Wiley & Sons.

Brown, A., & Woodhead, L. (2016). *That was the Church that was: How the Church of England lost the English people*. London: Bloomsbury.

Bruce, F.F. (1984). *The Epistles to the Colossians, to Philemon, and to the Ephesians*. Grand Rapids, MI: William. B. Eerdmans Publishing Company.

Bruce, S. (2008). *Fundamentalism*. Cambridge: Polity.

Bryan, J. (2016). *Human being: Insights from psychology and the Christian faith*. London: SCM Press.

Buchanan, C., Craston, C., Gregg, D., Gunstone, J., Howard, C., & Pattison, D. (1981). *The charismatic movement in the Church of England*. London: The Central Board of Finance of the Church of England.

Burman, E. (1994). Interviewing. In P. Banister, E. Burman, I. Parker, M. Taylor, & C. Tindall (Eds.), *Qualitative methods in psychology* (pp. 49–71). Buckingham: Open University Press.

Bushman, B.J., & Baumeister, R.F. (1998). Threatened egotism, narcissism, self-esteem, and direct and displaced aggression: Does self-love or self-hate lead to violence? *Journal of Personality and Social Psychology, 75*(1), 219–229.

Butler, J. (1990). *Gender trouble: Feminism and the subversion of identity*. London: Routledge.

Butler, J. (1993). *Bodies that matter: On the discursive limits of sex*. London: Routledge.

Butt, R. (2011, May5). Archbishop of Canterbury appoints flying bishops. *The Guardian*. https://www.theguardian.com/world/2011/may/05/archbishop-canterbury-flying-bishops.

Caldwell, R. (2007). Agency and change: Re-evaluating Foucault's legacy. *Organization, 14*(6), 769–791.

Caldwell, S. (2021, October 14). Dr Michael Ali-Nazir, former Anglican Bishop of Rochester, joins the Catholic Church. *Catholic Herald*. https://catholicherald.co.uk/dr-michael-nazir-ali-former-anglican-bishop-of-rochester-joins-the-catholic-church/.

Carey, G. (2004). *Know the truth: A memoir*. London: HarperCollins.

Carlson, N., Martin, G., & Buskist, W. (2000). *Psychology*. Harlow: Pearson Education Limited.

Carpenter, J. (2014). What's new about the new evangelical social engagement? In B. Steensland & P. Goff (Eds.), *The new evangelical social engagement* (pp. 265–279). Oxford University Press.

Chadwick, O. (1972). *The Victorian Church (Part II)*. London: Adam and Charles Black.

Chadwick, O. (1990). *The spirit of the Oxford Movement: Tractarian essays*. Cambridge University Press.

Chandler, M. (2003). *An introduction to the Oxford Movement*. New York: Church Publishing Incorporated.

Chapman, R. (Ed.). (2006). *Firmly I believe: An Oxford Movement reader*. Norwich: Canterbury Press.

Church of England. (2020, May 14). *Churches could "re-open in July"*. https://www.churchnewspaper.com/82384/archives.

Church of England. (n.d.). *Understanding discernment*. https://www.churchofengland.org/life-events/vocations/preparing-ordained-ministry/understanding-discernment.

Church of England Glossary. (2018a). *Bishop*. https://www.churchofenglandglossary.co.uk/dictionary/definition/bishop.

Church of England. (2018b). *Anglo-Catholic*. https://www.churchofenglandglossary.co.uk/dictionary/definition/anglo_catholic.

Clarke, V., Braun, V., & Hayfield, N. (2015). Thematic analysis. In J.A. Smith (Ed.), *Qualitative psychology: A practical guide to research methods* 3rd edition (pp. 222–248). London: Sage.

Cornwall, S. (2015). Laws "Needefull in later to be abrogated": Intersex and the sources of Christian theology. In S. Cornwall (Ed.), *Intersex, theology and the Bible: Troubling bodies in Church, text, and society*. Hampshire: Palgrave Macmillan.

Coston, B.M., & Kimmel, M. (2012). Seeing privilege where it isn't: Marginalized masculinities and the intersectionality of privilege. *Journal of Social Issues, 68*(1), 97–111.

Cowie, L.J., Greaves, L.M., & Sibley, C.G. (2019). Sexuality and sexism: Differences in ambivalent sexism across gender and sexual identity. *Personality and Individual Differences, 148*, 85–89.

Crandall, C.S., & Eshleman, A. (2003). A justification-suppression model of the expression and experience of prejudice. *Psychological Bulletin, 129*(3): 414–446.

Craston, C. (1988). *Biblical headship and the ordination of women*. Bramcote: Grove Books.

Crenshaw, K.W. (2017). *On intersectionality: Essential writings*. New York: The New Press.

Crocker, J., Luhtanen, R.K., Cooper, M.L., & Bouvrette, A. (2003). Contingencies of self-worth in college students: Theory and measurement. *Journal of Personality and Social Psychology, 85*(5), 894–908.

Crocker, J., & Knight, K.M. (2005). Contingencies of self-worth. *Current Directions in Psychological Science, 14*(4), 200–203.

Dawkins, R. (1989). *The selfish gene*, 2nd edition. Oxford University Press.

Day, A. (2017). *The religious lives of older laywomen: The last active Anglican generation*. Oxford University Press.

Delap, L. (2013). "Be strong and play the man": Anglican masculinities in the twentieth century. In L. Delap & S. Morgan (Eds.), *Men, masculinities and religious change in twentieth century Britain* (pp. 119–154). Basingstoke: Palgrave Macmillan.

Dixon, J., Durrheim, K., & Tredoux, C. (2005). Beyond the optimal contact strategy: A reality check for the contact hypothesis. *American Psychologist, 60*(7), 697–711.

Dovidio, J.F., Allen, J.L., & Schroeder, D.A. (1990). Specificity of empathy-induced helping: Evidence for altruistic motivation. *Journal of Personality and Social Psychology, 59*(2), 249–260.

206 Bibliography

Dovidio, J.F., Gaertner, S.L., & Kawakami, K. (2003). Intergroup contact: The past, present, and the future. *Group Processes and Intergroup Relations*, 6(1), 5–21.

Drury, C. (2001). The pastoral epistles. In J. Muddiman & J. Barton (Eds.), *The Oxford Bible commentary: The Pauline epistles* (pp. 244–263). Oxford University Press.

Dunn, J. (1998). *The theology of Paul the apostle*. Grand Rapids, MI: William B. Eerdmans Publishing Company.

Eisenberg, N., & Miller, P.A. (1987). The relation of empathy to prosocial and related behaviors. *Psychological Bulletin*, 101(1), 91–119.

Eldredge, J. (2001). *Wild at heart: Discovering the passionate soul of a man.* Nashville, TN: Thomas Nelson.

Eldredge, J., & Eldredge, S. (2005). *Captivating: Unveiling the mystery of a woman's soul.* Nashville, TN: Thomas Nelson.

Ellemers, N., Kortekaas, P., & Ouwerkerk, J.W. (1999). Self-categorisation, commitment to the group and group self-esteem as related but distinct aspects of social identity. *European Journal of Social Psychology*, 29(2–3), 371–389.

European Institute for Gender Equality (2020). *Gender Equality Index.* https://eige.europa.eu/gender-equality-index/compare-countries.

European Union (2006). *On establishing a European Institute for Gender Equality (Regulation (EC) No. 1922/2006).* https://eur-lex.europa.eu/legal-content/EN/TXT/PDF/?uri=CELEX:32006R1922&from=EN.

Fairweather, E.R. (Ed.). (1964). *The Oxford Movement.* Oxford University Press.

Faught, C.B. (2003). *Oxford Movement: A thematic history of the Tractarians and their times.* University Park, PA: Pennsylvania State University Press.

Fausto-Sterling, A. (2000). *Sexing the body: Gender politics and the construction of sexuality.* New York: Basic Books.

Fernández, M.L., Castro, Y.R., & Lorenzo, M.G. (2004). Evolution of hostile sexism and benevolent sexism in a Spanish sample. *Social Indicators Research*, 66(3), 197–211.

Ferns, S. (2014). *The five guiding principles: Guidance for candidates for ordination in the Church of England.* Ministry Division. https://www.churchofengland.org/sites/default/files/2017-10/the_five_guiding_principles.pdf.

Fletcher, W. (2013). There for the burials; there for the births: Women in leadership in the Anglican Communion. In K. Pui-lan, J. Berling, & J. Plane Te Paa (Eds.), *Anglican women on Church and mission* (pp. 55–75). Norwich: Canterbury Press.

Foucault, M. (1977). *Discipline and punish* (A. Sheridan, Trans.). New York: Pantheon.

Francis, L.J., & Robbins, M. (1999). *The long diaconate, 1987–1994: Women deacons and the delayed journey to priesthood.* Leominster: Gracewing Publishing.

Francis, L.J., Robbins, M., & Astley, J. (2005). *Fragmented faith: Exposing the fault lines in the Church of England.* Milton Keynes: Paternoster Press.

Frable, D.E., & Bem, S.L. (1985). If you are gender schematic, all members of the opposite sex look alike. *Journal of Personality and Social Psychology*, 49(2), 459–468.

Frijda, N.H. (1986). *The emotions.* Cambridge University Press.

Fry, A.D.J. (2019a). Justifying gender inequality in the Church of England: An examination of theologically conservative male clergy attitudes towards women's ordination. *Fieldwork in Religion*, 14(1), 8–32.

Bibliography 207

Fry, A.D.J. (2019b). *Gender attitudes amongst Anglo-Catholic and evangelical clergy in the Church of England: An examination of how male priests respond to women's ordination as priests and their consecration as bishops* (Doctoral dissertation, Durham University).

Fry, A.D.J. (2020, July 6). Religious 'fundamentalism': The origins of a dubious category. *Religion and Global Society.* The London School of Economics and Political Science. https://blogs.lse.ac.uk/religionglobalsociety/2020/07/religious-fundamentalism-the-origins-of-a-dubious-category/.

Fry, A.D.J. (2021a). Postfeminist, engaged and resistant: Evangelical male clergy attitudes towards gender and women's ordination in the Church of England. *Critical Research on Religion, 9*(1), 65–83.

Fry, A.D.J. (2021b). Clergy, capital and gender inequality: An assessment of how social and spiritual capital are denied to women priests in the Church of England. *Gender, Work & Organization, 21*(6), 2091–2113.

Furlong, M. (2000). *The CofE: The state it's in.* London: Hodder & Stoughton.

GAFCON. (2008). *The Complete Jerusalem Statement.* https://www.gafcon.org/resources/the-complete-jerusalem-statement.

GAFCON. (n.d.). *About GAFCON.* https://www.gafcon.org/about.

Gallagher, S.K. (2003). *Evangelical identity and gendered family life.* New Brunswick, NJ: Rutgers University Press.

Gallagher, S.K., & Smith, C. (1999). Symbolic traditionalism and pragmatic egalitarianism: Contemporary evangelicals, families, and gender. *Gender and Society, 13*(2), 211–233.

Ganiel, G., & Jones, P. (2012). Religion, politics and law. In L. Woodhead & R. Catto (Eds.), *Religion and change in modern Britain* (pp. 299–321). London: Routledge.

Garaigordobil, M. (2014). Sexism and empathy: Differences as a function of socio-demographic variables and relations between both constructs. In A. Columbus (Ed.), *Advances in psychology research, vol. 100* (pp. 59–80). New York: Nova Science Publishers, Inc.

Gatrell, C., & Peyton, N. (2019). Shattering the stained glass ceiling: Women leaders in the Church of England. In A-S. Antoniou, C. Cooper, & C. Gatrell (Eds.), *Women, business and leadership* (pp. 299–315). Cheltenham: Edward Elgar Publishing.

General Synod of the Church of England. (1988). *The ordination of women to the priesthood: A second report by the House of Bishops.* London: The Central Board of Finance of the Church of England.

Gilligan, C. (1993). *In a different voice.* Cambridge: Harvard University Press.

Glick, P., & Fiske, S.T. (1996). The ambivalent sexism inventory: Differentiating hostile and benevolent sexism. *Journal of Personality and Social Psychology, 70*(3), 491–512.

Glick, P., & Fiske, S.T. (1997). Hostile and benevolent sexism: Measuring ambivalent sexist attitudes toward women. *Psychology of Women Quarterly, 21*(1), 119–135.

Glick, P., & Fiske, S.T. (1999). The ambivalence toward men inventory: Differentiating hostile and benevolent beliefs about men. *Psychology of Women Quarterly, 23*(3), 519–536.

Glick, P., & Fiske, S.T. (2011). Ambivalent sexism revisited. *Psychology of Women Quarterly, 35*(3), 530–535.

208 *Bibliography*

Gonzales, A.L., & Hancock, J.T. (2011). Mirror, mirror on my Facebook wall: Effects of exposure to Facebook on self-esteem. *Cyberpsychology, Behavior, and Social Networking, 14*(1–2), 79–83.

Goodchild, S. (2002, March 10). *Church pays millions to clergy who walked out over women priests.* The Independent. https://www.independent.co.uk/news/uk/home-news/church-pays-millions-clergy-who-walked-out-over-women-priests-9196207.html.

Goodhew, D., & Cooper, A-P. (Eds.). (2018). *The desecularisation of the city: London's churches, 1980 to the present.* Oxford: Routledge.

Gray, J. (1992). *Men are from Mars, women are from Venus: A practical guide for improving communication and getting what you want in your relationships.* New York: Harper Collins.

Gray, J. (2011). *Men are from Mars, women are from Venus and children are from Heaven.* New York: Random House.

Guest, M. (2007a). *Evangelical identity and contemporary culture: A congregational study in innovation.* Eugene, OR: Wipf and Stock Publishers.

Guest, M. (2007b). In search of spiritual capital: The spiritual as a cultural resource. In K. Flanagan & P. Jupp (Eds.), *A sociology of spirituality* (pp. 181–200). Aldershot: Ashgate.

Guest, M., & Aune, K. (2017). Students' constructions of a Christian future: Faith, class and aspiration in university contexts. *Sociological Research Online, 22*(1), 1–13.

Guest, M., Aune, K., Sharma, S., & Warner, R. (2013). *Christianity and the university experience: Understanding student faith.* London: Bloomsbury.

Guest, M., Olson, E., & Wolffe, J. (2012). Christianity: Loss of monopoly. In L. Woodhead & R. Catto (Eds.), *Religion and change in modern Britain* (pp. 57–78). Oxford: Routledge.

Grady, M.P. (1998). *Qualitative and action research: A practitioner handbook.* Arlington, VA: Phi Delta Kappa International.

Graham, J.M. (2002, December).Review of *Slaves, women and homosexuals: Exploring the hermeneutics of cultural analysis,* by W. J. Webb. *Journal of the Evangelical Theological society, 45*(4), 678–679.

Grayzel, S.R. (1999). *Women's identities at war: Gender, motherhood, and politics in Britain and France during the First World War.* Chapel Hill, NC: University of North Carolina Press.

Grayzel, S.R. (2002). *Women and the First World War.* London: Pearson Education.

Green, T.K. (2007). Discomfort at work: Workplace assimilation demands and the contact hypothesis. *North Carolina Law Review, 86*(2), 379–440.

Green, J.C. (2014). New and old evangelical public engagement: A view from the polls. In B. Steensland & P. Goff (Eds.), *The new evangelical social engagement* (pp. 129–153). Oxford University Press.

Greene, A.M., & Robbins, M. (2015). The cost of a calling? Clergywomen and work in the Church of England. *Gender, Work and Organization, 22*(4), 405–420.

Greer, G. (1970). *The female eunuch.* London: MacGibbon and Kee.

Groppe, E. (2009). Women and the persona of Christ: Ordination in the Roman Catholic Church. In S. Abraham & E. Procario-Foley (Eds.), *Frontiers in Catholic feminist theology: Shoulder to shoulder* (pp. 153–171). Minneapolis, MN: Fortress Press.

Grudem, W.A. (1994). *Systematic theology: An introduction to biblical doctrine.* Nottingham: InterVarsity Press.

Bibliography 209

Grudem, W.A. (2002). The meaning of κεφαλή ("head"): An evaluation of new evidence, real and alleged. In W. Grudem(Ed.), *Biblical foundations for manhood and womanhood* (pp. 145–202). Wheaton, IL: Crossway.

Hackett, C. et al. (2016). *The gender gap in religion around the world: Women are generally more religious than men, particularly among Christians*. Washington, D.C.: Pew Research Center.

Hall, D. (1994). Muscular Christianity: Reading and writing the male social body. In D. Hall (Ed.), *Muscular Christianity: Embodying the Victorian age* (pp. 3–15). Cambridge University Press.

Halualani, R.T. (2008). How do multicultural university students define and make sense of intercultural contact? A qualitative study. *International Journal of Intercultural Relations, 32*(1), 1–16.

Handley, P. (2017, September 15). The Philip North Sheffield fiasco—and the question that simply wasn't asked. *The Church Times*. https://www.churchtimes.co.uk/articles/2017/15-september/news/uk/the-sheffield-fiasco-and-the-question-that-simply-wasn-t-asked.

Harari, Y.N. (2011). *Sapiens: A brief history of humankind*. London: Penguin Random House.

Harvey, G. and Vincett, G. (2012). Alternative spiritualities: Marginal *and* mainstream. In L. Woodhead & R. Catto (Eds.), *Religion and change in modern Britain* (pp. 165–172). London: Routledge.

Haslam, S.A., Reicher, S.D., & Platow, M.J. (2011). *The new psychology of leadership: Identity, influence and power*. East Sussex: Psychology Press.

Heelas, P., & Woodhead, L. (2004). *The spiritual revolution: Why religion is giving way to spirituality*. London: John Wiley & Sons.

Heeney, B. (1988). *The Women's Movement in the Church of England 1850s-1930*. Oxford: Clarendon Press.

Herek, G.M. (2004). Beyond "homophobia": Thinking about sexual prejudice and stigma in the twenty-first century. *Sexuality Research and Social Policy, 1*(2), 6–24.

Higgins, E.T. (1987). Self-discrepancy: A theory relating self and affect. *Psychological Review, 94*(3), 319–340.

Hindess, B. (1996). *Discourses of power: From Hobbes to Foucault*. Oxford: Baker Academic Press.

Hitlin, S., & Piliavin, J.A. (2004). Values: Reviving a dormant concept. *Annual Review of Sociology, 30*, 359–393.

Hollis, C. (1967). *Newman and the modern world*. London and Aylesbury: Compton Printing Ltd.

Hunter, J.D. (1987). *Evangelicalism: The coming generation*. New York: Barron's Educational Series.

Hylson-Smith, K. (1993). *High churchmanship in the Church of England: From the sixteenth century to the late twentieth century*. Edinburgh: T&T Clark.

Jagger, S. (2021). Mutual flourishing?: Women priests and symbolic violence in the Church of England. *Religion and Gender, 11*(2), 192–217.

Jenkins, D. (2005). "Letter from Richard Jenkins, Director of Affirming Catholicism to the Rt Revd Christopher Hill on the Provision for Those to the Admission of Women to the Episcopate." Received by Rt Revd Christopher Hill. In Rigney, J. with Chapman, M. (Eds.). *Women as Bishops* (pp. 131–138). London and New York: Mowbray, 3 Nov. 2008.

210 Bibliography

Joel, D. (2011). Male or female? Brains are intersex. *Frontiers in Integrative Neuroscience, 5.* 10.3389/fnint.2011.00057.

Johnson, E.A. (1993). *Women, earth, and creator spirit.* Mahwah, NJ: Paulist Press.

Jones, I. (2004). *Women and priesthood in the Church of England: Ten years on.* London: Church House Publishing.

Jost, J.T., & Banaji, M.R. (1994). The role of stereotyping in system-justification and the production of false consciousness. *British Journal of Social Psychology, 33*(1), 1–27.

Jost, J.T., Banaji, M.R., & Nosek, B.A. (2004). A decade of system justification theory: Accumulated evidence of conscious and unconscious bolstering of the status quo. *Political Psychology, 25*(6), 881–919.

Jost, J.T., Hawkins, C.B., Nosek, B.A., Hennes, E.P., Stern, C., Gosling, S.D., & Graham, J. (2013). Belief in a just God (and a just society): A system justification perspective on religious ideology. *Journal of Theoretical and Philosophical Psychology, 34*(1), 1–26.

Kay, A.C., Gaucher, D., Napier, J.L., Callan, M.J., & Laurin, K. (2008). God and the government: Testing a compensatory control mechanism for the support of external systems. *Journal of Personality and Social Psychology, 95*(1), 18–35.

Kirk, T. (1993). *The polarisation of Protestants and Roman Catholics in rural Northern Ireland: A case study of Glenravel Ward, County Antrim 1956 to 1988* (Doctoral dissertation, Queen's University, Belfast).

Knox, E.A. (1933). *The Tractarian Movement, 1833–1845: A study of the Oxford Movement as a phase of the religious revival in Western Europe in the second quarter of the nineteenth century.* London: Putnam.

Krosnick, J., & Petty, R. (1995). Attitude strength: An overview. In R. Petty & J. Krosnick (Eds.), *Attitude strength: Antecedents and consequences* (pp. 1–14). New York: Psychology Press.

Kumra, S., & Vinnicombe, S. (2010). Impressing for success: A gendered analysis of a key social capital accumulation strategy. *Gender, Work & Organization, 17*(5), 521–546.

Laqueur, T.W. (2012). The rise of sex in the eighteenth century: Historical context and historiographical implications. *Signs: Journal of Women in Culture and Society, 37*(4), 802–813.

Larsen, T. (2006). *Crisis of doubt: Honest faith in nineteenth-century England.* Oxford University Press.

Leafe, S. (2012, November 21). Why I voted no to women bishops. *The Independent.* Retrieved from https://www.independent.co.uk/voices/comment/why-i-voted-no-to-women-bishops-8340833.html.

Leary, M.R. (2005). Sociometer theory and the pursuit of relational value: Getting to the root of self-esteem. *European Review of Social Psychology, 16*(1), 75–111.

Leary, M.R., & Baumeister, R.F. (2000). The nature and function of self-esteem: Sociometer theory. In *Advances in Experimental Social Psychology, 32,* 1–62.

Legislation. (2010). *Equality Act 2010.* http://www.legislation.gov.uk/ukpga/2010/15/contents.

Legislation. (n.d.). *Sex Discrimination Act 1975.* https://www.legislation.gov.uk/ukpga/1975/65.

Lobel, T.E. (1994). Sex typing and the social perception of gender stereotypic and nonstereotypic behavior: The uniqueness of feminine males. *Journal of Personality and Social Psychology, 66*(2), 379–385.

Bibliography   211

Lyon, D. (2000). *Jesus in Disneyland: Religion in postmodern times*. Cambridge: Polity Press.

MacCulloch, D. (2009). *A history of Christianity: The first three thousand years*. London: Penguin.

Macquarrie, J. (1990). *Jesus Christ in modern thought*. London: SCM Press.

Maiden, J. (2018, February 19). *The charismatic turn of the long 1960s: Contexts and characteristics* [Paper presentation]. Contemporary Religion in Historical Perspective: Publics and performances. Milton Keynes, United Kingdom.

Maltby, J. (1998). One Lord, one faith, one baptism, but two integrities? In M. Furlong (Ed.), *Act of Synod- act of folly? Episcopal Ministry Act of Synod 1993* (pp. 42–58). London: SCM Press.

Mantle, G. (1991). *Archbishop: The life and times of Robert Runcie*. London: Sinclair-Stevenson Ltd.

Marsden, G. (1991). *Understanding fundamentalism and evangelicalism*. Grand Rapids, MI: William B. Eerdmans Publishing Company.

Martin, B. (1976). *John Keble: Priest, professor and poet*. London: Croom Helm Ltd.

Martin, J.L. (2017). *Thinking through methods: A social science primer*. Chicago and London: University of Chicago Press.

Martin, J., & Lembo, A. (2020). On the other side of values. *American Journal of Sociology, 126*(1), 52–98.

Masser, B.M., & Abrams, D. (2004). Reinforcing the glass ceiling: The consequences of hostile sexism for female managerial candidates. *Sex Roles, 51*(9–10), 609–615.

Maxwell, J.A. (2004a). Using qualitative methods for causal explanation. *Field Methods, 16*(3), 243–264.

Maxwell, J.A. (2004b). Causal explanation, qualitative research, and scientific inquiry in education. *Educational Researcher, 33*(2), 3–11.

Mayland, J. (2007). The ordination of women and the ecumenical movement. In J. Wootton (Ed.), *This is our story: Free Church women's ministry* (pp. 105–128). Peterborough: Epworth.

McCarthy Brown, K. (1994). Fundamentalism and the control of women. In J.S. Hawley (Ed.), *Fundamentalism and gender* (pp. 175–201). Oxford University Press.

McGrath, A. (1993). *The renewal of Anglicanism*. London: SPCK.

McLeod, H. (1999). Protestantism and British national identity, 1815–1945. In P. Van der Veer & H. Lehmann (Eds.), *Nation and religion: Perspectives on Europe and Asia* (pp. 44–70). Princeton, NJ: Princeton University Press.

McLeod, H. (2007). *The religious crisis of the 1960s*. Oxford University Press.

McLeod, H. (2012). The "Sportsman" and the "Muscular Christian": Rival ideals in nineteenth century England. In P. Pasture, J. Art, & T. Buerman (Eds.), *Beyond the feminisation thesis: Gender and Christianity in modern Europe* (pp. 85–96). Leuven: Leuven University Press.

Merino, S.M. (2010). Religious diversity in a "Christian nation": The effects of theological exclusivity and interreligious contact on the acceptance of religious diversity. *Journal for the Scientific Study of Religion, 49*(2), 231–246.

Ministry Division. (2014). *Criteria for selection for the ordained ministry in the Church of England*. https://www.churchofengland.org/sites/default/files/2017-10/selection_criteria_for_ordained_ministry.pdf.

Montefiore, H. (1978). *Yes to women priests*. Great Wakering: Mayhew-McCrimmon.

212 Bibliography

Mounce, W.D. (2000). *Word biblical commentary: Pastoral epistles*. Waco, TX: Thomas Nelson.

Mruk. C. (1995). *Self-esteem: Research, theory, and practice*. New York: Springer.

Nason-Clark, N. (1984). *Clerical attitudes towards appropriate roles for women in church and society: An empirical investigation of Anglican, Methodist and Baptist clergy in Southern England* (Doctoral dissertation, The London School of Economics and Political Science).

Nason-Clark, N. (1987a). Ordaining women as priests: Religious vs. sexist explanations for clerical attitudes. *Sociological Analysis, 48*(3), 259–273.

Nason-Clark, N. (1987b). Are women changing the image of ministry? A comparison of British and American realities. *Review of Religious Research*, 330–340.

Nathanson, A.I., Wilson, B.J., McGee, J., & Sebastian, M. (2002). Counteracting the effects of female stereotypes on television via active mediation. *Journal of Communication, 52*(4), 922–937.

Nazir-Ali, M. (2001). *Can women be bishops?* The Guardian. https://www.theguardian.com/world/2001/mar/31/religion.uk.

Noll, M.A. (1994). *The scandal of the evangelical mind*. Grand Rapids, MA: William B. Eerdmans Publishing Company.

Numbers, R. (2006). *The creationists: From scientific creationism to intelligent design*. Cambridge, MA: Harvard University Press.

Office for National Statistics. (2013). *Full story: What does the Census tell us about religion in 2011?* https://www.ons.gov.uk/peoplepopulationandcommunity/culturalidentity/religion/articles/fullstorywhatdoesthecensustellusaboutreligionin2011/2013-05-16.

Office for National Statistics. (2022). *Religion, England and Wales: 2021 Census*. https://www.ons.gov.uk/peoplepopulationandcommunity/culturalidentity/religion/bulletins/religionenglandandwales/census2021.

Ollard, S.L. (1963). *A short history of the Oxford Movement*. London: Mowbray.

Olsen, G.W. (1990). *Religion and revolution in early-industrial England: The Halevy thesis and its critics*. Lanham, MD: University Press of America.

Packer, J.I. (1973). Thoughts on the role and function of women in the Church. In C. Craston (Ed.), *Evangelicals and the ordination of women*. Bramcote: Grove Books.

Page, S.-J. (2010). *Femininities and Masculinities in the Church of England* (Doctoral dissertation, University of Nottingham).

Page, S.-J. (2013). Feminist faith lives? Exploring perceptions of feminism among two Anglican cohorts. In N. Slee, F. Porter, & A. Phillips (Eds.), *The faith lives of women and girls: Qualitative research perspectives* (pp. 51–63). Farnham: Ashgate.

Page, S.-J. (2014). The scrutinized priest: Women in the Church of England negotiating professional and sacred clothing regimes. *Gender, Work and Organization, 21*(4), 295–307.

Page, S-J. (2017). Anglican clergy husbands securing middle-class gendered privilege through religion. *Sociological Research Online, 22*(1), 1–13.

Peek, C.W., & Brown, S. (1980). Sex prejudice among white Protestants: Like or unlike ethnic prejudice? *Social Forces, 59*(1), 169–185.

Penning, J.M. & Smidt, C.E. (2002). *Evangelicalism: The next generation*. Ada, MI: Baker Academic.

Percy, E. (2017). Women, ordination and the Church of England: An ambiguous welcome. *Feminist Theology, 26*(1), 90–100.

Bibliography   213

Perkin, J. (1989). *Women and marriage in nineteenth-century England*. London: Routledge.

Perrin, R. (2016). *The Bible reading of young evangelicals: An exploration of the ordinary hermeneutics and faith of Generation Y*. Eugene, OR: Pickwick Publications.

Pettigrew, T.F. (1971). *Racially separate or together?* New York: McGraw-Hill.

Pettigrew, T.F. (1998). Intergroup contact theory. *Annual Review of Psychology*, *49*(1), 65–85.

Pettigrew, T.F., & Tropp, L.R. (2005). Allport's intergroup contact hypothesis: Its history and influence. In J. Dovidio, P. Glick, & L. Rudman (Eds.), *On the nature of prejudice: Fifty years after Allport* (pp. 262–277). Hoboken, NJ: Blackwell Publishing.

Pettigrew, T.F. (2008). How does intergroup contact reduce prejudice? Meta-analytic tests of three mediators. *European Journal of Social Psychology*, *38*(6), 922–934.

Peyton, N., & Gatrell, C. (2013). *Managing clergy lives: Obedience, sacrifice, intimacy*. London: A&C Black.

Pickering, W.S.F. (1989). *Anglo-Catholicism: A study in religious ambiguity*. London: Routledge.

Pilarski, A.E. (2011). The past and future of feminist biblical hermeneutics. *Biblical Theology Bulletin*, *41*(1), 16–23.

Piper, J., & Grudem, W. (Eds.). (1991). *Recovering biblical manhood and womanhood: A response to evangelical feminism*. Wheaton, IL: Crossway.

Piper, J., & Grudem, W. (2016). *50 crucial questions: An overview of central concerns about manhood and womanhood*. Wheaton, IL: Crossway.

Porter, M. (2011). *Sydney Anglicans and the threat to world Anglicanism: The Sydney experiment*. London: Routledge.

Press, A.L. (2011). "Feminism? That's so seventies": Girls and young women discuss femininity and feminism in *America's Next Top Model*. In R. Gill & C. Scharff (Eds.), *New Femininities: Postfeminism, neoliberalism and subjectivity* (pp. 117–133). Basingstoke: Palgrave Macmillan.

Putnam, R.D. (2000). *Bowling alone: The collapse and revival of American community*. New York: Simon and Schuster.

Radford Ruether, R. (1974). Misogynism and virginal feminism in the Fathers of the Church. In R. Radford Ruether (Ed.), *Religion and sexism: Images of woman in the Jewish and Christian traditions* (pp. 150–183). New York: Simon and Schuster.

Raven, C. (2009, March 30). *Bishop Michael Nazir-Ali—"Enough is enough"*. Virtue Online. https://virtueonline.org/bishop-michael-nazir-ali-enough-enough-charles-raven.

Redfern, C., & Aune, K. (2010). *Reclaiming the F word: The new feminist movement*. London: Zed.

Reed, J.S. (1996). *Glorious battle: The cultural politics of Victorian Anglo-Catholicism*. Nashville, TN: Vanderbilt University Press.

Research & Statistics. (2019). Statistics for mission 2018. *The Church of England*. https://www.churchofengland.org/sites/default/files/2019-10/2018StatisticsForMission_0.pdf.

Research & Statistics. (2020). Ministry Statistics 2020. *The Church of England*. https://www.churchofengland.org/sites/default/files/2021-07/Ministry%20Statistics%202020%20report%20FINAL.pdf.

214 Bibliography

Riessman, C.K. (2005). *Narrative analysis*. In N. Kelly, C. Horrocks, K. Milnes, B. Roberts, & S. Robinson (Eds.), *Narrative, memory and everyday life* (pp. 1–7). Huddersfield: University of Huddersfield.

Rkaina, S. (2014, November 2). *Feminist t-shirts worn by celebrities and MPs "made by sweatshop workers paid 62p per hour."* The Mirror. https://www.mirror.co.uk/news/uk-news/feminist-t-shirts-worn-celebrities-mps-4552364.

Robbins, M., & Greene, A.M. (2018). Clergywomen's experience of ministry in the Church of England. *Journal of Gender Studies, 27*(8), 890–900.

Ruddick, A. (2016). Complementarian ministry in the local parish church. In A. Gatiss (Ed.), *Positively Anglican: Building on the foundations and transforming the church* (pp. 55–66). Watford: Church Society.

Rudman, L.A. (2005). Rejection of women: Beyond prejudice as antipathy. In J.F. Dovidio, P.E. Glick, & L.A. Rudman (Eds.). *On the nature of prejudice: Fifty years after Allport* (pp. 106–120). Hoboken, NJ: Blackwell Publishing.

Saldaña, J. (2009). *The coding manual for qualitative researchers*. London: Sage.

Sani, F. (2005). When subgroups secede: Extending and refining the social psychological model of schism in groups. *Personality and Social Psychology Bulletin, 31*(8), 1074–1086.

Sani, F., & Reicher, S. (1999). Identity, argument and schism: Two longitudinal studies of the split in the Church of England over the ordination of women to the priesthood. *Group Processes and Intergroup Relations, 2*(3), 279–300.

Sani, F., & Reicher, S. (2000). Contested identities and schisms in groups: Opposing the ordination of women as priests in the Church of England. *British Journal of Social Psychology, 39*(1), 95–112.

Sayer, A. (2000). *Realism and social science*. London: Sage.

Schüssler Fiorenza, E. (1983). *In memory of her: A feminist theological reconstruction of Christian origins*. London: SCM Press.

Seybold, K.S. (2007). *Explorations in neuroscience, psychology and religion*. London: Routledge.

Smith, C. (2017). *Religion. What it is, how it works, and why it matters*. Princeton, NJ: Princeton University Press.

Smith, C. with Emerson, M., Gallagher, S., Kennedy, P., & Sikkink, D. (1998). *American evangelicalism: Embattled and thriving*. Chicago, IL: University of Chicago Press.

Spence, J.T. (1993). Gender-related traits and gender ideology: Evidence for a multifactorial theory. *Journal of Personality and Social Psychology, 64*(4), 624–635.

Stanton, G.N. (2001). Galatians. In J. Muddiman & J. Barton (Eds.), *The Oxford Bible commentary: The Pauline epistles* (pp. 151–169). Oxford University Press.

Starr, C.R., & Zurbriggen, E.L. (2016). Sandra Bem's gender schema theory after 34 years: A review of its reach and impact. *Sex Roles, 76*(9), 566–578.

Steensland, B., & Goff, P. (Eds.). (2014). *The new evangelical social engagement*. Oxford University Press.

Stephan, W.G., & Finlay, K. (1999). The role of empathy in improving intergroup relations. *Journal of Social Issues, 55*(4), 729–743.

Stewart, A.R. (2012). *Gender, faith, and storytelling: An ethnography of the charismatic internet* (Doctoral dissertation, University of Sussex).

Storkey, E. (1985). *What's right with feminism?* London: SPCK.

Strauss, D.F. ([1846] 2010). *The Life of Jesus, critically examined*. New York: Cosimo Inc.

Stringer, M.D. (1996). Towards a situational theory of belief. *Journal of the Anthropological Society of Oxford, 27*(3), 217–234.

Summerfield, P. (1998). *Reconstructing women's wartime lives: Discourse and subjectivity in oral histories of the Second World War.* Manchester: Manchester University Press.

Swingewood, A. (2000). *A short history of sociological thought*, 3rd ed. Aldershot: Palgrave.

Sykes, S.W. (1987). Introduction: Why authority? In S. Sykes (Ed.), *Authority in the Anglican Communion: Essays presented to Bishop John Howe* (pp. 11–23). Toronto: Anglican Book Centre.

Tajfel, H. (1974). Social identity and intergroup behaviour. *Social Science Information, 13*(2), 65–93.

Tajfel, H., & Turner, J.C. (1979). An integrative theory of intergroup conflict. *The Social Psychology of Intergroup Relations, 33*(47), 33–47.

Tajfel, H., & Turner, J.C. (1986). The social identity theory of intergroup behaviour. In S. Worchel & W.G. Austin (Eds.), *Psychology of intergroup relations* (pp. 7–24). Chicago, IL: Nelson Hall.

Tannen, D. (1990). *You just don't understand.* New York: Ballantine.

The Archbishops' Council. (2004). *Women Bishops in the Church of England? A report of the House of Bishops' Working Party on Women in the Episcopate.* London: Church House Publishing.

The Free Church of England (2018). *FCE History.* https://fcofe.org.uk/our-history/.

Theos. (2013). *The spirit of things unseen: Belief in post-religious Britain.* Theos. https://www.theosthinktank.co.uk/cmsfiles/archive/files/Reports/Spirit%20of%20 Things%20-%20Digital%20(update).pdf.

Thorne, H. (2000). *Journey to the priesthood: An in-depth study of the first women priests in the Church of England.* Bristol: Centre for Comparative Studies in Religion and Gender.

Thrall, M.E. (1958). *The ordination of women to the priesthood: A study of the biblical evidence.* London: SCM Press.

Toi, M., & Batson, C.D. (1982). More evidence that empathy is a source of altruistic motivation. *Journal of Personality and Social Psychology, 43*(2), 281–292.

Tooher, J. (2016). Overflowing with ministry opportunities! In Gatiss, L. (Ed.). *Positively Anglican: Building on the foundations and transforming the church* (pp. 67–72). Watford: Church Society.

Towsey, M. (2010). "Philosophically playing the Devil": Recovering readers' responses to David Hume and the Scottish Enlightenment. *Historical Research, 83*(220), 301–320.

Trzebiatowska, M. (2015). What theologians need to know: Contributions from sociology. In A. Thatcher (Ed.), *The Oxford handbook of theology, sexuality, and gender* (pp. 120–136). Oxford University Press.

Turnbull, R. (2007). *Anglican and evangelical?* New York: Continuum International Publishing Group.

Turner, J.C., & Oakes, P.J. (1986). The significance of the social identity concept for social psychology with reference to individualism, interactionism and social influence. *British Journal of Social Psychology, 25*(3), 237–252.

Turner, J.C., & Reynolds, K.J. (2012). Self-categorization theory. In P. Van Lange, A. Kruglanski, & E. Tory Higgins (Eds.), *The handbook of theories of social psychology: Self-categorization theory* (pp. 399–417). London: Sage.

216 Bibliography

Vanhoozer, K. (2004). Into the "Great Beyond": A theologian's response to the Marshall plan. In I.H. Marshall (Ed.), *Beyond the Bible: Moving from scripture to theology* (pp. 81–95). Ada, MI: Baker Academic Press.

Van Herk, K.A., Smith, D., & Andrew, C. (2011). Examining our privileges and oppressions: Incorporating an intersectionality paradigm into nursing. *Nursing Inquiry*, 18(1), 29–39.

Vasey-Saunders, M. (2015). *The scandal of evangelicals and homosexuality: English Evangelical Texts, 1960–2010*. London: Routledge.

Verter, B. (2003). Spiritual capital: Theorizing religion with Bourdieu against Bourdieu. *Sociological Theory*, 21(2), 150–174.

Village, A. (2013). Traditions within the Church of England and psychological type: A study among the clergy. *Journal of Empirical Theology*, 26(1), 22–44.

Vonk, R., & Olde-Monnikhof, M. (1998). Gender subgroups: Intergroup bias within the sexes. *European Journal of Social Psychology*, 28(1), 37–47.

Webb, W.J. (2001). *Slaves, women and homosexuals: Exploring the hermeneutics of cultural analysis*. Nottingham: InterVarsity Press.

Weiss, R.S. (1995). *Learning from strangers: The art and method of qualitative interview studies*. New York: The Free Press.

Westenberg, L. (2017). "When she calls for help"—domestic violence in Christian families. *Social Sciences*, 6(3), 71.

Williams, D.K. (2014). Prolifers of the left: Progressive evangelicals' campaign against abortion. In B. Steensland & P. Goff (Eds.), *The new evangelical social engagement* (pp. 200–220). Oxford University Press.

Wintour, P., & Davies, L. (2012, November 21). David Cameron: Church of England should "get on with it" on female bishops. *The Guardian*. https://www.theguardian.com/world/2012/nov/21/david-cameron-church-female-bishops.

Witherington III, B. (1987). *Women in the ministry of Jesus: A study of Jesus' attitudes to women and their roles as reflected in his earthly life*. Cambridge University Press.

Witherington III, B. (1990). *Women and the genesis of Christianity*. Cambridge University Press.

Wood, W. (2000). Attitude change: Persuasion and social influence. *Annual Review of Psychology*, 51, 539–570.

Wright, A. (2013). *Christianity and critical realism: Ambiguity, truth and theological literacy*. Oxford: Routledge.

Wright, J.H. (1997). Patristic testimony on women's ordination in Inter insigniores. *Theological Studies*, 58(3), 516–526.

Young, F. (2015). *Inferior office? A history of deacons in the Church of England*. Cambridge: James Clarke and Co.

Index

Page numbers followed by "n"

Abrams, D. 66
Act of Synod 39, 45, 76
agent(s) 13, 17; agency 13, 17–18,
    181, 198
Aldridge, A. 6–7, 62, 95–96, 177
Allen, J. L. 80
Allport, G. 65–66, 112, 174
Alsop, R. 20n2
Altglas, V. 192
ambivalence/ambivalent 7, 53, 55–56,
    60–61, 63, 66–69, 71–74, 93,
    135–136, 155, 158, 164–165,
    172, 178, 199n4
Ammerman, N. T. 47–48, 151, 157
Andrew, C. 93
Anglican(s)/Anglicanism 3, 6–7, 9, 14,
    26–27, 31–37, 41, 43, 45, 52, 63,
    65, 75–76, 91–95, 106, 110, 112,
    115–117, 128–129, 132–137,
    141–144, 152–153, 156, 158,
    161, 165–166, 173, 175, 178,
    181, 183, 185–186, 192,
    196–197
Anglo-Catholic(s)/Anglo-Catholicism
    3–4, 8, 10, 18–19, 20n8, 26, 28,
    34, 37–38, 42–45, 52–53, 60–63,
    72–75, 83, 86, 92–93, 96,
    109–110, 112–113, 120–125,
    128, 138–139, 141–144,
    146–147, 163–164, 166, 168n6,
    173, 175, 177–181, 187, 195
Antoun, R.T. 148
Appiah, K. 116, 136
Appleby, R. Scott 148
Archbishop(s) 1, 5, 34, 37, 41
The Archbishops' Council 41
Astley, J. 3

Atherstone, A. 148, 155
attitude(s) 6–8, 10–11, 13, 15–19,
    20n12, 21n16, 26–27, 29, 31–32,
    35–36, 40, 43–45, 46n3, 53, 55,
    58–60, 63, 66–69, 71, 74, 76, 80,
    85, 97–98, 108–109, 113–114,
    116–117, 124, 130, 132–133,
    135, 138, 156, 167, 172–178,
    180–181, 184, 191, 193–195,
    197–198; gender attitudes
    see gender
Aune, K. 29, 31, 45, 55–56, 58, 65,
    76n1, 130, 196
authority(ies) 1, 3, 5, 27–28, 32–33, 36,
    40, 42, 53, 61, 63, 70, 72, 75,
    103, 112, 115, 118, 121, 124,
    133, 148–150, 154, 159, 163,
    168n4, 175, 182, 185–186
Avis, P. 37, 158

Bagilhole, B. 6, 40
Baker, J. 42
Balmer, R. 27, 31, 148–150, 161, 186
Balz, H. 160
Banaji, M.R. 174, 194, 196
Baron-Cohen, S. 91
Barr, J. 148
Barticioti, F. 5
Barton, J. 154
Batson, C. D. 80
Baumeister, R.F. 174–175
Beattie, T. 33, 164
Bebbington, D. W. 3, 10, 14, 26, 36, 38,
    94, 133, 151–153, 155, 168n4
behaviour(s)/behave(s) 7–8, 13, 16,
    18–19, 45, 84, 87, 97, 102,
    112–114, 118, 123–124, 128,

218   *Index*

131, 133, 135, 140, 142, 144, 161–162, 167, 173, 176, 182, 192–193; behavioural 7–8, 16, 113, 115
belief(s)/believe(s)/believed 2–5, 7–8, 12–14, 16, 18–19, 20n14, 27, 29, 31, 34, 37–38, 40–42, 45, 52, 54, 56, 58–61, 67, 69–72, 73–75, 85–89, 91–92, 96–98, 102, 104, 111, 115, 117, 119–120, 124, 128–130, 132–134, 136, 139, 141–142, 146–148, 151, 155–157, 159–160, 164, 166–167, 173, 180, 188n4, 192
Bem, S. L. 84–86, 93, 99n1
Benn, W. 43
Bhaskar, R. 12
Bible 3, 32, 35, 38, 40–41, 53, 57, 75, 81–82, 94, 107, 134–135, 148–151, 153–157, 159–160, 162–163, 168n4, 195; biblical 14, 31, 32, 33, 35, 41, 54, 57, 75, 94–95, 116, 147–149, 151, 153–154, 159–160, 162–163, 186
Bielo, J.S. 178, 197
biology/biological/biologically 9, 12, 33–34, 58–59, 66, 69, 88, 91–92, 165, 191
bishop(s) 1–5, 8–9, 19, 20ns3, 10–11, 26–28, 34–35, 37–44, 52, 57, 61–63, 73, 106–107, 112, 115, 117, 122–123, 132, 134–135, 137, 142, 157, 161–162, 164, 177, 179, 185–186; consecration as (consecrate/consecrated/consecrating) 19, 26, 28, 35, 40–42, 44, 52, 61, 63, 73, 116, 157, 175, 179–180, 184–185, 187–188; flying bishops 39, 43, 112, 134, 136, 186
Bizman, A. 129
Blomberg, C. 32
Boden, J.M. 174
Boone, K.C. 149–150, 160
Bourdieu, P. 94, 97, 99n3, 130, 138
Bouvrette, A. 175
Brasher, B.E. 149–150, 156
Braun, V. 11
Brewer, W. F. 85
Brierley, P. W. 7, 196
British Social Attitudes 183
Brittain, C.C. 107

Brown, A. 2, 5, 29–30, 42, 63, 94, 152, 187
Brown, C. G. 29–30, 153, 157, 161, 184
Brown, D. 184
Brown, R. 80, 113, 179
Brown, S. 198
Bruce, F. F. 151, 154, 168n2
Bruce, S. 27, 147–148, 151
Bryan, J. 11
Buchanan, C. 34
Burman, E. 11, 97
Bushman, B.J. 174
Buskit, W. 7
Butler, J. 33
Butt, R. 43

Caldwell, R. 13
Caldwell, S. 41
Carey, G. 34, 37–38, 107, 185
Carlson, N. 7
Castro, Y.R. 193
causality/causation/cause/caused/causal 15–18, 54, 83, 113–114, 119, 136, 147–148, 167, 181, 183, 187, 193, 196
Chadwick, O. 4, 148
Chandler, M. 27
Chapman, R. 27
Christ 4, 27, 33, 41, 62–63, 139, 148, 158, 164–165, 188n4; *see also* Jesus
Christian/Christianity 3–4, 18, 20n9, 27–28, 30–35, 41, 43–44, 56, 58, 63, 73–76, 89, 91–92, 105, 110, 115, 120, 125, 126n2, 134, 148–153, 156, 162–164, 167, 186, 188n4, 192, 196–197
Clarke, V. 11
Collier, A. 12
Cooper, M.L. 175
Craston, C. 34
Crocker, J. 175
chronological/chronologically 11, 15–16
Church(s)/church(s) 3–4, 8, 10, 13, 20ns5 & 13, 26–45, 53–58, 61, 63, 65, 68–76, 81–82, 87, 89–90, 92–95, 97, 103, 106–112, 114–118, 120, 122–124, 126n3, 132, 134–135, 137–138, 140–142, 147–151, 153–154, 156–159, 161–163, 165, 173, 175, 177, 180–182, 184–187, 195–197, 199; Church of

England (CofE) 5–6, 9–10, 12, 14–15, 18–19, 26–29, 32, 34–46, 52–53, 57–61, 64, 73–74, 76, 81, 86, 90, 93–96, 104, 106–107, 110–111, 113–114, 116–122, 124–126, 126n3, 130, 133–136, 138, 140–142, 146, 152–153, 155, 158–162, 164, 167, 168n5, 172–173, 175, 177–179, 181, 183–188, 191, 194–197, 199; Established Church 1–2, 4, 6–8, 26, 34–36, 44–45, 65, 76, 107, 119, 126, 134–135, 152–153, 158, 161–162, 178, 181, 183–185, 187, 196–197

Church of England [as author] 184, 199

Cisgender 9, 191, 197

Clarke, V. 11

class(es) 4, 29, 31, 81, 93–96, 121, 136, 142, 147, 156, 177, 179, 183; clergy/clergyperson/clergymen 3–6, 8–10, 12, 14–15, 18–19, 27–28, 31, 33, 37, 38–40, 42–43, 52–53, 63–64, 71–72, 74, 79–81, 87, 94–96, 102, 104, 107, 110–112, 114–118, 122–125, 126n1, 128, 130–132, 134, 136, 138–139, 141–144, 161, 166–167, 172–173, 176–179, 181–184, 186–188, 191, 195–199

codes/coding 11–12, 17

communion 4–5, 20n6, 34–35, 37, 40, 43, 61, 106, 109, 111–112, 121, 134, 139, 158, 161, 165, 176, 180, 185–186

complementarian(s)/ complementarianism 53, 58, 68, 87, 89, 156, 160

contact 71, 102, 107–110, 112–115, 117, 119–121, 123–125, 128, 135–137, 139, 143–144, 172–173, 179–182, 184, 186–188, 192–193, 198; avoidance 105, 116–117, 122, 124–125, 128–129, 133, 135, 176, 178–179, 181–182, 188, 192–193–194; hypothesis 112, 128, 130, 143–144

Cooper, A-P. 184, 196

co-operation/co-operative/co-operatively 66, 80, 106, 108, 113–118, 120,

122, 130–131, 137–140, 143–144, 184–185

Cornwall, S. 13

Coston, B. M. 93, 96

Cowie, L.J. 199n4

Crandall, C. S. 68

Craston, C. 36

creation 53–54, 57, 151, 155–156; created 53, 58, 68–69, 87, 89, 155–156, 160

Crenshaw, K. W. 93

critical realism/critical realist 12–13, 16, 67, 74, 181, 183

culture(s)/culturally 8–9, 15, 28, 31–33, 40, 57, 84–85, 89, 91, 94, 96, 110, 116, 123, 141–142, 150–151, 153–154, 156, 158, 162–163, 166–167, 183, 185

data 8–12, 14–17, 19, 20n12, 20n14, 21n16, 21n17, 52, 65, 74, 79, 81, 86, 92, 97–98, 99n2, 112, 119, 122, 128, 144, 149, 157, 166, 168n6, 173–174, 179, 181, 183, 191, 195–196, 198–199, 199n3

Davies, L. 187

Dawkins, R. 88

Day, A. 2, 30

deacon(s) 2–6, 26, 34, 37, 39, 57, 61–62, 105, 126n3; deaconess 4–5, 29, 32, 34, 37, 109, 118; diaconate 4–6, 34, 37, 61, 108, 110–111, 125, 140; permanent 4–5, 37

Delap, L. 31, 91, 156

design/designed 53

diocese(s)/diocesan 3, 8–10, 20n7, 20n11, 43, 73, 102–103, 106–107, 109–112, 114, 118–120, 122–123, 126n1, 126n2, 131, 133–138, 141, 145n2, 155, 160–162, 185–186, 195

Dixon, J. 124

Dovidio, J. F. 80, 113

Drury, C. 159

dualism 32, 58, 60, 63

Dunn, J. 62, 186

Durrheim, K. 124

ecumenism/ecumenical 33–34, 42–43, 61, 95, 109–110, 120, 164

Eisenberg, N. 80

220 *Index*

Eldredge, J. 89, 156
Eldredge, S. 89, 156
Ellemers, N. 176
Emerson, M. 35, 75, 150, 152, 178, 183
emotion(s) 7, 18–19, 67–68, 79, 97, 102,
    113, 128–129, 131–134,
    136–137, 139, 141–144, 167,
    172, 174, 182, 192–193;
    agitation 129, 132, 134, 137,
    141, 193; dejection 129, 132,
    137, 141, 193
empathy/empathetic/empathise 79–84,
    91, 98, 108, 114; altruistic
    80–81; lack of 80–81, 83
enclave 28, 110, 112, 123
engaged orthodoxy 45, 56, 73–74, 123,
    150, 155, 158, 166, 173,
    178–179, 181, 188
episcopate/episcopacy/episcopal 2, 5, 63,
    104, 112, 131, 176
epistemology/epistemological 12, 20n14,
    180–181, 183, 194
Eshleman, A. 68
essentialism/essentialist 12, 33, 54, 60,
    63–64, 86–87, 98
Established Church *see* Church of
    England
ethics/ethical 10, 21n16, 74, 81
ethnographic observation(s) 11, 17, 93
Eucharist 3, 180
evangelical(s)/evangelicalism(s) 3–4,
    7–10, 14, 19, 20n15, 26, 29,
    31–36, 38–39, 41–45, 46n3, 52,
    55–58, 60, 64, 72–75, 83, 86–87,
    89–98, 103–109, 116–119,
    124–125, 132–138, 141, 143,
    146–163, 165–167, 173, 175,
    177–181, 184, 195–196;
    charismatic 3, 8, 10, 46n3, 53,
    56, 58–60–61, 71, 73–75, 82–83,
    86, 90–93, 95–98, 107–109,
    117–119, 124–125, 136–138,
    143, 146, 162–163, 173,
    179–180, 195–196; conservative
    4, 8–10, 20n15, 26, 38, 44–45,
    53, 56, 74–75, 86, 89–90, 93–94,
    96, 105–107, 116–118, 125,
    132–136, 141, 146, 149,
    151–156, 158–162, 175,
    177–179, 195; liberal 3, 14, 26,
    92, 151–152
explanatory power 7–8, 14, 19, 85, 97,
    128, 167, 181

Fairweather, E. R. 27
faith 2–3, 5, 11, 20n3, 27, 29–30, 33,
    35, 38, 41–43, 88, 116–117, 130,
    135, 156, 164
The Faith and Order Commission 43
family(ies)/familial 4, 10, 15, 27, 29–30,
    33, 52–55, 68–69, 73–74, 81,
    85–87, 89–90, 92, 94–96, 121,
    139, 142–143, 149, 151–152,
    156–157, 182, 188
Faught, C. B. 28
Fausto-Sterling, A. 33
female(s) 5–6, 9, 14, 20ns2, 14, 29–30,
    33, 36, 38–41, 53, 57, 59, 65, 68,
    70–71, 74, 80–81, 83, 86–88,
    90–91, 93, 102, 108–110,
    115–116, 118, 120, 123, 130,
    138–139, 141, 150, 155, 165,
    173, 179, 181–182, 186, 196;
    submission *see* submission
feminine/femininity 29, 54–55, 59, 64,
    70, 91–92
feminism 2, 12–13, 20n2, 27, 31–33, 44,
    53, 55–56, 58, 60–61, 63–65,
    69–73, 76n1, 81, 87, 92, 137,
    149, 155, 158, 164–166, 168n6;
    ambivalent attitudes towards
    see ambivalence: feminist(s) 1,
    12–13, 31–33, 41, 56, 63–66,
    70–74, 117, 137, 150, 159, 165,
    196; first wave 31; positives of
    53, 56, 60–61, 63–65, 69, 71–73,
    158–159, 165; negatives of 53,
    56, 60–61, 63–65, 69–73, 87, 92,
    158–159, 165; second wave 2,
    20n2, 31–32, 41, 44, 58; third
    wave 33
Fernández, M.L. 193
Ferns, S. 73, 116, 185
Finlay, K. 80
Fiske, S. 66–67, 72, 75, 174, 193–194
Fitzsimons, A. 20n2
Fletcher, W. 34–35, 158
Forward in Faith 10, 38, 63, 111–112,
    121–123, 139, 142,
    177–178, 180
Foucault, M. 103
Frable, D. E. 85
Francis, L. J. 3, 5–6, 37–39, 161
Free Church of England 106, 134, 161
Frijda, N.H. 129
Fry, A. D. J. 2, 18, 20n2, 31, 33, 54–56,
    69, 75, 76n1, 89, 94, 99n2, 112,

120, 123, 130, 139, 149, 156, 159, 173, 186, 187, 188n1, 195, 198

fundamentalist/fundamentalism 148–150, 151–152, 154–155, 160–161

Furlong, M. 4, 39, 44

Gaertner, S.L. 113
GAFCON 106, 133–134, 136, 161
Gallagher, S. K. 13, 27, 30, 35, 75, 149–152, 178, 183
Ganiel, G. 199
Garaigordobil, M. 80
Gatrell, C. 40
gender 2, 4, 9, 12–14, 19, 26–33, 35–36, 38–40, 42–45, 46n3, 52, 55, 57, 59, 63–67, 69–76, 79, 81, 84–93, 95, 97–98, 99n1, 102–104, 106, 109, 115–117, 119–121, 123–126, 132, 136, 138–142, 146–147, 149–151, 155–167, 172–173, 175, 181–187, 191–198, 199n3; attitudes 1, 6–8, 11, 15–19, 26–27, 29, 31, 36, 40, 43–45, 46n3, 52–53, 56–61, 64, 67, 73–76, 79, 85–86, 89–90, 95, 97, 102, 119, 121, 124–126, 131, 138, 146, 155–156, 158, 160, 162–167, 173, 175, 181–184, 187, 191–199, 199n3; equality/equal 1–2, 13, 32–33, 39, 41, 44, 56–58, 64, 87, 116–117, 150, 156–158, 163–164, 173, 177, 183, 185, 199; flexible 9, 26, 28–30, 33, 36, 37, 41, 44–45, 59, 71, 90, 182, 191, 193; gendered 6, 27, 32–33, 40, 58, 71, 84–86, 91; inequality 19, 39, 43, 55, 75, 81, 88, 114, 194–196; norms 7, 53, 56, 120–121, 126, 132, 149, 156, 162, 173, 177, 192, 197; roles 4, 26, 53, 59, 66, 68–72, 74, 86–88, 90, 95–97, 111, 126, 149–150, 155–156, 158, 160–161, 172–173, 191, 196; schemata/schema 79, 84–87, 89–93, 98, 99n1, 182, 191, 193, 199n3; values 7, 9, 14, 28, 30, 33, 39, 43–45, 54, 56, 73, 85, 89–90, 92, 106, 109, 119, 125,

132, 157, 161–162, 183, 187, 197

General Synod 5–6, 8, 20n10, 36–40, 42, 63, 161

General Synod of the Church of England 38

Gilligan, C. 89
Glick, P. 66–67, 72, 75, 174, 193–194
God 3, 13, 20n3, 20n8, 30, 33–34, 40, 54–55, 59, 62–64, 68–69, 82, 88–89, 94, 144n1, 147–148, 150, 153, 156–157, 160, 163, 168n3
Goff, P. 8
Goodchild, S. 5
Goodhew, D. 184, 196
Gonzales, A.L. 176
Grady, M. P. 11
Graham, J. M. 32
Gray, J. 88
Grayzel, S. R. 28–29
Green, T. K. 65
Greene, A. M. 6, 40
Greer, G. 89
Greaves, L.M. 199n4
Gregg, D. 34
Groppe, E. 33
group(s)s/grouping 8–13, 17–18, 27, 34, 36, 38, 41, 44, 46n2, 62, 66, 71–73, 80–81, 83, 92–98, 105, 107, 109–110, 113, 119, 121–123, 125, 128–130, 132–139, 141–144, 156, 161–163, 167, 173–174, 176, 178–179, 181–184, 192–194, 198–199, 199n1, 199n2
Grudem, W. A. 33, 54, 150, 154, 156, 160, 167
Guest, M. 8, 31, 33–35, 45, 55–56, 58, 65, 130, 136, 151, 178
Gunstone, J. 34

Hackett, C. 2
Hall, D. 31
Halualani, T. 97, 114, 124
Hancock, J.T. 176
Handley, P. 43
Harari, Y.N. 187
Harvey, G. 192
Haslam, S.A. 167
Hayfield, N. 11
head/headship 53, 55–57, 60, 87, 95, 118, 150, 154–156, 158

Index

Heelas, P. 192
Heeney, B. 27
Herek, G. M. 121
hermeneutic(s)/hermeneutical 31–32, 41, 95–96, 149, 153–154, 159–160, 162–163, 195, 198
heterosexual/heterosexuality 67, 72, 75, 93–95, 121–122, 182, 194, 199n4
Higgins, E.T. 129
Hindess, B. 13
history(ies) 26, 32, 41, 53, 59–60, 74–75, 83, 94, 118, 122, 125, 142, 146, 148, 152–153, 173, 177–178, 181; historic 1, 7, 35, 41, 62, 134; historical/historically 2, 8–9, 15, 18–19, 26, 28–31, 32–34, 45, 52–53, 55, 57–58, 63, 65, 74–76, 79, 81, 84–85, 87, 89, 94–97, 106, 112, 123, 125–126, 132–134, 136, 141, 146–148, 151–156, 158, 160, 162–164, 166–167, 173–177, 178, 181–182, 187–188, 192–193, 196
historical criticism/historical-critical/ biblical criticism 14, 62, 154, 159, 163
Hitlin, S. 7
Hollis, C. 27
homosexual(s)/homosexuality 71, 75, 93, 96, 107, 111, 119, 121, 138, 163, 194, 199n4
Howard, C. 34
Hunter, J. D. 29–30, 45
husband(s) 6, 27, 30, 33, 56–57, 69, 87, 94–95
Hylson-Smith, K. 4

identity(ies) 2, 6, 9, 13–14, 19, 20n14, 28, 31, 40, 45, 79, 86, 93–96, 98, 114, 116–117, 125, 129, 132–137, 141–144, 160, 167, 174–176, 178–182, 185, 187–188, 191–197, 199n4; social identity theory see social identity (theory)
inequality(ies) 6, 12, 19, 39, 43, 75, 93
Industrial Revolution 26–27, 147, 149, 151
influence(s)/influenced/influential 8, 11, 13–15, 17–18, 31, 36, 74, 76, 93,

125, 139, 146–148, 156, 163–164, 166–167, 194, 198
Ingroup 97, 113–114, 122, 140, 174, 176, 178, 181–182, 187, 192–193, 195
Intergroup 80, 102, 112–114, 117, 120, 123–124, 128, 140, 143–144, 172, 178–179, 181–183, 191–193, 195, 197
international/internationally 146–147, 162, 164, 166–167
intersectional/intersectionality 19, 79, 93, 97–98, 136, 143–144, 181, 188; intersecting 19, 182, 187, 192, 194
intersecting social strata 191–192
intersex 9, 20n14, 197
interview(s)/interviewed 9–12, 15, 21n17, 52–53, 60, 63, 65, 69, 79, 81, 94, 103, 105, 110, 119, 121, 123, 126, 128, 132, 136, 138, 142, 157, 162, 172, 177–179; semi-structured 10, 14, 17

Jagger, S. 54
Jenkins, D. 42
Jesus 3, 20n6, 38, 62–63, 144n1, 148, 163, 186; see also Christ
Joel, D. 91
Johnson, E. A. 32, 60, 63
Jones, I. 6, 8, 10, 38, 40, 123, 158, 161
Jones, P. 199
Jost, J. T. 18, 173–174, 194, 196

Kawakami, K. 113
Kay, A. C. 18
Keele 36, 73, 116, 118, 152–153, 162
Kennedy, P. 35, 75, 150, 152, 178, 183
Kimmel, M. 93, 96
Kirk, T. 113
Knight, K.M. 175
Knox, E. A. 28
Kortekaas, P. 176
Krosnick, J. 7
Kumra, S. 130

Laqueur. T. W. 33
Larsen, T. 27
lead/leader/leadership 53–54, 58–59, 68–71, 87, 90, 94–95, 107–109, 118–119, 124–125, 150–151, 155, 157, 159, 163, 165, 177, 180, 196

Leary, M.R. 175
Lease, S. 42
legislation 150, 161, 168n5
Lembo, A. 7, 20n12
Lennon, K. 20n2
liberalism/liberal 3, 9, 14, 36, 38, 73,
    102, 105–106, 112, 116–117,
    134, 136, 138, 140–141,
    148–149, 152–153, 160, 162,
    175; evangelicalism *see* liberal
    evangelicalism
Lobel, T. E. 85
Lorenzo, M.G. 193
Luhtanen, R.K. 175
Lyon, D. 192

MacCulloch, D. 30, 34, 148, 151
Macquarrie, J. 148
Maiden, J. 3, 34, 109
male(s) 4–6, 8–9, 12–13, 15, 20n2,
    20n14, 28, 31, 33, 36, 38–42, 53,
    55, 57–59, 61–62, 66, 69, 71, 80,
    83–84, 86–87, 90–91, 93, 95,
    102, 105, 110, 112, 118,
    120–122, 138–139, 149–150,
    154–156, 164–165, 167,
    172–173, 176–182, 188, 191,
    196–197; headship *see* head:
    male dominated 6–7, 28, 31, 40,
    110, 123; male power 6, 66
Maltby, J. 2, 5, 39, 158
Man 38, 54, 66, 139, 159, 191
Mantle, G. 37
Marsden, G. 148–149
Martin, B. 28
Martin, G. 7
Martin, J. 7, 20n12
Martin, J. L. 21n16
masculine/masculinity 31–32, 55, 70,
    84, 89, 91–92, 156
Masser, B. M. 66
Maxwell, J. A. 16–17, 21n17
Mayland, J. 34–35
McCarthy Brown, K. 148
McGrath, A. 4
McKinnon, A. 107
McLeod, H. 27, 30, 31, 35, 156
men 1–2, 4–9, 12–13, 27–31, 33, 36–37,
    39, 40, 42–43, 53–54, 56, 60, 64,
    66–72, 84, 87–92, 95–96, 105,
    108–109, 111, 115–116, 120,
    137, 140, 149–151, 156–157,

159–162, 175, 177–178,
    193–194, 197
Merino, S. M. 65
method(s) 11, 13–14, 16–17, 21n17,
    130, 151, 154, 160, 163, 195,
    197–199; methodology/
    methodologically 9, 15, 19, 53,
    74, 79, 85, 97–98, 102, 123, 128,
    143–144, 147, 166, 173, 177,
    180, 198
methodist/methodism 35, 153
Miller, P. A. 80
minister(s) 4, 14, 35, 40, 43, 62, 162,
    175, 184; ministerial 3, 20n4, 39;
    ministry 3–4, 8, 15, 31–32, 35,
    37, 39–40, 42–43, 55, 57, 76, 92,
    95, 102–103, 105–106, 109, 114,
    116–118, 120, 134–135, 140,
    149, 163, 180, 184–185
misogyny 13
modernity 26, 45, 146–149, 151, 155,
    158, 161, 163, 183
monograph 2, 7–10, 12–15, 18, 19,
    20n12, 20n15, 70, 86, 93,
    125–126, 144, 167, 172–173,
    180–181, 183–184, 191, 194,
    196–198, 199n3
Montefiore, H. 37
Mounce, W.D. 159
Mruk, C. 175

narrative(s) 11, 14–16, 18, 29, 36,
    52–58, 60, 63, 65, 68, 70–74, 82,
    84, 88, 90–93, 97–98, 102–103,
    106, 108, 112, 114–116,
    118–123, 126, 128, 131–135,
    137–141, 144, 146–147,
    154–157, 159–160, 162–164,
    166–167, 172, 174, 177, 183,
    185, 187, 196, 198
Nason-Clark, N. 4–5, 37, 97, 126
Nathanson, A. I. 85
nature/natural 53–55, 87, 89, 102, 104,
    111, 121, 124, 143,
    147–148, 191
Nazir-Ali, M. 41
New Testament 3, 36, 40, 54, 64, 83,
    154–155, 159, 163–164, 186
Noll, M.A. 152
Nosek, B.A. 173
Numbers, R. 155

224   *Index*

Oakes, P. J. 129, 135, 174
Olde-Monnikhoff, M. 65
Ollard, S. L. 28
Olsen, E. 8, 33–35, 136
Olsen, G.W. 153
ordination 3–4, 6, 8, 10–11, 26, 28–29,
    31, 34–42, 44–45, 52, 82, 94–96,
    98, 103–104, 107–109, 111, 117,
    120–121, 126n1, 131–132, 134,
    140, 152, 157, 177, 182; of
    women 3–10, 14, 18, 19, 26,
    28–29, 31, 34–42, 44–45, 52,
    55–59, 61–62, 82, 95, 98,
    104–108, 111, 113–116,
    118–120, 131, 134, 140,
    157–158, 161, 164–165,
    174–176, 178–180, 184, 188
outgroup(s) 65, 83, 102, 113–114, 117,
    120, 122, 124, 136, 140, 142,
    173–182, 187, 192–193, 195,
    198, 199n2
Ouwerkerk, J.W. 176
Oxford Movement 3, 27, 106

Packer, J. I. 36
Page, S-J 6, 12–13, 33, 126, 176
participant(s) 8–19, 20n14, 20n15,
    21n16, 21n17, 45, 46n3, 52–61,
    63, 65, 67–72, 74–76, 79–98,
    102–114–120, 122–126, 128,
    131–139, 141–144, 146–147,
    149, 153–167, 168n6, 172–175,
    177–181, 183–184, 187, 191,
    193, 195, 197–198, 199n3;
    selection/recruitment 9, 81, 113
patriarchy/patriarchal 31–32, 58, 67, 81,
    126, 150, 199
Pattison, D. 34
Peek, C.W. 198
Penning, J. M. 45
Percy, E. 44
Perkin, J. 27
Perrin, R. 35, 153–154, 159, 163
Pettigrew, T. F. 66, 113
Petty, R. 7
Peyton, N. 40
Pickering, W. S. F. 28
Pilarski, A. E. 20n2, 31, 136
Piliavin, J. A. 7
Piper, J. 33, 156
Platow, M.J. 167
plausible/plausibility/plausibility

structure 30, 55, 114,
    147–148, 166
Porter, M. 154
positivism/positivist 12, 16
postfeminist/postfeminism 56, 166
poststructuralism/poststructuralist 12
Powell, A. A. 80
Power 6, 7, 8, 14, 19, 33, 69, 72, 103,
    130, 140, 164, 196, 198
Press, A. L. 56
prejudice 9, 12, 19, 52, 65–66, 68, 71,
    75–76, 76n3, 79–80, 83–86,
    97–98, 102, 112–114, 116–117,
    119–120, 124–125, 128,
    143–144, 172–174, 179,
    181–183, 186–187, 193,
    197–198, 199n2; prejudice
    suppression 65, 68, 71–73, 75;
    prejudicial 9, 12, 21n16, 65,
    67–68, 71–72, 74, 80, 83, 93,
    97–98, 108–109, 112, 114, 117,
    119, 121, 125–126, 133, 144,
    172–176, 182, 193; reduction 71,
    80, 84, 113–115, 120, 124, 130,
    139, 179, 184, 187; undermining
    of 72, 114, 116, 119, 121, 123,
    125, 137, 142, 173, 179–180,
    182, 193
priest(s) 2, 3, 4, 5, 6, 10, 19, 20ns4, 5,
    10, 33, 36, 39, 57, 62, 93, 95,
    105, 107, 109–110, 117–118,
    121–123, 126n3, 139–142, 151,
    164, 172, 175–176, 178–181,
    185; priesting 4, 34, 37, 39–40,
    161; priesthood 4–5, 10, 28,
    33–34, 36–38, 40, 43, 61–63, 81,
    83, 92, 94–95, 103, 110–111,
    117, 120–121, 125, 139–140,
    152, 157, 164–165, 175–176,
    178, 182, 185; women
    see women priests
privilege/privileged 1–2, 6, 29, 93–94,
    96–97, 123, 161, 174–179,
    183, 187
process theory 15, 17
protestant(s)/protestantism 27, 32, 52,
    75, 147–148, 157, 178, 183, 186
Provincial Episcopal Visitor *see* flying
    bishops
psychology 7, 18, 199n3; psychological
    6, 8, 16, 19, 66, 84, 88, 98, 128,
    167, 181

Putnam, R.D. 130, 133, 143, 176

qualitative 11, 15–16, 18, 67, 97–98, 102, 124, 143–144, 172, 198–199; qualitatively 18–19, 198
quantitative 15–16, 18–19, 65–66, 86, 97, 102, 114, 124, 126, 144, 172, 179, 197–198

Radford Ruether, R. 75
rationalisation 147
Raven, C. 41
Redford, C. 55
Reed, J. S. 27
reflexive 12; reflexivity 14
reform 9–10, 20n15, 38, 53, 55–58, 60, 68, 70–74, 81–82, 88–89, 92, 95–96, 98, 102–103, 106–107, 109, 113–116, 123–125, 131–136, 143–144, 145n2, 155–156, 158–163, 173, 177–178, 180, 187
reformation 3, 28, 41, 147
Reicher, S.D. 6–7, 38, 63, 167, 174
religion 14, 19, 27, 147–148, 176, 186; religious 2, 10–11, 15, 18–19, 20n8, 26–30, 55, 65, 69, 75, 85–86, 88–91, 93, 95, 98, 110, 125, 128, 130, 143, 147–148, 151, 161, 165–167, 182–183, 186, 188, 192–193, 195–197
represent/representative 2–3, 9–10, 14, 17, 41, 43–44
resist/resisted/resisting/resistance/ resistant 5, 7–8, 10, 12, 26, 28, 36, 43–45, 46n3, 52, 63, 73–74, 92, 102–106, 112, 115, 119, 123–124, 131, 133, 137, 142, 144, 149, 151, 153–155, 160–162, 173, 177, 181, 192, 196
Reynolds, K. J. 80
Riessman, R. K. 11
Robbins, M. 3, 5–6, 37–39, 161
Roman Catholics/Roman Catholicism 3–4, 10, 14, 19, 27–28, 32–34, 37–38, 41–42, 44, 61–63, 65, 75, 96, 112, 134, 141–142, 146–147, 163–167
Ruddick, A. 43
Rudman, L. A. 65

Saldaña, J. 11
Sani, F. 6–7, 38, 63, 129, 174
Sayer, A. 12
schism/schismatic 102, 106, 128–139, 142–144, 161–162, 174, 182, 185, 193
Schneider, G. 160
Schroeder, D. A. 80
Schüssler Fiorenza, E. 32, 41
scripture 4, 31–32, 35, 40, 58, 69, 81, 94, 96, 150–151, 153, 156–157, 163, 165, 175; scriptural 14, 40, 159, 198
self-categorisation (theory) 128–129, 173–174, 176, 178
self-discrepancy (theory) 128–129
self-esteem/threatened self-esteem 174–183, 187–188, 191–194
sex/sexes 6, 9, 11–13, 20ns2, 14, 29, 32–33, 39, 41, 53, 57, 60, 63–67, 69, 71, 81–82, 84–88, 91–93, 118, 125, 151, 157, 160–161, 164–165, 182, 191, 193, 197; as binary 9, 20n2, 20n14, 29, 67, 84–87, 90, 93, 95, 98, 125, 144, 191, 197
sexism 6, 9, 13, 16, 19, 32, 52–53, 65–75, 76n3, 80, 83, 93, 96–98, 119, 121, 125–126, 166, 172, 174–175, 177–178, 180–181, 183, 185–186, 188, 191, 193–194, 196–198, 199n4; benevolent/benevolently 66–67, 193; hostile 66–67, 69–73, 75, 80, 83, 166, 193; indirect 68–69, 73, 75, 80, 121, 194, 199n3; sexist 13, 17, 76, 97, 114, 119, 131, 175–176, 178–179, 193–194, 197–198
Seybold, K. S. 13
shape(s)/shaped 7–8, 11, 15, 17–19, 26, 28, 34, 44, 52–53, 60, 85, 89, 91, 118, 146, 151, 154–155, 166–167, 172, 174–176, 178, 181–182, 191, 193–195; shaping 6, 16, 79, 98, 125, 162–164, 166–167, 181–183, 187
Sharma, S. 56, 58, 65, 130
Sibley, C.G. 199n4
Sikkink, D. 35, 75, 150, 152, 178, 183
Smart, L. 174
Smidt, C. E. 45

226 *Index*

Smith, C. 35, 75, 150, 152, 178, 183
Smith, D. 93
social capital 19, 102, 128, 130–131,
   133, 135, 137, 139–141, 143,
   173, 176, 179–182, 184–185,
   188, 192–193, 196, 198
social construction/socially constructed
   12–13, 20n14, 33
social context/social contexts 15–16, 75,
   79, 85, 124
social factors 15, 19, 53, 91, 146, 162,
   172, 191
social forces 13, 17, 126
social identity theory 174
social psychology 6–7, 18, 123; social
   psychological 8, 18, 19, 52–53,
   65, 74, 76n3, 79, 97, 102, 112,
   119, 126, 143, 172, 198
social scientific 6–7, 12, 13, 14, 19
social structures 17, 18
society(ies) 2–4, 6–9, 18, 20n15, 26–27,
   29, 31–32, 29, 43–45, 54, 56–57,
   67, 71, 74–76, 84, 88–92, 97,
   114, 125, 141, 143, 147,
   150–151, 153, 156, 158,
   161–162, 166–167, 174, 177,
   179, 187, 191–192, 194–196;
   societal 15, 44, 46n3, 56, 62, 74,
   87, 90–92, 148, 155, 165–166
sociology 74; sociological 8, 18–19, 53,
   74, 79, 85, 114, 123, 143, 148,
   167, 186
Spence, J. T. 85
spiritual capital 19, 102, 128, 130–131,
   133, 135, 137–141, 143, 173,
   176, 179–182, 184–185, 188,
   192, 198
Stanton, G. N. 64
Starr, C. R. 85
status(es) 65–66, 71, 87, 93–97,
   113–116, 118, 121–122, 130,
   136, 139, 148, 174, 175,
   177–178, 183, 193–194, 199
Steensland, B. 8
Stephan, W. J. 80
stereotype(s)/stereotyped/stereotyping/
   stereotypically 1, 66–67, 69–71,
   84–87, 93, 98, 99n1, 113, 116,
   138, 174, 182, 193
Stewart, A. R. 31
Storkey, E. 13, 32, 58, 97
stratification of reality 13, 16, 76n3,
   181, 194

Strauss, D.F. 148
Stringer, M.D. 119
structured observations 11–12, 17, 195
submission/submit/submitting/
   submissive 6, 33, 36, 41, 53–54,
   63, 68, 70, 81, 87, 156, 159;
   subordination 32, 38, 54, 57–58;
   subservient 110
Summerfield, P. 29, 157
Swingewood, A. 17, 177
Sykes, S. W. 75
symbolic boundaries 45, 46n2, 46n3,
   116, 119, 123, 173, 181, 188,
   191–192
symbolic meaning 116–117, 123, 175

Tajfel, H. 13, 97, 117, 122, 174, 176
Tannen, D. 89
thematic narrative analysis 11
theme(s) 11–12, 17, 53, 60, 82, 87, 90,
   102, 104, 108–110, 112, 115,
   128, 131, 137–138, 143, 155,
   162–163, 165
theology 8–10, 14, 27–28, 31–32, 35,
   37, 41, 43, 53, 56–60, 62, 73–74,
   95, 104–106, 108, 110, 118,
   131–134, 138, 140, 142,
   147–148, 157–161, 164–165,
   180, 186; theologies 4, 14, 41,
   53, 117, 137, 150; theological 4,
   8–11, 13, 14, 28, 32, 35–36,
   38–39, 40, 42, 56, 59, 61, 63–64,
   69–70, 72, 88, 94, 103–112, 115,
   118, 123–124, 132–138, 142,
   148, 151, 153–154, 156,
   159–161, 163, 165, 168n4, 175,
   180, 184–186, 196; theologically
   3, 9, 11, 14–15, 36–37, 39, 53,
   105–106, 115–116, 122,
   131–134, 136, 140, 161, 197;
   theologically conservative,
   theological conservative(s) 11,
   53, 106, 112, 134, 141, 167, 173,
   177, 181, 188, 191, 196;
   theological liberalism
   see liberalism
Theos 192
Thiselton. A. C. 54
Thorne, H. 29, 31, 36–37
Thrall, M. E. 32, 161
Toi, M. 80
Tooher, J. 43
Towsey, M. 149

Index 227

Tractarians 27–29, 63, 110, 112, 165
tradition 3–4, 6–11, 13–15, 17–19, 26, 28, 31–35, 39, 41, 43–45, 53, 59–60, 62, 73–76, 83, 89–91, 93–96, 98, 102–105, 107–112, 115, 117–119, 122–123, 125–126, 130, 132, 135, 137–138, 141–142, 146–150, 153, 155, 157, 160, 163, 165–167, 173, 175–182, 184–186, 188, 192–193, 195–196–197; traditional 1, 3–5, 9–10, 14, 19, 26, 28–30, 35, 37–39, 42–43, 45, 55–56, 59, 66–67, 69–70, 72–75, 84, 86–87, 90–91, 98, 99n1, 104, 109, 117, 119, 121, 125, 132, 134, 141–142, 147–150, 152, 156–158, 166, 175, 178, 180, 191, 195–197; traditionalist(s) 5, 7–9, 14, 38–40, 42–44, 60–61, 69, 95–96, 104, 106, 112, 123, 125, 139, 141–142, 151, 173, 182, 185–187; traditionally 9, 28–29, 92, 99n1
train/trained/training 3, 10, 40, 42, 94–96, 102–105, 108–111, 115, 117–118, 120–121, 131–134, 136–139–141, 154–155, 160, 163, 177, 184–185, 188n1, 196
transmute/transmuted 84–85, 87
Tredoux, C. 124
Treyens, J. C. 85
Tropp, L. R. 65, 113
Trzebiatowska, M. 15
Turnbull, R. 153
Turner, J. C. 80, 97, 129, 135, 174, 176

value(s) 7–8, 15, 18, 20n12, 26, 28, 30, 32–33, 39, 43–45, 52, 56, 68, 75, 85, 87, 89, 113, 119, 132, 135, 155, 175, 192; gender values *see* gender

Van Herk, K. A. 93
Vanhoozer, K. 32
Vasey-Saunders, M. 26, 75, 178
Verter, B. 130
Village, A. 3
Vincett, G. 192
Vinnicombe, S. 130
volition 13, 17
Vonk, R. 65

Warner, R. 56, 58, 65, 130
Webb, W. J. 32, 163
Weiss, R.S 15
Westenberg, L. 54
wife/wives 6, 30, 56–57, 59–60, 69, 71, 87, 90, 94–95, 110
Wintour, P. 187
Witherington III, B. 14, 35
Wolffe, J. 8, 33–35, 136
woman/women 1–10, 12–14, 18–19, 20n2, 26–45, 52–64, 66–71, 73, 74, 76, 80–84, 87–93, 95–96, 102–103, 105–111, 114–115, 117–121, 124–125, 128–130, 131, 137–142, 144, 149–151, 156–157, 159–166, 172–173, 177, 180–182, 184–185, 187, 191, 193–194, 196–198; priests 3, 5, 19, 26, 28, 32, 34–41, 44, 52, 80–83, 95, 102, 110, 116–120, 122, 128, 133, 138, 141–142, 174–175, 177, 179
Wood, W. 7
Woodhead, L. 2, 29–30, 63, 94, 152, 185, 187, 188n2, 192
Worldview 13, 27, 123, 147, 192
Wright, A. 12

Yinon, Y. 129
Young, F. 4, 5

Zurbiggen, E. L. 85